Innovations in
learning technologies for
English language teaching

Edited by Gary Motteram

ISBN 978-0-86355-713-2

Contents

Foreword

Martin Peacock

I remember as a fledgling teacher in the British Council teaching centre in Hong Kong listening to the Director of Studies giving a welcome speech to teachers at the start of the new academic year. The centre had begun investing heavily in computers and had just opened its 'Classroom of the Future' – a classroom with specially adapted furniture which gave students relatively painless access to computers built into desks. The Director of Studies was talking about the role of technology in the future of language learning and rather dramatically made his point by closing with the following epithet: 'The British Council needs teachers who are confident with technology. You are either into technology or you are in the way and had better start looking for a new job.'

Strong words indeed – and at the time quite a wake-up call for a number of teachers in the room who looked nervously around at their colleagues and no doubt made mental notes to get to grips with this new-fangled email malarkey.

Times have changed, teachers have evolved, and we now have a new breed of learning technologists. As in Hong Kong, the first changes began in the classroom itself – new technologies such as overhead projectors, interactive whiteboards, laptop computers and wireless internet have opened up the classroom to the outside world. Teachers who spent their lives managing with a textbook, a tape recorder and a blackboard are now adept at using PowerPoint to present grammar, playing podcasts to practise listening skills, pulling texts off the world wide web to introduce reading skills and perhaps most ground-breaking of all – empowering students by giving them access to a wide range of web-based tools that allow them to publish work and engage with live audiences in real contexts.

And that is just the beginning – because just as technologies have begun to change the way that English is learned in the classroom, even bigger changes seem to be taking place outside it. In fact, the digital revolution in learning now threatens to undermine the classroom completely as a place of study. Learning English through mobile devices gains credibility every day and the increasing popularity and rapidly diminishing cost of tablet devices reinforce this by providing a format that really is capable of delivering courseware. Factor in the growing interest in Massive Open Online Courses (MOOCs), providing large-scale (and free) learning interventions, and it is clear that technology still has much to offer ELT.

This is why I am delighted to introduce *Innovations in learning technologies for English language teaching*, the latest volume in the British Council's Innovations series. The volume provides a systematic and comprehensive overview of the current use of technologies to support English teaching and learning. Systematic in the sense that each chapter looks at a key segment of the ELT market – young learners, adults, English for specific purposes, English for academic purposes, assessment and teacher training and provides a view on the current state of technological intervention. Comprehensive because the view is a wide one, supported by numerous case studies which serve to keep the volume grounded in the realities of practising teachers using technologies in innovative and exciting ways. I am sure that this volume will be of practical interest to teachers and researchers in search of teaching ideas and examples of good practice, and provide food for thought for policy makers and school administrators studying the potential of learning technologies in transforming the ELT sector.

I would like to finish by thanking all the contributors who have written chapters for the volume and the teachers and researchers who have contributed case studies. And a special thanks to Gary Motteram for his tireless work, both as a contributor and volume editor, in making this publication a reality.

Martin Peacock
Head of English Product Development, British Council

Acknowledgements

I would first like to thank the British Council for giving me the opportunity to work on this book and particularly Adrian Odell for his support when it took longer than we had both anticipated.

I would also like to thank all the writers for working with me and helping to make what I believe is a novel and exciting contribution to the field of CALL.

All of us would like to thank the teachers who have generously supplied all of the case studies that are the core of what we have written about. All of the case study contributors who wanted to be named are included in a summary of the chapters in the Introduction.

Very special thanks from me should go to Juup Stelma, my colleague at Manchester University, who has helped enormously to make my own chapters better, and has also given professional advice on another.

Gary Motteram
Senior Lecturer in Education (TESOL)
University of Manchester

Introduction

Gary Motteram

In this early part of the 21st century the range of technologies available for use in language learning and teaching has become very diverse and the ways that they are being used in classrooms all over the world, as illustrated in this book, have become central to language practice. We are now firmly embedded in a time when digital technologies, the focus of this book, are what Bax has referred to as 'normalised' (2003, 2011) in daily life in many parts of the world, although not amongst all people as there are digital divisions everywhere (Warschauer, 2003), and still not always in the world of education. However, digital tools, or what I will describe in Chapter 7 as 'technical cultural artefacts' have long been a feature of the world of education (Bates, 2005), and particularly language education (Salaberry, 2001). These digital tools are, of course, central in what I would argue is the established and recognised field of computer assisted language learning (CALL), but are also increasingly a core part of English language teaching (ELT) in general.

People continue to debate the use of the term CALL itself, asking whether it is still relevant. Levy and Hubbard making the argument for (2005), whilst Dudeney and Hockly (2012) are rather less convinced. In a world where we increasingly see laptops, tablet computers, or mobile phones as the technology of choice, it might be argued that we are at a tipping point when this common term will soon disappear. However, in this chapter at least I will refer to the discipline as CALL, because along with the names of the different special interest groups and the predominant journals in the field, this continues to be the most common referent. A useful definition of CALL comes from Levy: 'the search for and study of applications of the computer in language teaching and learning'. (1997: 1) and this is what this book presents, albeit in a new way of thinking about the field. This fresh approach sees it as one that has significantly diversified, illustrates real practice with a considerable number of authentic case studies and then in the final chapter shows how CALL makes an increasingly significant contribution to the general world of ELT.

CALL has its origins in the development of the first mainframe computers (Levy, 1997; Beatty, 2010; Davies et al., 2013) and articles about the use of computers in language education started appearing in earnest in the 1980s, over 30 years ago, at the same time as early desktop computers started to make an appearance. At the time of going to press there are 11 organisations listed in the entry on CALL on Wikipedia starting with the Asia Pacific Association for CALL (APACALL) and ending with WorldCALL, an umbrella group which runs an overarching conference every five years (in 2013 in Glasgow). There are also a number of dedicated journals that focus on the field of technology and language learning including: *CALICO, CALL, International Journal of Computer Assisted Language Learning and Teaching, Language Learning and Technology* and *ReCALL*. CALL is also written about in journals that take a more general focus on technology in education, for example, *Computers in Education*, or the *British Journal of Educational Technology* and arguably more significantly for the general acceptance of the discipline, there are a number of journals in the language teaching field that also regularly feature articles on CALL. *English Language Teaching Journal* (ELTJ), arguably one of the most influential practitioner oriented journals in the TESOL field, in a recent special issue has an article by Dudeney and Hockly (2012) in which they review the 30 years of technology in language teaching, and Nicky Hockly continues a tradition started by David (Diana) Eastment in each issue of producing a short article on technology in language learning. In the special issue of ELTJ just mentioned, the topic is mobile learning. You will also see other general language journals referenced throughout this book.

CALL has then moved from being a niche field practised by a few early adopters, to being mainstream and arguably having significant impact with two of the journals mentioned above, *Computers in Education* and *Language Learning and Technology* being ranked in the top 20 most influential journals in education.

The diversification of CALL

CALL is no longer one subject; in fact, Arnó-Macià (2012) has argued that we are now in the realm of a definite division between computer mediated communication as one branch of the world of educational technology and ELT and CALL, as another. I would argue for further sub-divisions of CALL, for the teaching and learning of specific purposes languages as well as CALL for younger learners, and you will find chapters on each of these areas in this book. We can also appreciate these developments in the creation of special interest groups in organisations like EuroCALL and CALICO.

In very recent times we have also seen a growth of overview articles in journals that address these very specific domains. In *Language Teaching* there has been a recent review of CALL for young learners (Macaro, Handley and Walter, 2012); in the *Modern Language Journal* there was an overview of ESP (Arnó-Macià, 2012), which acted as an introduction to a special issue. We have seen for a while more specificity in books too, with Kern and Warschauer starting the trend with *Network Based Language Teaching* (2000), Dudeney on the *Internet and the Language Classroom* (2000 and 2007), an ESP book on technology (Arnó, Soler and Rueda, 2006), O'Dowd on online intercultural exchanges (2007), a book on social media in language learning (Thomas, 2009), Mawer and Stanley on digital games (2011) and an expected glut around mobile learning in the next few years. However, there are still influential general books in the field, for example, Levy and Stockwell (2006), Thomas, Reinders and Warschauer (2013), this latter forming part of a series which is always a good sign of a healthy field, as are second editions, for example Beatty (2010).

Most of the books that have been published so far are general introductions, collections of more formal reports of research conducted by a series of writers, or resource books for teachers which give ideas about how teachers can engage with technology often based only on classroom practice, with little or no connection to language teaching theory. Teachers then take these ideas and adapt them to their own classrooms, but we very seldom hear how these adaptations went, or what happened to the teachers when they tried out these ideas. This is where the reports that were created for the Cambridge University Press project that are discussed in

Chapters 3 and 7 and the case studies that have been assembled for this book differ. In the chapters here we find actual descriptions of practice, we see the technological choices that the teachers make in the different contexts of activity. In some cases we see why they choose to do what they do, in some cases we learn more about the role of the institution or other colleagues.

Issues of methodology and technology

Since computers started to be introduced in language learning (and in education in general) people have rightly asked whether the investment we are making in these technologies gives us value for money. As digital technologies have taken a hold in society in general, this particular question is not asked quite so often, but it is still important to make sure that the technologies that we have available are used effectively. People are always tempted to try to make an argument for technology having an impact on the development of pedagogy and in many cases we can see that the use of technology has enabled teachers to re-think what they are doing. We also see people trying to populate this domain by talking about notions like the 'flipped classroom', ostensibly a methodology that sees input as occurring at 'home' and physical classrooms being used as spaces to explore what has been presented in the input. This is far from being a new idea, but these agendas are pushed for a while and then disappear again. What is a contender for a methodology that is central to the world of technology and language learning is that of blended learning (Motteram and Sharma, 2009). We see this methodology still being developed, but when handled best it is the most likely candidate for a starting point for getting teachers to work with technology in their practice. It is still the case that most teachers work in physical classrooms and looking at ways that these spaces can be augmented with digital technologies is a very good starting point. In our recent project for Cambridge University Press, Diane Slaouti, Zeynep Onat-Stelma and myself added the idea of the extended classroom to the notion of blended learning (see Chapter 3 for further discussion). An extended classroom is one that allows learners to engage in material beyond the regular class period, so while a blended classroom is looking at ways that an activity might be enhanced by a technology, we also see technologies being used to make it possible to cover areas of the curriculum that there is just not enough time for in the busy world of formal education, particularly in primary and secondary schools. Thorne and Reinhardt (2008) have also proposed the notion of 'bridging activities', which simplistically is about getting learners to talk about how learners are using technology in their 'out of class lives' in the classroom. Thorne and Reinhardt (2008) are interested in fan fiction, the sort of narrative material that is created around digital gaming. What they propose is that teachers encourage learners to bring this activity into the classroom with them and they use it as the foundations of lessons. I explore this idea of the transformations of language learning through technology further in the final chapter (Chapter 7).

The range of technologies

At the beginning of this introduction I talked about the range of technologies that are now regularly used in classrooms throughout the world. In the research that I mentioned above: Motteram, Onat-Stelma and Slaouti (2008), we surveyed teachers of adults about the technologies that they use with their learners and we saw a very wide range. What we found was that it wasn't always the case that new technologies replaced old ones. In some cases, when a newer technology is not always available, what drove teachers' choices was the needs of the lesson and the perceived needs of the learners. This diversity of technologies is replicated in this book in the chapters that follow and in Table 1.1 I have listed all of the technologies that are presented in the cases studies discussed in the chapters. Some of the chapters do feature discussion of further digital technologies, but these are not listed in Table 1.1, although links to these technologies and descriptions of their use are provided in the body of the chapters.

Table 1.1: Cases and technologies, chapter by chapter

Case study title and context	Technologies discussed
Chapter 1: Primary education	
Case Study 1.1: Travelling through arts – Spain and Canada – Melinda Dooly and Dolors Masats	Blogs (e.g. www.wordpress.com; www.blogger.com) Wikis (e.g. www.pbworks.com; www.wikispaces.com) Second Life – virtual world Online exhibition via Glogster (www.glogster.com)
Case Study 1.2a: Developing spoken language skills and cultural understanding – Japan and Australia – Nagata Shigefumi and Hiroko Arao	Video conferencing (Polycom) with whiteboard facility PowerPoint (Google now offers its own presentation software and on Apple machines there is Keynote)
Case Study 1.2b: Picture book reading – Taiwan – Jane Chien	Video conferencing (JoinNet)
Case Study 1.3: Cross curricular story writing – Turkey – Özge Karaoğlu	Interactive books (Adobe Creative Suite) iBook – Bubble and Pebble (www.bubbleandpebble.com)
Case Study 1.4: Talking books – Hampshire Ethnic Minority and Traveller Achievement Service – England – Anwen Foy	Talking pens and stickers (Mantra Lingua)
Case Study 1.5: Edugaming – Barcelona – Kyle Mawer	No5 (3wish – www.3wish.com)
Case Study 1.6: WriteOnline – England – Chris Pim	WriteOnline
Case Study 1.7a: Mobile games – England	Anspear
Case Study 1.7b: Lifeplayer – South Africa – Caroline Grant and Phil Sambati	Lifeplayer (Lifeline Energy)

Chapter 2: Secondary education	
Case Study 2.1: Telecollaboration at a secondary school – Egypt – Ayat Al-Tawal	Teacher's own laptop Projector Skype (www.skype.com) Private Facebook group (www.facebook.com) Photopeach.com – photo-based slide shows MP3 Skype recorder (www.voipcallrecording.com) Edmodo (www.edmodo.com) Voxopop (www.voxopop.com)
Case Study 2.2: Sharing the experiences of webtools – Brazil – Ana Maria Menzes	Learner podcasts Teacher feedback videos (www.educreations.com) Voki (www.voki.com) Edmodo (www.edmodo.com) used as a portfolio or PLN Songify – iPad app
Case Study 2.3: Digital storytelling – Argentina – Vicky Saumell	Wiki for project work (www.wikispaces.com) Windows Movie Maker Zimmer Twins (www.zimmertwins.com)
Case Study 2.4: Mobile learning inside and outside of the classroom – Turkey – Karin Tıraşın	Learners own mobile phones School Wi-Fi Website creation tool: Doodle Kit (www.doodlekit.com) Fotobabble (www.fotobabble.com) for uploading pictures Animated cartoons using Go Animate (www.goanimate.com) Cartoon strips using Toon Doo (www.toondoo.com) and Bit Strips (www.bitstrips.com) Voki (www.voki.com) Quick Response (QR) codes Audio blog software VocalPost (www.vocalpost.com) Online grammar quizzes Dictionary app
Chapter 3: General adult language education	
Case Study 3.1: ESOL in further education – England – Susan Blackmore-Squires	Interactive Whiteboard PowerPoint VLE – Moodle (www.moodle.org) Google (www.google.com) Audacity Word processing (Word is now just one example of many ways of making text on digital devices) (http://audacity.sourceforge.net)

Case Study 3.2: English for Sociology – Slovenia – Vida Zorko	Moviemaker
	Wiki (www.pbworks.com)
Case Study 3.3: General intermediate level English at a University – Czech Republic – Ivana Pekarova	Materials printed from the web, tracked down using Google image search
	YouTube
	Learn English website (http://learnenglish.britishcouncil.org)
	Online dictionary
	Moodle (www.moodle.org)

Chapter 4: English for Specific Purposes (ESP) and Business English (BE)

Case Study 4.1: English for politicians – Germany – Cornelia Kreis-Meyer	Teleconferencing – Skype (www.skype.com) Audio and video conferences and text chat
	Sound Studio for recording Skype conversations
	Telephone
Case Study 4.2: Business English – Uruguay – Mercedes Viola	Skype (www.skype.com)
	Email
	Virtual conferencing rooms
	Online dictionaries
Case Study 4.3: English for advertising – Taiwan – Ayden Yeh	Yahoo Groups
	A blog
	PowerPoint
	Slideshare
	Google Drive (Formerly Docs)
	Document archiving service (www.thinkfree.com)
	Video servers (Blip TV and YouTube)
	Digital audio and video recorders
	Media Player
	Windows Movie Maker

Chapter 5: English for Academic Purposes (EAP)

Case Study 5.1: Concordancing in the classroom – Canada – Andy	Concordancers
	Corpora
	www.lextutor.ca
Case Study 5.2: Using a wiki to provide additional cultural support to EAP learners – Canada – Beth	Wiki (www.wikispaces.com)
Case Study 5.3: Using an LMS in an EAP classroom – Germany – Sarah	Learning Management Systems (LMS), e.g. Moodle or Blackboard

Chapter 6: Assessment

| Case Study 6.1: Recorded group discussions – Peru – Antonio | VoiceThread (www.voicethread.com) |

Case Study 6.2: Using a virtual learning environment to support reflective writing assessment – Turkey – Yrma G	Virtual Learning Environment Moodle (www.moodle.org)
Case Study 6.3: Developing written fluency through discussion topics – Tunisia – Mouna	Edmodo (www.edmodo.com)
Case Study 6.4: Improving presentation skills with PowerPoint – England – Russell Stannard	myBrainshark (www.brainshark.com) PowerPoint
Case Study 6.5: Developing speaking skills – England – Russell Stannard	Vocaroo (http://vocaroo.com)
Case Study 6.6: Language improvement for language teachers – England – Russell Stannard	Blogs (www.wordpress.com; www.blogger.com)

In many of the teaching resource books that are produced, we do not get a real insight into how teachers actually make use of the technologies to support the learning outcomes of the classes. What we tried to do in the Cambridge project and what we have tried to do here is to provide good examples of teacher practice embedded in a broader understanding of what happens in the classrooms, so the Cambridge project produced a series of detailed case studies of teacher activity that you can find and read on the web (http://blogging.humanities.manchester. ac.uk/CUP/). This book continues this trend, but it broadens the database of cases on display. The CUP project focused on the adult world, whereas this book includes chapters that discuss a wider and more detailed view of the world of ELT, which also reflects the broader uses of technology in the world.

The chapters in this book cover the following more specialist topics: Chapters 1 and 2 are concerned with those who in ELT are often referred to as 'young learners'. For many years most learners only started languages once they left basic education. This is no longer the case and primary language learning has become a central focus of language teaching and learning. This is not only the case in ELT, but in the teaching of other languages all over the world. Chris Pim covers the primary area and Graham Stanley covers secondary. Chris, who works as a freelance teacher and teacher trainer in the UK, provides a useful overview of language teaching in the primary sector and presents a large group of case studies covering a broad range of technologies. Graham, who has spent many years working with learners face-to-face in Barcelona, but in recent years also online with both learners and teachers, shows how the secondary sector has developed to include an increased emphasis on technology in language education. His chapter also shows how teachers can collaborate through digital technologies to provide better access to language for their learners, or who re-think the whole process of the way that languages should be developed in the classroom across a whole school.

Chapter 3 takes us on to the adult world and Diane Slaouti, Zeynep Onat-Stelma and myself provide a chapter that shows teachers using technology in interesting and effective ways in the language classroom. This chapter also acts as a bridge to the subsequent adult chapters by providing an overview of how adults learn with an introductory discussion of 'andragogy'.

Chapter 4 is concerned with ESP and Business English. Nergiz Kern defines what we mean by ESP and Business English, but also explores three cases that illuminate the increasing role that technology plays in this area of ELT. Because of the very specialist nature of ESP, it is inevitable that teachers have had to create their own materials and we can see in this chapter how helpful digital technologies can be in this respect.

EAP is the focus of Chapter 5, and Jody Gilbert gives us an insight into what is a core activity for many teachers in the further and higher education sectors around the world. With the increasing role that technology plays in academic life in general, its growing use in EAP is inevitable and here we see case studies reflecting typical activity in this sector of ELT.

Chapter 6 is concerned with assessment in language teaching and Russell Stannard and Anthony Basiel approach this topic not from the perspective of the electronic summative test, but the role of assessment to promote language development in the classroom.

Chapter 7, my own chapter, provides a final summation, but also approaches technology and language teaching in its role of providing tools that can develop language teaching. Technology is no longer at the periphery of the ELT field, but at its centre, providing teachers with the means to enhance the teaching of languages in classrooms all over the world.

References

Arnó Macià, E (2012) The Role of Technology in Teaching Languages for Specific Purposes Courses. *The Modern Language Journal* 96 s1: 89–104.

Arnó Macià, E, Soler Cervera, A and Rueda Ramos, C (eds) (2006) *Information technology in languages for specific purposes: Issues and prospects.* New York: Springer.

Bates, AW (2005) *Technology, e-learning and distance education.* London: Routledge.

Bax, S (2003) CALL – Past, present and future. *System* 31/1: 13–28.

Bax, S (2011) Normalisation revisited: The effective use of technology in language education. *IJCALLT* 1/2: 1–15.

Beatty, K (2010) *Computer Assisted Language Learning.* London: Longman.

Davies, G, Otto, SEK and Rüschoff, B (2013) 'Historical perspectives in CALL', in Thomas, M, Reinders, H and Warschauer, M (2013) *Contemporary computer assisted language learning.* London: Bloomsbury.

Dudeney, G (2000 and 2007) *The Internet and the language classroom.* Cambridge: Cambridge University Press.

Dudeney, G and Hockly, N (2012) ICT in ELT: how did we get here and where are we going? *English Language Teaching Journal* 66/4: 533–542.

Kern, R and Warschauer, M (2000) *Network-based language teaching: concepts and practice*. Cambridge: Cambridge University Press.

Levy, M (1997) *Computer-Assisted Language Learning*. Oxford: Clarendon.

Levy, M and Hubbard, P (2005) Why call CALL 'CALL'? *Computer Assisted Language Learning* 18/3: 143–149.

Levy, M and Stockwell, G (2006) *CALL dimensions: Options and issues in computer-assisted language learning*. London: Routledge.

Macaro, E, Handley, Z and Walter, C (2012) A systematic review of CALL in English as a second language: Focus on primary and secondary education. *Language Teaching* 45/1: 1–43.

Mawer, K and Stanley, G (2011) *Digital play: Computer games and language aims*. Peaslake Delta Publishing.

Motteram, G and Sharma, P (2009) Blending learning in a web 2.0 world. *International Journal of Emerging Technologies & Society* 7/2: 83–96.

Motteram, G, Onat-Stelma, Z and Slaouti, D (2008) *Technology in ELT: Survey report*. Cambridge: Cambridge University Press.

O'Dowd, R (2007) *Online intercultural exchange*. Clevedon: Multilingual Matters.

Salaberry, MR (2001) The use of technology for second language learning and teaching: A retrospective. *The Modern Language Journal* 85/1: 39–56.

Thomas, M (ed) (2009) *Handbook of research on web 2.0 and second language learning*. Hershey, PA., New York and London: Information Science Reference.

Thomas, M, Reinders, H and Warschauer, M (2013) *Contemporary computer assisted language learning*. London: Bloomsbury.

Thorne, SL and Reinhardt, J (2008) 'Bridging activities', new media literacies, and advanced foreign language proficiency. *CALICO Journal* 25/3: 558–572.

Warschauer, M (2003) Demystifying the digital divide. *Scientific American*, 289/August: 42–47.

Emerging technologies, emerging minds: digital innovations within the primary sector

1

Emerging technologies, emerging minds: digital innovations within the primary sector

Chris Pim

Introduction

With English reportedly the most commonly 'learned' second language around the world (Crystal, 1997; Special Eurobarometer, 2006: 243), this chapter explores how information and communication technologies (ICT) can be used to support the process of English language learning for those in the very early stages of education. It asks: what innovative approaches to language development can be employed to meet the needs of a new generation of young technocrats growing up within an increasingly globalised world?

This chapter examines exemplary use of technology for primary English language teaching and learning around the world and, like the other chapters in this volume, makes use of case studies to illustrate why these approaches are effective within the contexts in which they are used. Evidence suggests that there can be significant variability in practitioner and pupil confidence with ICT (Wild, 1996; Lam, 2000; Ertmer and Ottenbreit-Leftwich, 2010, Ertmer et al. 2011), although this is a rapidly changing picture as new generations of pupils who have grown up in a digital world come into classes, and graduates who don't remember a time when they didn't have a mobile phone train to be teachers and enter the school systems around the world. There is also unequal access to the technology itself and while there is increasing access to technologies throughout the world there are still 'digital divides', both in, and between, countries (Warschauer, 2003). Throughout the chapter, it is accepted that a 'one size fits all' approach to using technology is neither desirable nor practical. Each situation demands a specific approach to English language learning and these circumstances dictate not only when technologies are introduced to young learners, but how they are implemented. It is also apparent that whilst technology has the power to utterly transform learning, there are occasions where it can actually serve to reinforce linguistic, social and cultural hegemonies, rather than challenging them (Rasool, 2000).

It is not surprising, however, that an examination of exemplary practice in the use of ICTs throws up some common themes. For example, technology-mediated language learning seems to be most successful when the technology is seamlessly integrated into the overall activity and where it is used as a cross-curricular tool (Leask, 2001), rather than being an additional skill-set that must be acquired prior to, or during, learning. Practitioners frequently comment how ICTs facilitate collaboration whilst also offering the potential for personalised, scaffolded learning (Sutherland, et al., 2004). There is also the recognition that there is a place for computer assisted language learning (CALL), particularly for independent, self-paced learning via assessable assets such as language games and drilled activities. This type of learning can be particularly effective due to the immediate feedback that is offered to the user, and indirectly the teacher, a highly significant attribute of 'visible learning' (Hattie, 2009). Outcomes for children are likely to be most successful, most 'visible', when teachers are able to see learning through the eyes of their children and where children understand that teaching and all that it entails is key to their own continued progression. Broadband-related technologies have particular significance, enabling learners to communicate with each other over distance, bringing native speakers into contact with non-native speakers and providing opportunities for developing intercultural understanding (Kern, Ware and Warschauer, 2008; Whyte, 2011). These projects started mainly in universities. However, with many schools around the world having access to broadband technologies or mobile tools with good internet access, we see many new projects being developed, mainly within the European Union (see the Dooly example later), but also across the world with support from organisations like the British Council (http://schoolsonline.britishcouncil.org).

Use of technology for English language learning does not appear to be restricted to any particular age group as is confirmed by the range of chapters offered in this volume and the case studies presented here suggest that practitioners are increasingly using ICT innovatively within the early years. In many contexts, learners are being exposed to a range of technologies from a very early age in the home and by the time they reach nursery age many have developed at least some of the digital skills that enable them to participate in technology-driven activities as soon as they start school (Battro, 2004; Facer et al., 2003). Even where the use of certain ICT outstrips the current skill level of the children, there is evidence that practitioners can provide scaffolding in the overall language-learning objective. See the 'Travelling through Arts' case study later in the chapter.

Tech-savvy teachers have also begun to embrace children's interest in 'digital play', creating language learning opportunities through the use of computer games within an educational context – this is sometimes known as digital games-based learning (DGBL). See Kyle Mawer's 'digital games' case study.

Technology continues to be used for all sorts of specific language learning activities, such as oral practice and reading and writing skills development. However, ICT seem to be particularly successful when integrated into project-based language learning (ProjBLL)[1] (Beckett and Miller, 2006), where English can be acquired naturally through themed activities and different subject disciplines. A typical scenario within the primary sector might consist of a sequence of content-driven, language-based activities that culminate in a significant event such as an oral presentation, or a specific task like writing a letter or essay. Children might engage in a teacher-led question and answer session, watch a video, research using books and the internet,

---

[1] This acronym is chosen to distinguish it from PBL (problem based learning), which, although it has many characteristics in common, is rather different in how it plays out in the classroom.

take part in a role play or debate and experience any number of other activities in preparation for the final task. Throughout, learners will inevitably dip in and out of using ICT – an approach often termed 'blended learning'.

The trend towards introducing English teaching at primary level

The question of when the best time to start learning English is remains a much debated subject. This conundrum has been the subject of intense scrutiny for many years and continues to vex policy makers all over the world.

Much of the early debate around the early introduction of language learning into schools centred on the critical period hypothesis (CPH) which, broadly stated, 'is a causal explanation for the differential success in acquisition of a second language by younger and older learners', (Bialystok and Hakuta, 1999: 162). However, a longitudinal study in the UK on the teaching of French in both primary and secondary schools conducted by Burstall et al. (1974) showed that apart from improved pronunciation there appeared to be no significant difference between attainment for learners who started earlier and those that started later. This meant that, in the state sector in the UK at least, foreign languages were not taught in the primary sector for many years. The research and the debate have continued, but no definitive answer has been forthcoming. Kirsch (2008: 4) summarising our current understanding in this area suggests the following:

- research into the optimum age for language learning is inconclusive
- an early start has a positive impact on children's attitudes
- the only advantage of an early start is the total amount of time spent actively on learning a language.

However, the growth of globalisation of trade and the predominance of English in the media, particularly on the internet, have been responsible for driving change in language education policy and there is a global trend towards introducing English language teaching into the primary sector.

Within a politically charged educational environment, some policy makers have decided that the creation of a well-educated, English speaking workforce may be one route out of the current global economic downturn. Parents often consider academic excellence in English to be the number one priority in terms of access to higher education, university accreditation and economic prosperity for their children. Consequently, in many countries, children now begin their study of English at primary level.

What's in a name?

There are numerous terms to describe the process of learning English. In many English speaking countries it is often referred to as 'English as an additional language' or 'English language learning'. The distinctive position in these contexts is for learners to acquire English alongside other subjects. This approach has proved very popular in the US, Canada, Australia and the UK, where over 25 years of research has informed a political agenda that promotes inclusion.

In other areas, such as the Middle East, the term 'English as another language' has been coined to reflect the notion of children from minority ethnic backgrounds, who already have experience of using their own home languages and are learning the official language of the country, as well as learning English.

In many other countries around the world, readers are likely to be familiar with the concept of learning 'English as a foreign language', where learning of English takes place in a non-English speaking context. In EFL classrooms there is a general aspiration for exposing learners to English as a 'living language', providing natural opportunities to practise target language through the use of authentic texts and exposure to real models of spoken English. In this case, the role of technology can provide a significant addition to the other more conventional tools (blackboards, textbooks, cassette players) that are found in classrooms around the world. Technologies like the internet can provide access to large quantities of authentic input material and at the same time can provide opportunities for practice. Teachers and learners are no longer isolated from the target language or culture and can '... participate in the socially mediated practices of [the target language] community.' (Kirsch, 2008: 46). Even if learners do not have direct access to the internet in their classrooms, or at home, teachers often do have and can provide additional resources to supplement the material offered via conventional means.

Technological change – from consumers to producers

Over the last 20 years, there has been a tremendous shift in the way that users integrate technology into their personal lives. These changes have taken time to filter down into the educational sector, but slowly teachers have realised the need to adapt their practice in order to reflect the changing nature of technological use in the wider world.

In the past, technology has predominately been used to source and consume information, whereas today's learners have become particularly adept at creating and collaboratively developing content for a wide variety of purposes, for example so-called Web 2.0 tools such as blogs, forums and wikis. Moreover, children and young people are now becoming increasingly interested in the concept of 'content curation' – selecting, sifting, showcasing and sharing content with friends, family and peers.

The change from a 'read Web' to a 'read/write Web' has encouraged teachers to become increasingly inventive in their approach to engaging technologically savvy learners who want to publish their work within an ever expanding arena.

> *When students write or speak for a broader and more international audience, they pay more attention to polishing their work, think more deeply about the content they produce, and consider cultural norms more thoughtfully...*

Ramirez (2010: 1)

What is the most appropriate approach for teaching young learners?

There is no right answer to this question, as it will depend on many factors: the age of the children, class size, the competency of the teacher, availability of resources, the school context and the framework constructed by bodies that create the educational landscape for the locality.

Should oral development precede reading and writing? There is a school of thought that suggests children learn best by hearing language being effectively modelled by skilled teachers, and having natural opportunities to use language in productive activities, before embarking on robust learning of literacy. However, the relative success of this type of approach may lie in the oral competency of the teacher and easy access to appropriate resources.

In some contexts it may make more sense to expose children early to reading, learning phonics and the explicit teaching of grammar. Clearly, it makes little sense to be teaching reading and writing in a second language beyond what has been achieved in a first language, although it may be possible for the two languages to develop at similar rates. However, older learners may have knowledge of literacy to transfer over from a stronger first language. In many contexts, schools are measured by how many children pass academic exams, which may necessitate and encourage a 'teaching to the test' mentality amongst teachers. However, this could mean that the more important aspects of learning are neglected.

The significance of oral competency

When learners of English are immersed in the target language, for example children studying in English medium schools or where the dominant language of the locality is English, as in the UK, the development of oral competency naturally tends to precede a more specific focus on reading and writing. However, when we are talking about foreign language learning the decision is more complex.

A useful framework for viewing learning a foreign language can be seen in Figure 1.1.

Figure 1.1: Dividing up language for child foreign language learning
(Cameron, 2001: 19)

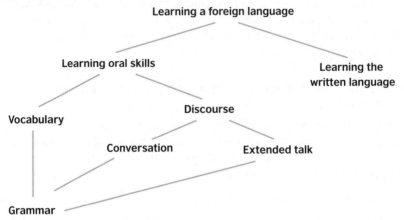

Cameron separates learning the written language, not necessarily because she sees this as coming later in a child's development, but because the written language needs to be explicitly taught by the teacher; the process needs planning and the teacher needs to understand what is involved in doing this. However, this does not mean that written language is divorced from spoken language, but for the young language learner, language is presented, practised and learned through speaking and listening. As the result of activities that take place in the class, children learn the meaning of words and grammar 'emerge[s] from the space between words and discourse' (Cameron, 2001: 18) and supports the development of meaning.

Technologies to support oral skills

For younger learners effective classroom strategies have traditionally involved use of songs, rhymes and traditional stories with repeated language structures. The internet can be a rich source of authentic oral models via recorded songs, talking electronic books, podcasts and video clips that help learners with pronunciation as well as acquisition and reinforcement of new vocabulary. These tools can also help to support teachers who don't feel as confident with their own language skills. Technology also affords children the opportunity to record themselves for playback at a later time. Learners report that the ability to listen and play back recordings helps identification of grammatical errors and inaccuracy in pronunciation, encouraging self-improvement.

Young children can use Flip, or other video cameras to record their mouth movements to develop phonetic accuracy; recordings can subsequently be compared with standard models sourced from the internet. Learning resources, such as songs and poems, can be downloaded from the internet and practised as a whole class via an interactive whiteboard prior to a live performance that can be filmed for posterity. Taking a karaoke-style approach, children are able to digitally visualise rhymes and songs through freeze-frame photography, artwork and text-based legends that can be synchronised to the words.

Audio recorders like talking tins, pegs or cards can be used to reinforce the learning of traditional rhymes or to record the singing of popular songs. Talking photo albums have been successfully used to create stories or non-fiction texts with an oral narrative. Here photos and text can be inserted into each page of the album and the user can subsequently record a corresponding narration. For further examples look here: www.segfl.org.uk/spot/post/recordable_talking_devices/

Recording devices like these are cheap, portable and simple enough to be used by even the youngest learner, where being able to overwrite recordings multiple times is essential to allow learners to achieve relative success in their oral work. Audio recorders have also been used to encourage reticent speakers to use oral language more openly in the classroom; a child makes a recording in isolation and plays this back in the classroom, validating their voice to their peers (Howard and Pim, 2007).

Recording devices also have a key role to play in assessment (see Chapter 7 for more information on technology use in assessment), where examples of oral work can be saved and revisited at a later time in order to show progression in learning. See: www.talkingproducts.com/

e-tools that facilitate language practice

What we have said so far in our discussion of the needs of young language learners suggests that they need to be offered opportunities to practise target language in as many ways as possible. What is missing for them in many EFL contexts is access to other language users with whom they can practise. Technology has the potential to overcome this limitation and provide learners with the opportunity to communicate with others, often native speakers of the language they are learning, or other learners studying the same language, but who don't share the same home language, so they are forced to make use of English to communicate. Synchronous solutions like video-conferencing (Phillips, 2010) and face-to-face interaction through online virtual worlds (Hew and Cheung, 2010; Zheng et al., 2009) are becoming increasingly popular as vehicles to promote language learning. Video conferencing is being used to bring learners together over distance so that they can communicate in a common language and share cultural experiences. Virtual worlds like Second Life, Active Worlds and Open Sim afford learners the possibility of 'living' within a 3D space, collaboratively developing content and interacting with peers through virtual experiences: debates, role play, exhibitions, performances and the like. Asynchronous tools like email, blogging and the collaborative development of wikis (Terrell, 2011; Wang and Vásquez, 2012; Woo et al., 2011) also have a significant role to play in facilitating the co-creation of content, where learners interact with peers by composing, editing and exchanging texts. These technologies offer learners the opportunity to engage in activities that produce comprehensible output and where meaning has to be negotiated. It has been argued for some time that in order for learners to develop competent language skills they need to engage in comprehensible output (Swain, 1985). It had been argued by Krashen (1981) that input would be enough, but Swain and colleagues, based on the work that they have done with Canadian bilingual learners, showed that without engagement with language and feedback, learners do not develop productive skills. Over the years since this original research, a considerable range of studies have explored this area. Technology allows learners who would not normally have as many opportunities to use the language they are learning in productive ways to communicate with other speakers of the target language.

Case studies from a range of countries have been chosen to illustrate how different technologies can be used to increase learners' access and participation as well as supporting their development of oral competency, reading and writing. In this first case study we see how Web 2.0 tools and virtual worlds can facilitate natural opportunities for language development between peers who are separated by large distances.

Case Study 1.1: Travelling through arts

At the Faculty of Education, Universitat Autònoma de Barcelona, researchers Melinda Dooly and Dolors Masats have been working with trainee teachers to investigate how computer mediated communication (CMC) can facilitate English language learning between children based in two different countries. The research has been triangulated through a close partnership with an internship school (CEIP Sant Jordi) and the specialist teacher, Maria Mont. Randall Sadler, of the University of Illinois Urbana Champaign (USA), collaborated in the materials development. The project is financed by the Spanish Ministry of Science and Innovation (EDU2012 17859; http://pagines.uab.cat/pads/en).

In the first year of the project, six-year old Catalan speakers were linked with peers in a Canadian school in order to work collaboratively on a cross-curricular project, integrating art, social science and language learning. Children in each school worked independently to research the life of a local artist by visiting galleries and examining the artist's work at first hand. This variously supported aspects of the curriculum: physical geography, transport, historical events and artistic style. Each school was subsequently able to share their findings asynchronously via blogs and wikis as well as through the more immediate 'face-to-face' context of a virtual world.

An ingenious method was chosen to bring children together in order to discuss the work of both local artists, as well as share each school's independent research. A virtual exhibition of artwork was created on a secure island in a virtual world called Second Life. Using a non-threatening 'Snoopy' avatar controlled by the teacher, the children were encouraged to use simple English commands to direct their virtual guide around the gallery, to inspect the exhibits and answer their questions. This proved to be an extremely successful way of teaching English, particularly instructional and descriptive language.

In order to bind the learning together in a suitable finished format, both schools worked together to produce an e-book based on an imaginary meeting between the two artists from each country. This e-book and other details about the project were showcased via a Glogster exhibit entitled 'Travelling Through Art'.

http://teachertefl.edu.glogster.com/travellingthruart/

This type of work shows how 'blended learning' can be particularly successful as it enables flexible working, where children can pursue projects through more traditional approaches that can subsequently be shared more widely with peers via communicative e-tools. Exploring common themes provides a natural context in which to develop target language through the sharing and co-creation of content.

This case study also illustrates the benefits of children acting as digital collaborators. They need to pay particular attention to the function and form of their oral and written contributions as well as ensuring that it is fit for purpose. Working with peers, particularly those from another cultural background, requires children to carefully consider the sophistication of their contributions as well as the socio-cultural nature of the content, in order to ensure that they, along with the recipients, get the most from the experience.

Video conferencing

Video conferencing (VC) continues to be a highly efficient way of inviting visitors into classrooms and for enabling learners to collaborate with each other at distance. In certain situations this can be one of the few methods available for exposing learners to native English speakers and for facilitating cultural exchanges. VC can also bring specialist English teachers into classrooms for direct teaching as well as modelling good practice for the mainstream teacher. Teachers themselves can also link up using the technology for more in-depth teacher training sessions.

Whilst excellent VC results can be achieved with professional equipment, great results can be obtained with a simple web camera, microphone and reliable internet connection. There are many free solutions available, such as Skype, ooVoo, iChat and FaceTime or Flash Meeting. In the case of low cost solutions, such as Adobe Connect, which allow more protection for young learners, and which are free from advertising, usually only one establishment needs to purchase the system and then the 'host' can invite participants to join a VC free of charge. This resource can then easily be shared between a number of institutions.

The quality of video and audio is obviously the number one priority, but it is clear that the most useful VC systems offer participants an array of additional tools such as shared whiteboards, text chat facilities, private meeting rooms and polling functionality. Here are two case studies that focus on VC: one from Japan and one from Taiwan.

Case Study 1.2a: Video conferencing – Developing spoken language skills and cultural understanding

Recently, Japan has made the teaching of English compulsory in all its elementary schools. This has posed significant challenges for schools and teachers, not least because many teachers lack the necessary oral competency to deliver lessons through English as well as providing effective speaking models for their students.

At Mie University, Nagata Shigefumi, a researcher in the field of social studies and Hiroko Arao, a researcher in English education, formulated a four-year international school linking project to facilitate learning between local students and peers from schools in other countries.

In the pilot project, Year 6 children from Kitarissei Elementary School visited Mie University for video conferencing sessions with children in Australia. The focus of the work was to develop oral competency for the Japanese children as well as sharing cultural experiences. In preparation, both classes researched a topic of interest to share with each other during the Polycom VC sessions; these included environmental and nutritional themes.

Each session followed a similar pattern:

1. Greetings and introductions from both schools.

2. Japanese children did a presentation followed by a question and answer session.

3. Australian presentation followed by a question and answer session.

Each class used the VC whiteboard facilities to show a PowerPoint, aiding the flow of their presentations. During follow-up discussion, the Kitarissei children mostly communicated in Japanese – a Japanese interpreter present in the Australian classroom subsequently translated this during the sessions.

Evaluations that have been conducted so far show that the confidence and motivational level of the Kitarissei children rose from the experience of using authentic oral language with the native speakers from the Australian schools. Children also developed a keener interest in global issues, as well as stating a desire to find out more about Australia. Interestingly, the children also reported that they needed to pay special attention to their oral presentations, ensuring that they were both clear and interesting to their peers. One student commented that 'I tried to use simple sentences matching the PowerPoint slide shows' and another that 'I thought of the ways of sending our message clearly'.

Case Study 1.2b: Video conferencing

As part of a recent promotion of 'picture book reading' in Taiwan, Jane Chien at the National Taipei University of Education has been using video conferencing to support schools and teachers in their delivery of this initiative.

According to Jane, in Taiwan there has not always been a culture of high-quality English picture book sharing between parents and children, because, of course, home reading is mostly done in Mandarin. Additionally, many teachers expressed their need to have a shared platform on which picture book reading activities and worksheets may be readily available to them and where more innovative teaching activities can be shared. This has obvious implications for younger children who are learning English.

Using a VC system called JoinNet, classes of 5th Grade children (11 years old) in Kelong district and in Taipei city were linked up with experienced primary teachers for a series of book readings. Three texts were chosen; *An old lady who swallowed a fly, Joseph had a little overcoat* and *We're going on a bear hunt*. Each book was delivered over three sessions.

Each session was considered to be highly motivating for the children because they were able to experience a book reading led by an expressive English user synchronously, whilst at the same time viewing the page spreads on the computer screen. They were also able to interact with the reader by asking and answering questions in their own first language about the plot, characters and events in the story. The teacher was able to specifically focus on English vocabulary, upload worksheets incorporating listening and spelling activities, such as cloze procedures, as well as utilising the system's polling function to elicit responses from the children.

Jane is clear that whilst the children gained a huge amount from these VC sessions, the major beneficiaries were the class teachers. They were able to see an effective book reading modelled by a skilled English speaker and identify techniques for engaging the listener, as well as learning how to enable children to think and talk around a story in order to maximise comprehension.

This second case study focuses on the way that technical tools can serve a variety of functions, and links together the development of oral skills and reading and writing. It also picks up on the theme that technology can provide effective teacher support where teachers lack confidence in their abilities with different aspects of the curriculum. It also links us to the next section where we explore the links between reading and writing.

Developing reading and writing

The interdependence of reading and writing cannot be over-emphasised; 'reading makes the writer' (Corbett, 2008: 1). This is a simple notion, yet the teaching of reading, in the worst cases, can lead to children who are able to decode, but are unable to comprehend or appreciate the full purpose of a piece of text. Whilst this would be an anathema for teachers of a first language, all too often this can be the case for children learning English as a foreign language. This might happen when reading is forced too early and becomes a purely mechanistic process, or if there are few engaging texts to interact with and where there is a lack of exposure to authentic oral models.

Reading can be severely compromised by limited access to appropriate texts and the internet itself offers texts that are often too sophisticated for many learners of English. However, there are places on the web where more accessible English can be found, for example, Simple English Wikipedia (http://simple.wikipedia.org/) that supports texts with a high content level, but reduced literacy demand.

Nowadays, digital literacy is particularly significant, as children are bombarded daily by an array of digital texts, and it is particularly important that they learn to understand the nuance of media-types that surround them in the physical world as well as on the internet.

Wordle (www.wordle.net) is a good example of a web-based tool that can help cement the interface between reading, writing and the significance of visual literacy in a 21st century world. The tool produces word clusters based on the frequency of words occurring in a sample of writing. Practitioners can use Wordle to help older children compare texts from different genres and ages, analyse the formality in writing or simply focus on key vocabulary from a particular topic. Children producing their own Wordles can also play around with shape, colour and styling in order to consider the impact of their work on different audiences.

Digital texts and electronic books (e-books), particularly when accessed on cool, portable technologies, can inspire children to read. Many offer effective oral modelling via text-to-speech synthesis and access to other tools like electronic dictionaries. Specialised software can record, measure and track progress in reading, and interactive fiction (IF) promotes active reading by enabling learners to affect outcomes in stories, maximising engagement in the storytelling process. Children are also motivated by their own personal writing and there are many tools available to support writing and allow them to author for different audiences – multi-modal digital narratives like cartoons, storyboards, presentations, blogs, websites and extended prose.

Talking texts

Books are a natural starting point for language learning at whatever age the process starts, particularly where the written form can be linked to an oral equivalent. Oral versions of a text can increase access for those whose current reading proficiency lags behind their ability to read. Moreover, well-produced talking books bring texts alive through the quality of voice characterisation, intonation and expression and in many cases can be one of the few ways of modelling authentic oral language to an English language learner.

Many professionally produced reading schemes offer audio CDs or online oral versions of the texts. Some companies, like Mantra Lingua (http://uk.mantralingua.com/), produce pointing devices that can play audio by scanning texts or interfacing with microdots printed onto paper. Digital texts can also be imported into e-book readers that can render text orally through text-to-speech synthesis. Using software screen-readers and standalone text-to-speech applications can also be an option.

Creating talking books

Children love sharing their knowledge about a favourite hobby or relating personal life experiences, such as the details of their last family holiday. They also enjoy playing around with traditional or familiar stories as well as inventing their own. It can be particularly motivating for learners to be responsible for creating and publishing their own digital texts, as this requires them to use language for a specific purpose and audience; for example authoring for peers, younger children or their parents.

At their most simple, talking books can be created in presentation software, specialist software like 2Simples's Create-a story (www.2simple.com), dedicated authoring programs like iBooks Author (www.apple.com/ibooks-author/), apps like Book Creator (http://itunes.apple.com/gb/app/book-creator-for-ipad/id442378070?mt=8) or even more professional software like Adobe Creative Suite (www.adobe.com/). Finished products can subsequently be published on blogs, websites or released in e-book format for playback on a range of different devices.

Whether texts are largely picture-based or contain significant quantities of text, meaning can be made more explicit when children record additional audio elements like sound effects, speech and narrative.

Here is a case study that brings together some of these ideas on using software to promote reading skills.

Case Study 1.3: Cross curricular story writing

At Terakki Foundation Schools, Istanbul, a class of five- and six-year old children worked on a year-long cross-curricular story writing project. Although initiated and sustained during English classes by teacher Özge Karaoğlu, practitioners from the art and ICT departments were also involved. The collaboration built upon a strong tradition at the school of using ICT to promote creativity, particularly using children's artwork to produce digital animations.

As in many early language learning contexts, Özge teaches English through fun-based activities centred on common themes, such as colours, numbers, food and the like. The children decided to consolidate their learning of new vocabulary by creating an audio-enabled talking book based on the characters of two imaginary children, 'Bubble' and 'Pebble'. The children were particularly motivated by the notion of becoming digital publishers and authoring an e-book to share with friends, family and the wider world.

Özge gave her children free rein to develop their own collaborative story, providing them with storyboards to support the flow of their ideas. During English lessons, teaching was always conducted in the target language, whilst the majority of dialogue between children took place in Turkish. Alongside this work, during art classes, the children were provided with a number of different character models and other assets upon which to design their animations for the story.

Özge supported the children to develop a written narrative, ensuring that they were mindful of the need to integrate 'learned' vocabulary repetitively throughout the story. The narrative was subsequently recorded by a few of the more confident speakers in the class using a 'sound recorder' on the computer. Finally, Demet Küyük created the book using Adobe Creative Suite 5.5 and then published it as an e-book ready for reading via iBooks (for example on a mobile device such as an iPad).

Bubble and Pebble e-book: http://itunes.apple.com/us/app/bubble-and-pebble-story/id444909635?mt=8

The successful creation of an electronic talking book not only helped consolidate new language for the children but also proved transformative in terms of extending learning through a follow-up project. With teacher support, the class produced a website of language games to help other children learn English. Based upon the characters of Bubble and Pebble who 'introduce' the activities, the games were designed to teach familiar topic vocabulary like colours, shapes, food, numbers and animals. The children imaginatively designed each game with a different concept in mind, such as learning the names of food by concocting a recipe to make popcorn.

Bubble and Pebble interactive games: www.bubbleandpebble.com

'Bubble and Pebble' illustrates well how technology can be harnessed to unite the different elements of the Cameron framework presented above. It is also illustrative of the ideas that underpin content and language integrated learning (CLIL), in which a number of departments within a school work together to support language development. In addition, it gives the opportunity for children to become digital publishers, thus developing their digital literacy. Authoring for a specific audience encourages children to think carefully about the suitability of the language they are using as well as ensuring that the activities make sense, are culturally appropriate and will be engaging enough to sustain interest.

Bringing sound to paper using technology

Over the last few years there has been an explosion in the development of different types of portable technology that can bring sound to paper. These 'pointing devices' have in-built scanners that interface with microdots on paper to trigger the release of audio content stored on flash memory or tiny hard disks. Many of these devices are capable of recording speech, songs and other ambient sounds ready for playback at a later time, which is particularly useful for assessment purposes. Some devices can be used to create interactive resources. Clever software within the device can register a user's actions, enabling the development of reading comprehension exercises that offer Boolean feedback – correct/wrong interactivity. The applications for language learning are numerous.

Using a device like Mantra Lingua's (http://uk.mantralingua.com) PENpal and phonics tiles (Talking Phonics Pack 1), children can learn phonics by playing interactive matching games and experiment with word building and segmenting activities.

PENpal can also support reading development by reinforcing the correspondence between the spoken word and the written form. Talking books enable a user to listen to a story, in more than one language if they wish, at the same time as leafing through a picture book; this is beneficial for individuals, small groups of children and even young children alongside a parent. It is a truly multi-modal approach: paper-based texts, supported by strong visuals, delivering professionally recorded sound through touch.

There is also the opportunity for learners to play around inside texts, for example recording a reading of a text, retelling the story or producing dual-language versions. The ability to transfer knowledge and skills from one language to another sits well with current theories of language acquisition: 'When children continue to develop their abilities in two or more languages throughout their primary school years, they gain a deeper understanding of language and how to use it effectively', Cummins (2001: online).

Case Study 1.4: Talking books

In the UK, Hampshire Ethnic Minority and Traveller Achievement Service (EMTAS) embarked on an early intervention in reading initiative, aimed principally at pre-school children from families where English was not the first language of the home. Evidence shows that many children from 'bilingual' homes start school in the advantageous position of 'living within' two or more languages, including English. They may have also been variously exposed to a number of written languages through their immediate print environment and exposure to books. However, some children can start school with under-developed speaking and listening skills in English, partly due to under-exposure to English in the home and the community, as well as inexact modelling from parents and peers. In addition, first language literacy rates amongst adults in families can vary widely. This sometimes impacts the development of oracy and early literacy, particularly at bedtime with knowing how to share a book with a child.

Working with the School Library Service, EMTAS sourced ten well-known books aimed at pre-school and nursery age children (children aged between three and five). The project set out to record readings and retellings in English and ten other languages commonly spoken within local communities. Recordings for each book were made by bilingual assistants, using Mantra Lingua's TalkingPENs and their removable Talking Stickers. Each bilingual book was subsequently made available for loan through local children's centres, so that a parent and child could orally share a book in English and the home language, using the supplied TalkingPEN.

During the preparation of the 'talking stories' it was also possible to record general ideas for parents (English and home language) on how to share a book with their child. This was reported as being immensely useful by some parents.

Reading practice

Technology and associated software affords early readers the opportunity to practise reading in a non-threatening, supportive environment, where the quality of feedback has been shown to be particularly beneficial.

TextHelp's Fluency Tutor (www.texthelp.com/UK) is a sophisticated reading programme that records a user's reading of a text and offers a quick quiz to test their understanding of what they have read. This enables a teacher to mark a learner's efforts online against a range of indicators such as mispronunciation, hesitation, omission, substitution, repetition, transposition and self-correction. The pupil can review the comprehensive feedback provided by the teacher at their leisure. The system tracks a user's achievements as they move through increasingly sophisticated texts, presenting progress via a range of information charts.

Other systems, like Pearson's Rapid Reading programme (www.pearsonschoolsand fecolleges.co.uk/Primary/Literacy/AllLiteracyresources/RapidReading/RapidReading. aspx), offer speech recognition, providing real-time feedback to a user as they read a text into a microphone connected to a computer. The software corrects mispronunciation and word errors, improving spoken English and building vocabulary. Such a system can be motivating for learners who benefit from synchronous feedback and the opportunity to practise in private.

It should be noted that the effectiveness of a reading programme lies within the appropriateness of the chosen texts. Technology can motivate learners by recording, measuring and feeding back progress with decoding and comprehension skills, but may not necessarily confer enjoyment in reading. As Leung (2005) points out, reading must be purposeful and is a multi-layered, multi-modal process. Thus, chosen texts should be engaging, relevant, visual and explore a variety of genres in order to genuinely meet the needs of 21st century learners.

Digital game-based learning (DGBL)

Most children in many parts of the world who have grown up with computers and gaming consoles and increasingly 'smart' mobile phones are highly conversant with the notion of using them for 'digital play'. Some educators are capitalising on their children's involvement with this type of technology by integrating video games into their lessons.

Tech-savvy teachers, who have in most cases grown up gaming themselves, have also begun to embrace children's interest in 'digital play', creating language learning opportunities through the use of computer games within an educational context – this is sometimes known as digital games-based learning (DGBL).

Digital games, in particular, are proving popular because they can be successfully used to facilitate teachable moments: curriculum content, core skills and language acquisition. Such games can be highly engaging to the user, featuring strong narratives via a range of rich-media types such as text, audio, video and animation.

They also tend to incorporate elements of problem solving that promote pupil collaboration. When children work together to solve problems there are opportunities for teachers to develop well-structured language learning activities.

Ironically, the engaging nature of digital games can sometimes be a distraction from the overall learning objective, because pupils get caught up in the notion of 'solving the problem' or 'winning the game'. At times, therefore, teachers may need to place specific restrictions on their learners in order to maximise the potential of using digital games for language learning. However, they will also need to develop activities 'which promote the practice of language but which do not take the fun out of playing the game...' Mawer and Stanley (2011: 15).

Case Study 1.5: Edugaming

Recently Kyle Mawer, an EFL teacher based in Barcelona, embarked on a short 'Edugaming' programme with a primary class consisting of 12 nine- to ten-year old B2 level language learners. Kyle chose an online game called N°5 from a company called '3wish' (www.3wish.com/game/game.htm) to use with his primary class. His criteria for choosing a game from this particular series was based on the fact that they are easily accessible online, they are free, the graphics are cartoonish and appealing and the content appropriate for his learners.

In preparation, Kyle decided to write a 'walkthrough' of the game for his children – this is a simple set of instructions (with screenshots) for completing a challenging puzzle game. He found a screen capture video of someone playing the game (on YouTube) and then wrote a walkthrough, down-grading the English appropriately. The challenge for writing a walkthrough is generally to avoid the word 'click', thus increasing the range and complexity of the language content for the children. Kyle also prepared a worksheet for a pre-game task, identifying language elements within the walkthrough that he considered might pose difficulty for his children; in this case a words and pictures matching game.

Along with the walkthrough, Kyle gave each pair of students some key comprehension questions to consider during game play. This helped focus attention on descriptive language and prepositions of place; language that should be within their immediate grasp such as 'it's above my head', or 'the book is on the shelf'. Each pair was also encouraged to engage in 'play dictation', where learners work in pairs to relay useful information to their gaming partner. Preventing mime and gesture, by getting the child who is relaying the information to sit on their hands, can be useful to prevent partners simply pointing at the screen, defeating the purpose of the task.

This careful staging enabled completion of the game in a relatively short space of time. Fortunately the game sits within a series, and fast finishers were directed to a walkthrough for the next game in the series, which had been written out and placed on a wiki page for easy access by the children.

This case study illustrates the potential for using digital games for language learning. Their strong narratives and inherent capacity to promote problem-solving encourage learners to use oral language for a shared task, namely completing the game. They encourage longer extended talk about topics that learners are interested in and can also help with vocabulary development. Carefully constructed written walkthroughs require users to internalise chunks of language and repurpose them as a set of succinct instructions during 'play dictation'. This gives them practice with grammar. It shows them how words are glued together with grammar (Sinclair, 1991) and how by transforming grammatical structures different meanings can be made.

There's no reason why the responsibility for writing a walkthrough needs always to be with the teacher. In controlled open class situations a walkthrough can be elicited from a class and peer dictated. Children may also be playing their own games at home; this can provide a natural opportunity for children to independently produce their own walkthroughs which they can later share back in class. Walkthroughs produced by others can also be found online and can be adapted by the teacher, or if at the right level used directly by the learners.

Kyle and his colleague Graham Stanley run a long-standing blog which is regularly updated with ideas for digital game-based playing: www.digitalplay.info/blog/

Promoting active reading through interactive fiction (IF)

A related activity to DGBL is interactive fiction (IF). IF is a purely text-based digital game in which the readers participate in the storytelling process by becoming the main protagonist, directly influencing how the narrative unfolds in the choices they make during the interactive reading process. Learners report that IF is particularly fun and engaging (Pereira, 2012), because users have control over the plot and need to solve puzzles along the way.

Children need to be properly prepared for an IF activity. Pre-reading tasks should introduce key vocabulary to the participants as well as teaching the basic range of commands that can be understood by the software.

When working with computers, good practice, and often the pragmatics of the available facilities, suggests that children be organised into appropriate working pairs so that they can be guided into exploratory talk, learning and reasoning together (Wegerif, 2004). Paired reading of IF helps to develop oral skills as the children discuss how the story should proceed. In order to affect the course of the text-based game, the reader types commands according to the context at that moment in the narrative. Participation at intervals throughout an IF requires active reading, thus developing comprehension. Action commands must adhere to a general set of logical rules but tend to fit a natural language pattern, consequently developing vocabulary and grammar skills. Upon completion of an IF, there is also the potential to develop follow-up reading and writing activities.

One of the main strengths of IF is the wide variety of texts freely available on the internet; however, it is important to match the linguistic challenge of the text to the English reading proficiency of the children.

In addition to using pre-made texts, teachers can prepare IFs for their learners. It can also be beneficial to encourage English learners to design their own IFs, either for peers or perhaps a younger audience. Choose the most up-to-date language interpreters (parsers), as this will help children with constructing their language input. At the time of writing two of the best include 'Quest 5' and 'Inform 7'. More information about IF can be found on the following websites:

www.ifdb.tads.org

http://inform7.com/

http://quest.codeplex.com/

www.theswanstation.com/wordpress/

http://iatefl.britishcouncil.org/2012/sessions/2012-03-22/learn-language-using-interactive-fiction-digital-game-based-language-learning

Supporting writing

Writing supports built into modern word processors can be tremendously useful for emergent writers. However, spelling and grammar checking tools will only make sense when users have been taught the specific conventions of mistake-marking, like red and green underlining of text (Davies, 2004). Indeed, other tools, like integrated dictionaries and thesauri, will only be useful to those more advanced learners of English who will not become overwhelmed by the variety of alternatives offered to them by the software.

Some software, like Cricksoft's WriteOnline (www.cricksoft.com/uk/products/tools/writeonline/default.aspx) and TextHelp's Read&Write Tutor (www.texthelp.com/UK/Our-products/Readwrite/features-PC), offer an additional set of tools, like text-to-speech synthesis as a user types, word prediction and contextual vocabulary, that can be inserted into a document at the click of a mouse.

This can be well illustrated by an example from Pim (2012: 113–114) on the use of WriteOnline. Hakim has been studying English for about two years and has been asked to write a few paragraphs about different types of energy in a science class.

Case Study 1.6: WriteOnline

As Hakim begins to write he has access to a layout of menus and tools similar to other word processors he has used before. Once he has written his first sentence the in-built text-to-speech synthesis automatically plays back his writing, providing him with an authentic oral model and assisting him with mistake and error checking. As he has problems with spelling the red underlining focuses his attention on incorrectly spelled words. He can right-click and have access to lists of alternative words that are also audio-enabled.

Hakim notices that to the right of the page words begin to appear in a list as he types. This word prediction allows him to quickly select the word he needs from a list and paste it into his writing. Moreover, because he still sometimes attempts phonetic spelling, 'physical' appears in the list as he types 'fizical'. Word prediction also presents words contextually, rather like a writing frame. As he thinks how to start his next sentence he is presented with words that naturally appear at the beginning of sentences, and when he needs a specific grammatical construct, a list of appropriate words become available.

Hakim also uses an 'energy' topic word bar that has been created by his teacher. The word bar presents a set of alphabetically ordered keywords and phrases at the bottom of the screen – this reminds him to use more academic language in his science writing.

Computer assisted language learning (CALL)

The endlessly patient and non-judgemental nature of computers (Wegerif, 2004) makes them perfectly suited to enabling repetitive language learning activities that provide instantaneous feedback to the user. In an EFL context, learners can really benefit from self-directed vocabulary and grammar-based exercises, particularly those that monitor voice input and assess the accuracy of pronunciation. Some learners have found English learning software like Rosetta Stone (www.rosettastone. co.uk/) and Eurotalk (http://eurotalk.com/en/) effective for swift acquisition of surface language.

However, 'drilling and skilling' can sometimes lack context in the way that information is presented to the user, potentially limiting long-term acquisition of language. More sophisticated CALL, like Education City's 'Learn English' software (http:// us.educationcity.com/us/content/learn-english-ell-teaching-resources), developed for US and UK markets, introduces children to themed-based multi-modal activities, where learners can interact within typical scenarios. The narratives are built around familiar settings like the school, family and neighbourhood, allowing children to internalise contextualised vocabulary and learn simple grammatical rules through fun-based repetitive exercises built around each scenario. Meaning is made explicit through a family of characters set within familiar settings and typical storylines. Full audio-visual support and synchronous feedback to a user, makes this type of CALL particularly successful for language learning.

However, like any product targeted at a specific market, some of the content will inevitably be culturally loaded. Teachers will need to think carefully about only selecting media and resources from one cultural domain as this may skew learners' perceptions of what standard English is, or should be.

CALL: do it yourself activities

The internet can be a vast treasure trove of English learning games and activities, but teachers should not underestimate the potential for making their own games for their learners. Indeed, there is also huge potential to enable learners to become 'game-developers' and publish for their peers. Language games and activities not only provide a framework for reviewing existing language but can also be used to explore and acquire new language (Dalton, 2005).

There are numerous online tools for developing games and activities as well as standalone packages such as '2Simple's 2Do It Yourself' (https://www.2simple.com/2diy/) software, which is easy enough for younger learners to use as well as providing enough complexity to keep older learners engaged. Here is a useful blog posting about creating language learning games: http://larryferlazzo.edublogs.org/2008/04/21/the-best-websites-for-creating-online-learning-games/

Mobile technologies

Portable devices such as tablet computers, smart and feature phones and MP3 players have particular resonance for English teaching in situations where practitioners move between different locations and where learning occurs in isolated contexts. These technologies have the potential to deliver high quality multimedia stored on internal drives or removable memory cards or that can be accessed over wireless and telecommunication networks. Many portable devices feature long-lasting batteries, particularly important where power supplies are only available during certain times of the day. Moreover, some can be powered using solar cells or charged via wind-up mechanisms.

Touch sensitive screens and simple menu systems may also be of particular benefit in situations where a lack of familiarity with mice, keyboards and operating systems might inhibit learning.

Many mobile devices sport one or more cameras and where there is a reliable internet connection, users can communicate over distance using simple video conferencing tools. GPS functionality and internal compasses also enable users to access and interact with powerful mapping tools. Front facing cameras allow learners to be creative as well as enabling them to trigger the release of information, for example by scanning QR codes (a type of barcode). In-built audio recording functionality allows children to record their thoughts about an area of learning or perhaps interview peers or family members prior to a task.

Mobile phones and other 'smart' devices are perfect for developing mobile assisted language learning (MALL) activities. Clever software can facilitate the delivery of multi-modal content as well as offering the potential to register user interaction, provide feedback and track progress.

Case Study 1.7a: Mobile games

In the UK, Anspear has developed English learning materials for mobile phones. The content is organised into themes related to English culture, featuring exercises for practising vocabulary, spelling, word associations, speaking and listening, reading and writing, and grammar in context. Through rich multimedia the software presents game-based activities to a user, recording progression and manually uploading achievements at regular intervals to the company's servers.

In one family learning project the technology was used with newly arrived Eastern European parents and their pre-school children to facilitate home–school communication and support their acquisition of English.

Youngsters enjoyed working with their parents on the game-based activities. Adult participants using the system reported that they felt more confident in their writing abilities and were more equipped to engage in community-based activities and in communicating with their children's schools.

Case Study 1.7b: Lifeplayer

Cheaper mobile solutions are available that can be highly effective in certain circumstances. Lifeline Energy, a South African-based company, has developed a clever device called a 'Lifeplayer'. This is an MP3 player, radio and audio recorder that stores interactive learning content on memory cards. It contains batteries that can be recharged conventionally, as well as by solar power and a wind-up mechanism.

The British Council has recently initiated an Open University-evaluated project to support the South African government's latest English language learning initiative. This 'First Additional Language' policy requires all schools to teach English from Year 1 onwards. Specifically targeting multi-grade schools in remote areas, the British Council has begun a programme to deliver 'Lifeplayers' containing preloaded interactive audio-based English learning materials to support both children and their teachers.

In most circumstances, students in these target schools use a first language other than English in the home: Zulu, Sesotho and Xhosa amongst others. English is taught principally as a foreign language, in situations where there can be wide variability in teacher confidence and expertise.

Existing British Council learning materials have already been pre-loaded onto the Lifeplayers and new materials are under development. For example, a local company has been commissioned to make audio commentary to accompany official Department for Education English workbooks. In addition, materials are being developed to support trainee teachers undertaking a Certificate in the Practice of ELT (*CPELT*). Materials like these aim to cover teacher pedagogy as well as offering comprehensive guidance on linguistics. Another idea involves the recording of traditional stories in English, from which to develop follow-up teaching materials.

One other useful feature of the Lifeplayer is that specially designed software can be integrated with learning materials so that a user's responses can be recorded. The memory card can subsequently be removed, inserted into a mobile phone and then a user's achievements can be uploaded to a central area for assessment purposes.

Mobile apps

'Smart' devices (both phones and tablets) feature dedicated software applications (apps) that can be used to assist language learning.

Certain apps help promote creativity: *'Toontastic'* and *'Puppet Pals'* enable younger learners to create stories using animated characters and recorded speech, as well providing opportunity for them to share their creations online. More sophisticated apps like *'Comic Life'* enable children to take photographs with the mobile device's in-built camera and incorporate them into cartoon-style templates, alongside written narrative. Others like *'Phoster'* provide a framework for developing posters so that children can play around with text and images in order to assess their visual impact on an audience.

Many apps have the more specific purpose of helping to develop reading and writing. In-built text to speech synthesis can open up access to texts for English language learners and can also serve as an effective model of oral language, particularly in the absence of native speakers. There is a multitude of dictionary apps available to support users in their acquisition of new vocabulary. Translation apps also have a role to play in enabling users to transfer knowledge and skills across from a stronger first language to their learning of English. In addition, there are numerous apps that support the development of vocabulary, grammar and colloquial language, as well as contextualising language through cultural contexts that make meaning clear.

The British Council has been developing a range of mobile apps in the recent past and you can find out more about them on the following website: http://learnenglish. britishcouncil.org/en/apps

Summary

It can be seen from the case studies and illustrative examples in this chapter that technology has a significant role to play in enhancing the delivery of English language teaching and learning in the primary sector. The range of technologies now available can support teachers in a variety of ways both inside the young learner classroom, but also increasingly in the home environment and while learners are on the move about their daily lives. Technological use is clearly 'situated', dependent on context and predicated on the notion that what works in one context may not be entirely replicable in another. However, creative practitioners will always be able to see the potential for an idea and are particularly adept at customising approaches to meet the individual needs of their learners.

With the continuing reduction in manufacturing costs, greater coverage and increasing speeds of communication networks and the development of a 'read/write Web', English language teachers have an unparalleled opportunity to ensure their curricula and teaching styles genuinely meet the needs of their 21st century learners.

References

Battro, AM (2004) 'Digital skills, globalization and education', in Suárez-Orozco, M and Qin-Hilliard, D *Globalization: Culture and Education in the New Millenium*. University of California Press.

Beckett, GH and Miller, PC (2006) *Project based second and foreign language learning: Past, present and future*. USA: Information Age Publishing.

Bialystok, E and Hakuta, K (1999) 'Confounded Age: Linguistic and Cognitive Factors in Age Differences for Second Language Acquisition', in Birdsong, D (ed) *Second Language Acquisition and the Critical Period Hypothesis*. Mahwah, N.J.: Lawrence Erlbaum Associates.

Burstall, C, Jamieson, M, Cohen, S and Hargreaves, M (1974) *Primary French in the balance*. Slough: National Foundation for Educational Research.

Cameron, L (2001) *Teaching languages to young learners*. Cambridge: Cambridge University Press.

Corbett, P (2008) *Good writers in Talk for writing*. London: DCSF.

Crystal, D (1997) *English as a global language*. Cambridge: Cambridge University Press.

Cummins, J (2001) *Bilingual Children's Mother Tongue: Why is it important for education?* Available online at: http://iteachilearn.org/cummins/mother.htm

Dalton, S (2005) *Language Learning Games: Why, When, and How*. Southern New Hampshire University. Available online at: http://gaeacoop.org/dalton/publications/LanguageGames.pdf

Davies, N (2004) Not just how but why: EAL and ICT in the multilingual classroom. *NALDIC Quarterly* 1/4.

Ertmer, PA, Newby, TJ, Liu, W, Tomory, A, Yu, JH and Lee, YM (2011) Students' confidence and perceived value for participating in cross-cultural wiki-based collaborations. *Educational technology research and development* 59/2: 213–228.

Ertmer, P and Ottenbreit-Leftwich, A (2010) Teacher technology change: How knowledge, confidence, beliefs, and culture intersect. *Journal of Research on Technology in Education* 42/3: 255–284.

Facer, K, Furlong, J, Furlong, R and Sutherland, R (2003) *Screenplay: Children and computing in the home*. London: Routledge Falmer.

Hattie (2009) *Visible learning: A synthesis of over 800 meta-analyses relating to achievement*. London: Routledge.

Hew, KF and Cheung, WS (2010) Use of three-dimensional (3-D) immersive virtual worlds in K-12 and higher education settings: A review of the research. *British Journal of Educational Technology* 41: 33–55.

Howard, L and Pim, C (2007) Animating the curriculum: Developing and preserving traditional stories through online collaboration and digital publishing. *NAACE Computer Education*, Issue 115.

Kern, R, Ware, P and Warschauer, M (2008) 'Network-based language teaching', in Van Deusen-Scholl, N and Hornberger, NH (eds) *Encyclopedia of Language and Education*, 2nd edition, Volume 4. New York: Springer Science+Business Media LLC.

Kirsch, C (2008) *Teaching foreign languages in the primary school*. London: Continuum.

Krashen, S (1981) *Principles and practice in second language acquisition*. London: Prentice-Hall International.

Lam, Y (2000) Technophilia vs. technophobia: a preliminary look at why second-language teachers do or do not use technology in their classrooms. *Canadian Modern Language Review/La Revue canadienne des langues vivantes* 56/3: 389–420.

Leask, M (ed) (2001) *Issues in teaching using ICT*. London: Routledge Falmer.

Leung, C (2005) *Developing reading in EAL*. NALDIC. Available online at: www.naldic.org.uk

Mawer, K and Stanley, G (2011) *Digital Play: Computer games and language aims*. Peaslake: DELTA Publishing.

Pereira, J (2012) 'Beyond hidden bodies and lost pigs: Student perceptions of foreign language learning with Interactive Fiction', in Baek, Y and Whitton, N (eds) (2012) *Cases on Digital Game-Based Learning: Methods, Models and Strategies*. New York: IGI Global.

Phillips, M (2010) The perceived value of videoconferencing with primary pupils learning to speak a modern language. *The Language Learning Journal* 38/2: 221–238.

Pim, C (2012) *100 ideas for supporting learners of EAL*. London: Continuum.

Ramirez, L (2010) *Empower English language learners with tools from the web*. London: Corwin.

Rassool, N (2000) Contested and contesting identities: Conceptualising linguistic minority rights within the global cultural economy. *Journal of Multilingual and Multicultural Development* 21/5: 386–398.

Sinclair, J (1991) *Corpus, Concordance, Collocation*. Oxford: Oxford University Press.

Special Eurobarometer 243 (2006) Europeans and their languages. Available online at: http://ec.europa.eu/languages/documents/2006-special-eurobarometer-survey-64.3-europeans-and-languages-report_en.pdf

Sutherland, R, Armstrong, V, Barnes, S, Brawn, R, Breeze, N, Gall, M, Matthewman, S, Olivero, F, Taylor, A, Triggs, P, Wishart, J and John, P (2004) Transforming teaching and learning: embedding ICT into everyday classroom practices. *Journal of Computer Assisted Learning* 20/6: 413–425.

Swain, M (1985) 'Communicative competence: Some roles of comprehensible input and comprehensible output in its development', in Gass, S, Madden, C (eds) *Input in Second Language Acquisition.* Rowley, Mass. Newbury House.

Terrell, SS (2011) Integrating online tools to motivate young English language learners to practice English outside the classroom. *International Journal of Computer-Assisted Language Learning and Teaching* (IJCALLT) 1/2: 16–24.

Wang S-G and Vásquez, C (2012) Web 2.0 and Second Language Learning: What Does the Research Tell Us? *CALICO Journal* 29/3: 412–430.

Warschauer, M (2003) *Technology and Social Inclusion: Rethinking the Digital Divide.* Cambridge, MA: MIT Press.

Wegerif, R (2004) The Role of ICT as catalyst and support for dialogue. *NALDIC Quarterly* 1/4: 4–12.

Whyte, S (2011) Learning to teach with videoconferencing in primary foreign language classrooms. *ReCALL* 23/3: 271–293.

Wild, M (1996) Technology refusal: Rationalising the failure of student and beginning teachers to use computers. *British Journal of Educational Technology* 272: 134–143.

Woo, M, Chu, S, Ho, A, and Li, X (2011) Using a wiki to scaffold primary-school students' collaborative writing. *Educational Technology & Society* 14/1: 43–54.

Zheng, D, Young, MF, Wagner, MM and Brewer, RA (2009) Negotiation for action: English language learning in game-based virtual worlds. *The Modern Language Journal* 93: 489–511.

Integrating technology into secondary English language teaching

2

Integrating technology into secondary English language teaching

Graham Stanley

Secondary education

English language teaching at secondary level generally takes place during the school day, at schools either funded by the state or privately financed, and after school in language academies, where learners are sent by their parents for additional English classes, usually to reinforce the English being learned at school, or to help the learners prepare for a specific examination.

For the purposes of this chapter, the term *secondary education* is used to refer to learners aged 11–18. According to UNESCO's *International Standard Classification of Education* (ISCED), secondary education can be divided into two parts: lower secondary (ISCED 2), and upper secondary (ISCED 3). Lower secondary education usually begins when children are aged 11–12 and lasts four years. The entrance age to upper secondary education to 'is typically 15 or 16 years' and lasts from 'two to five years of schooling' depending on the country. Teaching at lower secondary is typically subject-focused and aimed at preparing students for entry directly into working life or for upper secondary education, whereas the focus of upper secondary education is on preparing students for entry directly into working life or for tertiary education (UNESCO, 1997).

Growth of technology use

There has been a tremendous growth of information communication technologies (ICT) across the board in recent years. An overwhelming majority of teachers in Europe (90 per cent) use ICT to prepare their lessons (Empirica, 2006). All European Union (EU) countries have invested in ICT in schools and this has included spending on 'equipment, connectivity, professional development and digital learning content' (Balanskat, Blamire, and Stella, 2006: 2). Furthermore, the European Union has also set targets for enhancing digital literacy, skills and inclusion (European Commission, 2012).

Outside the EU, the story seems to be the same. In the US, the Office of Educational Technology (OET) has developed a 'National Educational Technology Plan' (OET, 2010) for transforming education through the power of technology. Across East Asia, 'enthusiasm for the use of computers and other information and communication technologies in education is undeniable and widespread (Trucano, 2012: 101); Tella et al. (2007: 5) report that 'the use of ICT in ... African countries generally is increasing', although they complain of limited access, and in Latin America, ICT is also appearing in secondary schools, albeit unevenly (Garcia-Murillo, 2003).

In fact, it is now difficult to disagree with Mark Pegrum's view 'that technology and education have a tightly intertwined future' (Pegrum, 2009: 5). The increase in investment in ICT by education departments around the world since 1998 has been well documented (Macaro, Handley and Walter, 2012; Becta, 2004), but how is it being implemented and what are teachers using ICT for?

In one study of the effect of ICT implementation in schools, Ilomäki (2008: 67) found two types of 'ICT stories'. The first saw expectations for ICT being overestimated in the majority of cases, with the process of implementation being top-down and 'without a strong commitment of the schools or the teachers'. In some cases, however, success came when the focus was placed on the needs of a specific school and was supported by internal improvement of that school. The effect of supporting teachers and on training teachers to use ICT can also not be underestimated.

Things, then, have come a long way since Levy wrote (1997: 3) 'CALL remains a peripheral interest in the language teaching community as a whole, still largely the domain of the CALL enthusiast, and there is scant evidence to suggest CALL has really been absorbed into mainstream thinking, education, and practice.'

Teacher training and continuing professional development and ICT

Research indicates that 'Training in ICT skills is crucial in implementing ICT integration in the teaching and learning of English' and 'the extent to which teachers are given time and access to pertinent training to use computers to support learning plays a major role in determining whether or not technology has a major impact on achievement.' (Samuel and Zitun, 2007: 10).

In many cases, however, this training is not given, and more likely than not, teachers are left to their own devices. More and more, it is a certain type of individual teacher who takes the initiative and implements technology into their classrooms. The case studies included in this chapter reflect this. Generally, these teachers are using readily available, free online tools and are finding out how to use them through social networks and online *communities of practice* (Lave and Wenger, 1991: 98). These teachers build their own *personal learning network* (Couros, 2008) and connect with other teachers around the world to share what they know and help others learn.

Personal learning networks (PLNs) developed out of the idea of building a *personal learning environment* (PLE), which is built out of a collection of web tools set up and owned by the learner. In this way, the 'management of learning migrates from the institution to the learner' and learning also 'evolves from being a transfer of content and knowledge to the production of content and knowledge' (Downes, 2007: 19). Since 2007, the focus has shifted to PLNs to reflect that most of the learning in a PLE comes from connecting to other people. An example of the increased interest in using PLNs in language teaching is the *aPLaNet* project (www.aplanet-project.eu), which aims to help teachers build their own PLNs for professional development.

As Perkins reflects, *continuing professional development* (CPD) 'is very personal...' and is 'an excellent barometer of the level of passion' a teacher has for their chosen career (Perkins, 2002: 97). Often, as the case studies here show, teachers who connect to colleagues online in this way and learn how to implement technology readily become involved in the ICT training of colleagues. Being part of a large online network of ICT-using language teachers means you regularly receive information from practising teachers about classroom technology, about what works and what does not work, and about what other teachers recommend you use in which situation.

Of course, not all secondary teachers have access to technology they can use at school, but, as our first case study shows, the 'so-called "digital divide" is as much a literacy issue as an economic one' (Pegrum, 2009: 4), with the teacher in question overcoming the lack of technology by bringing her own laptop computer to class.

The teacher in question is Ayat Tawel, a secondary school teacher in Cairo, Egypt, who has been using *telecollaboration* to connect her students' language learning to the real world outside the classroom.

Telecollaboration is 'a shared teaching and learning experience that is facilitated through the use of internet technology between distanced partners in institutional settings' (Dooly, 2008: 21). Collaborative learning can increase students' interest in learning (Dooly, 2008: 22), especially when the students are actively exchanging and negotiating ideas, engaging in discussion and taking responsibility for their learning. It is important for there to be *group goals* and *individual accountability* (Slavin, 1989: 231) and that each member of the group be responsible for a concept necessary for completing the task. Social interaction when working together can lead to students performing at higher intellectual levels than when working individually (Vygotsky, 1978: 84).

Another important aspect of telecollaboration in language learning is the intercultural one. Cultural awareness is, as Byram and Fleming (1998: 4) state, 'a significant aspect of language learning', so much so, that 'without cultural awareness, a language cannot be properly understood'. Corbett argues that intercultural language learners 'need to acquire an understanding of how interaction works, and how individuals relate more generally to those around them and to society at large' (2010: 2) and cites the benefits the internet can bring to the intercultural classroom, with its 'rich opportunities for "authentic" language use and comparison of different cultural practices' (2010: 7). Guth and Helm (2010: 121) suggest that it is important to view telecollaboration in a broader sense, taking into account the intercultural aspect rather than focusing purely on pedagogical practice. The teachers in our first case study have done this with their project.

The first case study is one example of how some English language teachers are opening up their classrooms to the real world and inviting guest speakers to engage their learners through intercultural telecollaboration. Hoffman identified this ability to link language learners with other language users as being possibly 'the most compelling appeal of computer networks' because it offers learners 'the exposure to authentic communicative language use that is so often missing in the micro-world of the classroom' (Hoffman, 1996: 68).

Research by Swain (1985) on what has been called 'the output hypothesis' suggests that collaborative tasks may be the best way to get students to produce comprehensible output, because when working together students need to negotiate meaning, and as a result are supported in producing comprehensible output beyond their own individual level of competence. Social interaction can lead the learners to language development through interactional exchanges and negotiation of meaning. Technology can facilitate this by making it easier for different groups of learners from different parts of the world to talk to each other, especially through telecollaboration.

Case Study 2.1: Telecollaboration at a secondary school in Egypt

Ayat Al-Tawel has been a teacher of English for more than ten years and teaches at the Baby Home Language School in Cairo, Egypt. She teaches English to lower secondary learners, with the average class size being 28–30 students and the language level of the learners ranging from pre-intermediate to intermediate level. There is an internet-enabled computer lab in the school, but Ayat doesn't have a computer in the classroom, so she uses her own laptop. Recently, the school bought a projector which she sometimes uses in class with her laptop.

Ayat first became interested in using technology with her learners when she joined the TESOL (Teachers of English to Speakers of Other Languages) Electronic Village Online (EVO) session 'Becoming a Webhead' (BaW) in January 2011. The TESOL EVO is organised by TESOL's CALL Interest section and run by volunteers. For five weeks at the beginning of the year, participants can engage with experts in collaborative, online discussion sessions or hands-on virtual workshops of professional and scholarly benefit. The BaW EVO session is an introduction to Webheads in Action, a long-standing Community of Practice of language teachers worldwide which developed out of a session in the first TESOL EVO. Since then (in 2002), 'the Webheads in Action community members continued to interact and learn from each other, prompting work on projects of mutual interest in spontaneous development of what we have come to call a community of practice' (Stevens, 2004: 204). Since taking the EVO session, Ayat has done a number of projects with her learners, and became a moderator of the BaW EVO session in January 2011.

Ayat is a firm believer in lifelong learning, and thinks that one of the best ways of developing professionally is by sharing with colleagues around the world that she has met online. Ayat's interest in using learning technology is based on her belief that language learning should be as communicative as possible, and that the learners should have a real reason for communicating in English. She believes that 'A language is to use', meaning that 'it is not enough to just teach in class for students to study and pass a test', but the learners should 'have to use the language in real-life situations'. As for ICT, Ayat feels that as the use of technology is increasing, both in

Egypt and elsewhere, and because young students are fond of trying and using this new technology, there is a place for it in the classroom.

Her main interests are in using blended learning and Web 2.0 tools to enhance the learning environment and inspire creativity in the classroom. For this reason, she has started a number of projects that involve her bringing guests into her classroom using the internet telephony programme Skype (www.skype.com).

During the hands-on online workshop BaW in 2011, Ayat met and started a friendship with a colleague, Maria Bossa from Argentina, and together, at the end of March 2011, they came up with the idea of an intercultural project with their lower secondary school learners. They decided to each be a guest in the other teacher's class and let the class interview them using Skype. In a podcast discussion about the project, Ayat said they chose Skype 'because it's a synchronous web tool which allows real-time live discussion and it extends the walls of the traditional classroom and it engages students to communicate with an authentic audience, and having an authentic atmosphere in class is something very important and it's not always there, we have to seek it' (Bossa, Stevens and Tawel, 2012).

One thing Ayat is clear about is the need to carefully manage the telecollaboration, which Corbett (2010: 7) states is a very important factor if online exchanges are to be effective. The exchanges were also planned to be as authentic as possible, and although they involved substantial teacher preparation, they can be claimed to be authentic as defined by Higgins (1991: 5) as 'anything not created by a teacher for the purpose of demonstrating language at work'.

To prepare for the interviews, each teacher thought of a context for the language practice so that it would fit with their syllabus. In Ayat's case, there was a unit in the coursebook she was using with her learners on global warming, with one section covering rainforests. She decided to start there, and asked her students about countries where rainforests could be found. They mentioned Chile, Argentina and Brazil. Ayat then asked them what Argentina was famous for and finished by asking the students what they thought about interviewing someone from Argentina. They were all positive about this opportunity.

Ayat's class then started to prepare questions. She encouraged the learners to ask any questions they wanted. She compiled these questions and sent them to the other teacher in advance. Before the first interview, Ayat said that the students didn't seem that interested. She thinks this was because they 'couldn't really imagine how they were going to be able to have an interview live'. However, once they entered the computer lab and started the activity, they were 'thrilled and motivated' when they saw the other teacher live on the screen and realised they were able to talk to her directly. Ayat conducted the interview with two classes of lower secondary learners. The second class did the interview after they had heard about the experience of the first class, so they were more motivated beforehand, and even decided they wanted to prepare something in Spanish to tell the other teacher.

Ayat collected feedback directly afterwards, asking the learners to rate the activity (from 1–10) and write a comment about what they thought. She usually asks her learners for their instant feedback after a new classroom activity 'to get their real feelings of how the experience was' (Tawel, 2012). Analysing this afterwards, she believes it clearly demonstrated the educational and cultural value of the experience. Here is a sample of what the learners wrote:

- 'We learned a lot of things about Argentina and had a great deal of fun'.
- 'It's good to know about other countries ... I hope we can do it with other countries'.

Ayat then asked the learners to do some writing based on the interview. The learners chose the genre. Some of them wrote it in the form of a dialogue, or as a diary entry, others as a biography, or a story.

The activity was so successful with the classes of both teachers that they decided to continue the collaboration. Another reason why the teachers wanted to extend the project is because the students 'wanted so much to communicate with the other teacher's students – not just the teacher' and they also didn't want the experience to end. Because of time differences, a Facebook group was chosen for the next stage of the learners' communication, and the teachers set up a private group (www.facebook.com/groups/argentegypt), to let the learners communicate with each other online. The teachers chose Facebook because the students already used this social network, spending lots of time on it. The learners joined the group voluntarily, asking each other questions about a range of topics, and sharing information about their own lifestyle, culture, traditions, festivals, some linguistic points, idioms or expressions etc. Ayat and Maria believed that it was very important to set a rule that all communication in the group should be in English, which was an important objective to practise the language. However, later on they allowed some Spanish and Arabic words because the learners in both classes wanted to know some basic words of the other language.

Ayat documented the interview with photographs and used the web tool Photo Peach (http://photopeach.com) to create a record of the interview as a video presentation which she was able to share with the learners, colleagues and parents. Sharing these documents on Photo Peach with her PLN means that she receives comments from colleagues and friends from around the world, which help to motivate and inspire her learners, who find it very rewarding as well as exciting that what they do in their classroom has an audience in the real world outside.

Because of the success of this project, Ayat decided she wanted to continue using Skype to invite guests to her classroom, to give her learners the chance to use English to speak to someone from abroad and to find out about their culture, especially if the learners were studying the country the guests were from.

After the first round of interviews, she realised that it would be beneficial to make recordings of the conversation. Since then, Ayat has used *MP3 Skype* Recorder (http://voipcallrecording.com/) to make recordings of Skype interviews, which allow the learners to listen to the interviews afterwards and understand the information that they might have missed the first time round, during the live interview. As her experience in arranging these interviews has increased, Ayat has found she can better prepare her learners for them, and better take advantage of the language learning opportunities that these interviews lend themselves to.

Ayat has also discovered that 'Skype helps to improve listening skills as the user has to pay active attention to what the interlocutor is saying. It's also useful to practise vocabulary and everyday language in a natural way, it fosters improvisation and puts our knowledge to the test when you're trying to write or to speak' (Bossa, Stevens and Tawel, 2012).

It is clear that the learners appreciate this kind of activity. At the end of the Photo Peach presentations which documented a follow-up classroom guest interview using Skype (http://photopeach.com/album/xnv4bg and http://photopeach.com/album/dlcrbb) some of them added the following comments:

- 'Thank God for being my teacher this year, you r realy very excellent, I really enjoy english with u'.
- this was a very nice interview and I love ms ayat and I love english thankyou and goodbye.
- thankyou miss ayat for the interview and we are so lucky that you are our teacher.
- thank you miss ayat to make us share in an experience like this, I am so lucky to be one of your students.

Ayat has subsequently started a number of other cross-cultural projects, raising the awareness of her learners and motivating them to become involved in using the language to communicate with, and learn about, other people in different parts of the world. This year, after the success of the Skype project, she started a collaborative online book project with Bernadette Rego, a Canadian teacher, and her classes, concentrating on the book *Harry Potter and the Philosopher's Stone* by JK Rowling, and using *Edmodo*, a private social network (www.edmodo.com). Edmodo has proven to be an ideal safe environment where the students can meet and discuss the book as well as share information with the other class. Voxopop (www.voxopop.com), an audio forum tool has also been used, for recording introductions and sharing questions and answers.

Web 2.0

The case study above is a clear example of a secondary language teacher embracing the affordances of recent developments online. The term *Web 2.0* is often used as a label for these developments, and although it is a term that means different things to different people, for our purposes, we can think of it as 'a shift from what were primarily informational tools to what we might call relational tools – so that if Web 1.0 was the *informational web*, Web 2.0 is the *social web*.' (Pegrum, 2009: 18).

Web 2.0 tools have proliferated in recent years, and as most allow for some degree of content creation and communication, they are often ideal for language learning. At the heart of Web 2.0 is the *blog*, short for *web log*. At its most basic, a blog is an online journal that can be used by teachers to publish information about a course, links to resources and other information directed to learners or other teachers. Ease of use was identified as one of the most important factors behind 'the significant proliferation in the number of teaching blogs' used by secondary school teachers in a recent study (Lai and Chen, 2011), and there is no doubt that the *push button publishing* first promoted by *Blogger* (www.blogger.com) has encouraged many teachers to embrace online publishing who otherwise would not have done so. Many teachers also now encourage their learners to blog, publishing their written work and projects online in ways that go beyond sharing their work with an audience beyond the teacher, and which help prepare learners 'for the digitally-driven post-industrial world into which they'll graduate – a world where our understanding of knowledge, culture, truth and authority are in the process of being rewritten.' (Pegrum, 2009: 28).

The other popular online publishing platform that has become well-used by secondary school teachers and learners is the *wiki*. The term comes from the Hawaiian for 'quick' and a wiki is a collaborative web space allowing for pages that can be created and edited by multiple users easily without any knowledge of web design. The wiki is similar to the blog in that it allows for quick and easy publishing, but the more flexible structure of the wiki means that it is good for project work, whilst the blog is better as an ongoing record of classwork as the latest work is always displayed at the top of the page.

Another development of Web 2.0 is the podcast, which comes from the combination of the words *iPod* and *broadcast*. Podcasts are audio or video files that are broadcast via the internet and can be downloaded and listened to on a computer or mobile device. Apart from software allowing the creation and sharing of podcasts, there are many other Web 2.0 tools that make use of audio, and to many users *podcasting* now refers to any creation and sharing of audio online.

Our next case study is an example of a teacher who uses Web 2.0 tools, especially audio, with her classes.

Case Study 2.2: Sharing the experience of web tools in Brazil

Ana Maria Menzes is an English teacher, teacher trainer and head of the Edutech Department at Cultura Inglesa, a language institute in Uberlândia, Brazil. She teaches mainly classes of teenagers. Ana is convinced of the value of using Web 2.0 with teenagers in particular, and thinks that one of the benefits is providing extra skills practice for the learners to do at home. She believes that although many teachers have integrated technology into their classroom practice, far fewer ask their learners to use technology for language learning at home. Ana has tried out a lot of web tools and makes a point of selecting the tools depending on the skills she wants her students to work with. Her learners have all said they prefer this type of homework.

Internet-based project work group activities which 'lend themselves to communication and the sharing of knowledge, two principal goals of language teaching itself. The use of projects encourages co-operative learning, and therefore stimulates interaction.' (Dudeney and Hockly, 2007: 44)

Let's look at a typical project of hers; one that she has recently started with a class of upper-intermediate students aged 15–16. Her objective is to provide the learners with extra writing, reading, listening and speaking practice at home.

Each week one volunteer learner creates a short text (50 words) for a listening dictation with the content being chosen by the learner from a previous lesson done in class. The teacher corrects the text, the learner then makes recordings of the text and shares it with the others in the class. Next, all the learners listen to the recording and transcribe the text. This means that every week, there is a different listening activity created by the learners and Ana says that 'from what I have observed, students have been taking great care pronouncing as best as they can, making sure their classmates understand what they say.'

Originally, Ana thought she would have the learner write their first draft, which she would correct and give them back on paper, but she decided instead to record a screencast while she corrected the text, explaining the learner's mistakes, at the same time providing a pronunciation model of how to read the text. The learner could then watch this video, change their texts according to the teacher's suggestions and then later record themselves reading their own texts. Not only does this method of corrective feedback take less time to record than it would to traditionally mark writing texts, 'the amount of information that can be provided by the teacher is much greater, and students feel it is the nearest thing to a one-to-one feedback session' (Stannard, 2006). The learner also gets additional listening practice. Ana is always looking for new ways to do things, especially when it comes to using technology to improve her classroom practice and help her learners. She also tests the efficacy of the tools and then shares her findings in her blog. For example, for the screencasting part of this project, she tried out the tool Educreations (www.educreations.com), which makes it easy to share videos with learners.

Ana strongly believes that publishing learner work online is motivating for learners, so the recordings the learners make are often posted online. As Hoffman found, having learners' work read by people other than teachers and classmates 'gives learner writing validity' and 'content, style and linguistic accuracy can be put on display before a variety of audiences meaning 'the writing that is shared becomes more than a demonstration of learning for a teacher: it is communication.' (1996: 64).

This shift in emphasis to collaborative writing and focus on learner created texts often leads to the textbook becoming 'much less important as a pedagogical focus than the writing which the students produce' (Barnes, 1989: 27), which is the case in Ana's teaching situation.

After gaining permission from her learners, Ana typically shares the work they do with her extensive PLN, via her Twitter account (www.twitter.com/anamariacult), on Facebook, and on her blog. For the project described above, she chose Voki (www.voki.com), which lets users upload audio and choose an animated avatar to go with it, adding an element of fun to the publishing process, such as in this example by one of her learners, who chose the topic 'Education in Brasil': http://bit.ly/T5nMar

Ana also uses the educational private network Edmodo (www.edmodo.com/) with her learners. This allows her to get to know the learners better, to share links to useful resources and information about the class, and allows the learners to chat with their classmates in English between classes. It also means that the work they do using web tools can be collected in one place, and the learners can look back and see the progress they have made since the start of the course. What the learners have created here, then, is something between an e-portfolio (i.e. a space used to display student work) and PLN, both of which can be 'individually tailored constructivist spaces built by and for learners' the difference being that 'while PLEs typically have a learning focus, e-portfolios may also serve display purposes.' (Pegrum, 2009: 28).

With this class and others, she has used other Web 2.0 tools, and has documented their use on her blog (http://lifefeast.blogspot.co.uk). One of the most popular of these was Songify[2]. She asked the learners to write sentences, and then using her iPad, recorded the students speaking to Songify, and then the app converted the sentences into songs. Ana said the learners had a lot of fun with this and probably spent more time practising the pronunciation of the sentences than they would have normally done.

Ana, like Ayat (Case Study 1), is also another example of a secondary teacher who has taught herself to use ICT and who also teaches others to do so. She has been using educational technology since 2006, when she attended a number of online courses held as part of the TESOL Electronic Village Online (http://evosessions.pbworks.com). She then volunteered to be a co-facilitator of 'Blogging for Educators' in the TESOL Electronic Village Online in 2008 and 2009 and has been sharing her experience and knowledge online with teachers ever since.

Research and practice

All of the case studies here show practitioners using their own networks, knowledge and resources rather than turning to classroom research for new ideas. With new tools appearing constantly, and the emergence of the 'perpetual beta' (Pegrum, 2009: 19), it is only normal to see research in learning technology trailing behind what is being done by innovative secondary school teachers. This is not new, however. As far back as 1977, Kemmis et al. stated 'CALL is practitioner led as opposed to research based' and 20 years later, Levy (1997: 4) stated that 'many developers rely on their intuition as teachers rather than on research on learning'.

At the heart of the issue here is the question whether the use of technologies in the classroom improves acquisition or development of language skills or if it is simply a distraction. In the systematic review of research undertaken by Macaro, Handley and Walter (2012: 15–20), the authors examined the evidence for this and concluded that 'some language learning benefits of CALL have been shown'. These include evidence that CALL helps secondary learners with listening and writing (particularly improvements in the amount of writing, length of texts and discourse features of

---

[2] Songify (http://itunes.apple.com/us/app/songify/id438735719?mt=8) is an Apple iPod/iPhone/iPad app that automatically turns spoken recordings into songs.

these texts), with some suggestion that speaking can also be improved. However, the research on whether CALL improves reading, and on the acquisition of grammar and vocabulary were inconclusive. As far as non-linguistic benefits are concerned, the research provides 'evidence of positive attitudes towards CALL' (2011: 21) and learners perceived an 'increase in confidence' in 'engaging in real learning experiences not found in books and speaking activities' (2011: 21).

One of the dangers of practitioners relying on intuition, and using technology in ways they see fit is that emphasis is placed more on the technology than the pedagogy, and Stockwell, reviewing studies from 2001–05 concluded that there was 'an element of failure to stipulate why a given technology was used in achieving learning objectives' (2007: 115). Reviewing the history of CALL (Delcloque, 2000), it also has to be noted that the field has been largely 'technology-driven rather than serving pedagogical needs' (Macaro et al. 2012: 2).

It is obviously impractical for teachers to wait for research to show whether a web tool is effective or not, but teachers can, as Chapelle (2001: 16) suggested, use ethnographic methods to investigate CALL effectiveness. Practitioners can ask not only whether a certain technology is effective, but also why it is effective. What also helps, and which can be seen in evidence in the case studies in this chapter, is teachers asking for feedback from learners and documenting the results of this, as well as stages of implementation in blog posts and in other publications (journals, newsletters, etc.) aimed at language educators.

Others believe that it is a question of time: 'Until technology becomes normalised, there's typically too much focus on the technology itself and not enough on how it's used pedagogically, socially, politically or ecologically' (Pegrum, 2009: 24).

Normalisation of ICT

Normalisation can be defined as the stage in which 'CALL finally becomes invisible, serving the needs of learners and integrated into every teachers' everyday practice' (Bax, 2003: 27). The concept was recently revisted (Bax, 2011), which was felt necessary because of the changes in technology use, especially the internet, which has become 'a high-stakes environment that pervades work, education, interpersonal communication, and, not least, intimate relationship building and maintenance' (Thorne and Black, 2007: 149).

While technology is, as research seems to indicate, not yet *normalised* in language education, and, as Thomas (2009: xxi) states:

...while those involved in educational technology often assume that their pursuits are central to what is happening in their institution, the reality is that a rather limited percentage of any given group of educators, either in the school or university sector, consistently integrate technology to any great effect...

There are definite 'signs of a more fully integrated approach to CALL emerging because of Web 2.0.' (Motteram and Stanley, 2011: ii).

Integration of ICT in secondary language teaching

Aside from Web 2.0, more traditional uses of ICT continue too. Jewell points out that many stand-alone applications such as word processing and presentation software (for example *Microsoft Powerpoint*) can be used effectively by secondary school learners to 'improve their language skills through research and by sharing their findings in oral presentations' which also 'provide real-world contexts and technological skills and enable students to develop confidence in their language abilities' (2006: 176).

Whether using established or emerging tools, it is when technology is utilised by teachers and learners and thoroughly integrated into the curriculum, as it is in the next case study, that wide-ranging benefits can be detected.

Case Study 2.3: Digital storytelling in Argentina

Vicky Saumell is co-ordinator of the EFL Department at Instituto San Francisco de Asís, a private school in Buenos Aires, Argentina that has 800 students at all levels, from kindergarten to secondary. Although private, the school is mostly funded by the state (to keep the fees low) and the students have three hours of English a week.

She has worked there for 20 years and has been using learning technology with learners and teachers for six years, first becoming interested through the Webheads in Action community of practice (http://webheadsinaction.org). Since then, she has developed from using ICT in her own classes to helping other teachers integrate technology into their classroom practice, training other teachers as well as being tutor of the module New Learning Environments for the Master's in ELT at Universidad de La Sabana, Colombia, where she has been teaching online since 2009. Vicky is also a materials writer, teacher trainer and is passionate about sharing her classroom practice with other teachers in Argentina and around the world, presenting at local, national and international conferences, as well as online events.

In 2008, while reviewing the way English was taught at the school, based on feedback from learners and teachers, Vicky became convinced that something needed to be changed. She 'started feeling that students, especially teens, were not being offered the best option for their learning' (Saumell, 2010). The problem was based on a number of things, but she determined that at the heart of the problem was the department's reliance on a coursebook to drive the English curriculum. There was a pressure on teachers to stick closely to the chosen coursebook, to finish it because it had been bought, but this meant teachers had little time to do other things, which they felt were more creative, fun or relevant. The coursebooks 'did not fully reflect the students' interests and culture or the language we wanted them to learn or how we wanted them to learn' and in general learners were not motivated by them, whereas the occasional projects that were undertaken 'were welcomed with enthusiasm and offered a more creative output, which resulted in increased motivation for both the teachers and the students.'

After consulting her colleagues, and ensuring consensus, the department decided to abandon using coursebooks in favour of designing their own curriculum and materials. The focus would be on project-based learning more directed at their students' interests and knowledge, in order to better engage them in the learning process. The new curriculum, for Grades 6 and above, was launched in March 2010.

The teachers design their own projects, taking into account the needs and interests of their students and the new syllabi. Vicky says this new direction embodies much of what she feels to be important about learning a language today, and is a combination of 'constructivism, connectivism, multi-literacies education for the 21st century, collaborative learning and the promotion of autonomous and lifelong learning.'

Teacher discussions were held about the role of the teacher in the classroom. Encouraging students to speak the language was made a priority, and giving them real-world, authentic tasks, often through using Web 2.0 tools, was encouraged. At the heart of this was a change from a teacher-centred paradigm to a more student-centred one. The key is giving learners more choice. Vicky says this is 'motivating for teenagers because they can express their individuality through their choices and they feel they are being taken into account and respected' (Benwell, 2010: online).

One of the major concerns when making the change was assessment. The idea was to shift 'from formal testing to continuous assessment through observation during the project development process and assessment of the final product.' (Saumell, 2010). A wiki (http://isfa.wikispaces.com) was set up to be used as a project repository and to keep a record of which projects were done with which class. This wiki was also used to provide help for teachers, with advice on implementing project-based learning and integrating technology into the curriculum, as well as links to guides and tutorials for Web 2.0 tools and any other supporting material.

Making the change proved to be a lot of hard work. Vicky discovered that it was necessary to provide constant teacher support and she set up a system to monitor progress through a system of periodic assessment so that any problems in the development of the project could be identified and solutions found to improve the program once issues had been analysed.

Vicky integrates technology on a daily basis with her own classes and she believes this has proved to be highly motivating for her learners. One of her recent projects, with three classes, of 20 learners, aged 17, has been using 'digital storytelling'. There are many different definitions of digital storytelling, but, as Robin (2006) says, 'they all revolve around the idea of combining the art of telling stories with a variety of digital multimedia, such as images, audio, and video'.

Barret (2005: 1) says that 'digital storytelling facilitates the convergence of four student-centred learning strategies: student engagement, reflection for deep learning, project-based learning, and the effective integration of technology into instruction'. According to Vicky, using digital storytelling with teenage learners is motivating because 'it gives the learners a voice as well as freedom and creativity to express themselves.' It is also a way for the learners to use English in a meaningful way on a project they have a say in, and, because it is published online, which they can share with their classmates, parents and any other interested parties.

She has used a wide range of different tools for digital storytelling. One example involved the learners creating 'Art Stories' collaboratively. For this, they worked in groups, chose a number of different famous paintings and wrote a narrative that linked the stories together. Finally, Windows Movie Maker was used to create an animated slideshow, with the learners recording a soundtrack of the story to go with the images. Another variation of this had the learners take photos of street art using digital cameras and their mobile phones and then again creating animated slideshows using Windows Movie Maker, but the soundtrack this time consisted of the learners discussing what they liked about the graffiti.

Another digital storytelling activity she did with learners involved them recreating part of the story of Shakespeare's *Midsummer Night's Dream* using various tools. Some of the learners made animated cartoon versions using animated movie-making software Zimmer Twins (www.zimmertwins.com) and recording a soundtrack. The finished work can be seen here: http://isfa.wikispaces.com/A+Midsummer+Night%C2%B4s+Dream

Apart from being for the benefit of her teachers, Vicky is happy that the school wiki (http://isfa.wikispaces.com), where work done by the learners is published, serves as a source of ideas for projects for other teachers around the world. Vicky also has a blog (http://vickysaumell.blogspot.com.es), which she updates regularly.

Digital literacy and mobile leaning

The incorporation of technology into school-wide teaching pedagogy as outlined above means that students will also develop *digital literacy skills* at the same time as acquiring a second language. It can be argued that because 'the ever expanding connectivity of digital technology is recasting social arrangements and relations in a more open, democratic and ultimately empowering manner' (Selwyn, 2013: 2), so 'teaching our students language in its traditional media is no longer enough' and 'increasingly, in everyday and professional life, people need the skills of electronic literacy.' (Healey et al., 2011: 9). Clearly, because 'learning and literacy are changing radically in the internet age' (Richardson, 2012: 15), a place must be found for digital literacy in education, but what does being *digital literate* entail?

There are many definitions of digital literacy, and what is interesting is the way the definitions have evolved to reflect the way the technology has changed. One definition, for example, states that it is 'the ability to understand and use information in multiple formats from a wide range of sources when it is presented via computers' (Gilster, 1997: 1), whereas a more recent definition expands it to '[a] person's ability to perform tasks effectively in a digital environment... Literacy includes the ability to read and interpret media, to reproduce data and images through digital manipulation, and to evaluate and apply new knowledge gained from digital environments.' (Jones-Kavalier and Flannigan, 2006: 1). One thing is certain, to be literate in the 21st century requires a more 'multimodal' (i.e. combining words, images, and sounds) approach because 'multimodality is more pervasive, diverse, and important today than ever before' (Gee and Hayes, 2011: 5).

One could also argue that digital literacy is more important now that more and more of our secondary learners come to school with mobile devices that have the potential to revolutionise what happens in the classroom.

Mobile Assisted Language Learning (MALL) is one of the most interesting emerging types of technology enhanced learning, especially now that mobile devices are carried by more and more people every day, and that the mobile phone 'has evolved from a simple voice device to a multimedia communications tool capable of downloading and uploading text, data, audio, and video – from text messages to social network updates to breaking news, the latest hit song, or the latest viral video' and that it can also 'be used as a wallet, a compass, or a television, as well as an alarm clock, calculator, address book, newspaper, and camera.' (Kelly and Minges, 2012: 11).

It is not just about the developed world, either: 'The developing world is now more mobile than the developed world' and 'the pace at which mobile phones spread globally is unmatched in the history of technology'. In 2003, 61 per cent of the world's population had access to a mobile cell signal, rising to 90 per cent by 2010. (Kelly and Minges, 2012: 9).

In secondary education this is important because 'nearly every student carries a mobile device, making it a natural choice for content delivery and even field work and data capture' (Johnson et al., 2009). This combination of available applications and a device that learners usually carry offers an opportunity to introduce learners to tools for study which could help them in later life, as well as new motivating ways of learning a language. Because of this, the implications for secondary education are dramatic.

However, in most secondary teaching situations, learners are not allowed to make use of these devices, even when, in many cases, these could be powerful aids to language learning. The final case study is an example of a teacher who has started to implement mobile learning in her classes, and how she and a colleague overcame resistance from the school and some of their colleagues.

Case Study 2.4: Mobile learning inside and outside of the classroom in Turkey

Karin Tıraşın is a secondary school teacher from Norway, who works at the private high school Sağlık ve Eğitim Vakfı (S.E.V., www.sevizmir.k12.tr) in Izmir, Turkey, where she has been a teacher for ten years.

In 2011, together with Çiğdem Uğur, a colleague at the school, she started a mobile project which shows a very innovative 'bring your own device' approach to using technology owned by learners in the classroom, with the learners making use of different functions of (mainly) smartphones (Tıraşın and Uğur, 2012).

In the first stage of the project, the learners worked in groups of three, using one phone per group. They used these phones on a field trip to a zoo. Once they were there, they used the phones as a data collection tool, taking pictures, recording videos (with or without sound), documenting the English they found in the zoo, taking special notice of any mistakes that had been made with translation.

Back at the school, each group then created a webpage using Doodle Kit (http://doodlekit.com), a free website builder. On the group websites (you can see one here: www.zoo.doodlekit.com/home) they posted their data using Web 2.0 tools such as Fotobabble (www.fotobabble.com), which allows audio to be added to images.

They also used other Web 2.0 tools, with the groups creating animated cartoons using Go Animate (http://goanimate.com); cartoon strips using Toon Doo (www.toondoo.com) and Bit Strips (www.bitstrips.com); and adding their voice to animated avatars using Voki (www.voki.com). The focus of this part of the project was to practise the language of animal idioms, and their work using these tools was also embedded on the group websites.

Use of mobiles on the field trip was successful, but not without its problems. Some of the learners' mobiles were older models, which meant there was some difficulty when transferring the photographs and videos. The battery life of the phones was a problem too. Registering for the websites in order to use the Web 2.0 tools was also time-consuming. However, Karin believes the results and the learners' feedback on the activity meant that this time was well spent.

The second part of the mobile project involved station work, with the learners working in groups of three in the classroom. There were a total of six stations, with each group using one mobile phone and spending an average of 12 minutes per station. Karin made use of a range of different smartphone applications for the activities. For many of them, the learners accessed the Web addresses (URLs) using a square barcode called a QR (quick response) code, which has become a popular way of delivering URLs to smartphones.

The learners were given worksheets and the activities consisted of:

- Listening. The learners used a barcode scanner application on their group's smartphone to scan a QR code. The information contained in the QR code led them to a recording of a poem. The learners then had to listen to the poem, complete a cloze activity and solve a puzzle hidden in the poem.
- Speaking/reading. The learners had to make a recording of a radio play script using the audio blog software VocalPost (http://vocalpost.com) and email it to their teacher.
- Writing. The learners scanned one of two QR codes, then watched a short video or cartoon. On their answer sheets they then had to write a paragraph retelling the story.

- Grammar. The learners scanned the QR code and were then sent to an online grammar quiz. After finishing this, the results were emailed to the teacher.
- Dictionary work. The learners used a dictionary app to complete one of the worksheets.
- Treasure hunt. The learners scanned another QR code, which led to a question and clue to a place in the school where they would find the next question. There was another QR code there, which had another question and clue and which led to a different location. This continued, with the learners running around the building and outside in the garden in order to answer all the questions.

Karin was able to have the learners use smartphones in this way only after determining several factors. The first of these was availability. Fortunately, at least one in three of her learners had smartphones they were happy to use in class for this activity. Access to the internet was through the school WiFi. Karin collected the mobiles at the beginning of the school day and they were added to the list of approved WiFi users by the school's IT department. She gave the phones back to the learners in the lesson and then collected them again at the end of the activity. At the end of the school day the mobile numbers were deleted from the WiFi list and the phones returned to the students.

Overcoming resistance to learners using mobile devices in class proved to be the biggest hurdle. The use of smartphones in the classroom had to be approved by the director of the school because learners are normally not allowed to bring any digital devices whatsoever onto the campus. To help her colleagues and the management of the school understand what they wanted to do, Karin and Çiğdem invited the teachers in the English Department (plus the school administration) to a Pecha Kucha presentation (i.e. 20 slides explained in 20 seconds) where they explained what they wanted to do, why they wanted to do it, and how they planned to do it. They also asked for help from their colleagues with the permissions required and helping them develop an acceptable use policy. During this meeting, the school also decided to produce a student checklist that would be consulted before publishing anything online and an internet safety learning programme for the learners (Tıraşın, 2011).

Permission was given on the condition that all parents signed permission slips agreeing to let their kids participate in the project, bring in their mobile devices, post photos/video/text of themselves on the internet, as well as use Web 2.0 tools and Facebook/YouTube whilst at school.

By presenting a very detailed plan for the project, and including the school in the planning, they overcame initial resistance. It also helped that they had carefully thought through and outlined objectives, had produced detailed lesson plans, and specified the reasons why, and how, the use of mobile devices would benefit the learning process.

Conclusion

There are a number of different conclusions that can be drawn from the case studies presented here:

- Using technology to enhance language learning, as Jewell mentions 'allows for increased learner autonomy and control, providing a more student-centred pedagogy' with learners at the centre of the learning process and 'more actively engaged in their learning than in traditional direct instruction methods' (Jewell, 2006: 178).

- Learning technologies are becoming more normalised in language classrooms, as Bax (2003) predicted, and teachers are beginning to 'stop seeing them as technologies and start seeing them as tools which suit some purpose and not others' (Pegrum, 2009: 23).

- Many teachers are self-directing their own learning when it comes to using technology, and are increasingly turning to online communities of practice, taking courses and building their own PLNs to act as a support system to help with the implementation of learning technology.

Finally, encouraging the use of educational technology in secondary language education has wider implications. As Dooly (2008: 23) mentions, '[i]f we are truly interested in preparing our students to be responsible citizens in an increasingly technologically advanced society, then our way of teaching our students must reflect this.'

References

Balanskat, A, Blamire, R and Stella, K (2006) *The ICT Impact Report: A review of studies of ICT impact on schools in Europe.* European Schoolnet. Available online at: http://ec.europa.eu/education/pdf/doc254_en.pdf

Barnes, LL (1989) Why is there a text in this class: Classroom teachers' (re)views of computer-assisted composition textbooks. *Computers and Composition* 7/1: 27–36.

Barret, H (2005) *Researching and evaluating digital storytelling as a deep learning tool Reflect round table.* Available online at: http://electronicportfolios.com/portfolios/SITEStorytelling2006.pdf

Bax, S (2003) CALL – past, present and future. *System* 31/1: 13–28.

Bax, S (2011) Normalisation revisited: The effective use of technology in language education. *International Journal of Computer Assisted Language Learning and Teaching* 1/2: 1–15.

Becta (2004) *Research report: Impact2: Pupils' and teachers' perceptions of ICT in the home, school and community.* Available online at: http://dera.ioe.ac.uk/1573/

Benwell, T (2010) *Vicky Saumell expands on project based learning.* Teflnet. Available online at: http://edition.tefl.net/articles/interviews/vicky-saumell

Bossa, M, Stevens, V and Tawel, A (2012) *Ayat Al-Tawel and Maria Bossa discuss their students' collaborations between Egypt and Argentina Learning2gether podcast.* Available online at: http://learning2gether.net/2011/06/12/ayat-al-tawel-and-maria-bossa-discuss-their-s/

Byram, M and Fleming, M (1998) *Language learning in intercultural perspective.* Cambridge: Cambridge University Press.

Chapelle, C (2001) *Computer applications in Second Language Acquisition.* Cambridge: Cambridge University Press.

Corbett, J (2010) *Intercultural language activities.* Cambridge: Cambridge University Press.

Couros, A (2008) *What is a PLN? Or, PLE vs. PLN?'* Open Thinking. Available online at: http://educationaltechnology.ca/couros/1156

Delcloque, P (2000) *History of CALL.* Available online at: www.history-of-call.org/

Dooly, M (ed) (2008) *Telecollaborative language learning. A guidebook to moderating intercultural collaboration online.* Bern: Peter Lang.

Downes, S (2007) 'Learning Networks in Practice' in Ley, DE (ed) *Emerging technologies for learning volume 2. London, BECTA.* Available online at: http://dera.ioe.ac.uk/1502/

Dudeney, G and Hockly, N (2007) *How to teach English with technology.* Harlow: Pearson Longman.

Empirica (2006) Benchmarking access and use of ICT in European schools. *Empirica,* European Union. Available online at: http://ec.europa.eu/information_society/eeurope/i2010/docs/studies/final_report_3.pdf

European Commission (2012) Digital literacy policies. *Digital Agenda for Europe.* Available online at: http://ec.europa.eu/digital-agenda

Garcia Murillo, M (2003) Patchwork adoption of ICTs in Latin America. *The Electronic Journal on Information Systems in Developing Countries* 15/1. Available online at: www.ejisdc.org/ojs2/index.php/ejisdc/article/viewFile/91/91

Gee, JP and Hayes, R (2011) *Language and learning in the digital age.* London: Routledge.

Gilster, P (1997) *Digital literacy.* New York: Wiley.

Guth, S and Helm, F (eds) (2010) *Telecollaboration 2.0: Language, literacies, and intercultural learning in the 21st century.* New York, NY: Peter Lang.

Healey, D, Smith, EH, Hubbard, P, Ioannou-Georgiou, S, Kessler, G and Ware, P (2011) *TESOL technology standards.* Alexandria: TESOL.

Higgins, J (1991) Fuel for learning: the neglected element of textbooks and CALL. *CAELL Journal* 2/2: 3–7.

Hoffman, R (1996) 'Computer networks: Webs of communication for language teaching', in Pennington, MC (ed) *The Power of CALL*. Houston, TX: Athelstan.

Ilomäki, L (2008) *The effects of ICT on school: teachers' and students' perspectives.* Doctoral dissertation. Department of Teacher Education: Annales Universitatis Turkuensis. Available online at: www.doria.fi/bitstream/handle/10024/42311/B314.pdf

Jewell, M (2006) 'Real-world contexts, skills and service learning for secondary school language learners', in Hanson-Smith, E and Rilling, S (eds) *Learning languages through technology.* Alexandria, VA: TESOL.

Johnson, L, Levine, A, Smith, R and Smythe, T (2009) *The 2009 horizon report: K-12 Edition.* Austin, Texas: The New Media Consortium.

Jones-Kavalier, BR and Flannigan, SL (2006) *Connecting the digital dots: Literacy of the 21st Century.* Available online at: http://connect.educause.edu/Library/EDUCAUSE+Quarterly/ConnectingtheDigitalDotsL/39969

Kelly, T and Minges, M (2012) *Maximizing mobile, information and communications for development.* The World Bank. Available online at: www.worldbank.org/ict/IC4D2012

Kemmis, S, Atkin, R, and Wright, E (1977) *How do students learn? Working papers on computer assisted language learning.* Uncal Evaluation Studies, Norwich: University of East Anglia.

Lai, H-M and Chen, C-P (2011) Factors influencing secondary school teachers' adoption of teaching blogs. *Computers and Education,* 56/4: 948–960.

Lave, J and Wenger, EC (1991) *Situated learning: Legitimate peripheral participation.* New York: Cambridge University Press.

Levy, M (1997) *Computer-Assisted Language Learning.* Oxford: Clarendon.

Macaro, E, Handley, Z and Walter, C (2012) A systematic review of CALL in English as a second language: Focus on primary and secondary education. *Language Teaching* 45/1: 1–43.

Motteram, G and Stanley, G (2011) Web 2.0 and the normalisation of CALL. *International Journal of Computer Assisted Language Learning and Teaching* 1/2: i–iv.

Office of Educational Technology (2010) National educational technology plan. *Office of Education,* US Department of Education. Available online at: www.ed.gov/edblogs/technology/netp-2010

Pegrum, M (2009) *From blogs to bombs.* Crawley: UWA Publishing.

Pennington, MC (1996) *The power of CALL.* Houston: Athelstan.

Perkins, A (2002) 'Continuing professional development: Sojourn or Odyssey?' in Edge, J (ed) *Continuing Professional Development: Some of our Perspectives.* Whitstable, UK: IATEFL Publications.

Richardson, W (2012) *Why school?* New York: TED Conferences.

Robin, B (2006) *The educational uses of digital storytelling.* Proceedings of the Society for Information Technology and Teacher Education International Conference 2006 (pp. 709–716). Chesapeake, VA: AACE. Available online at: http://faculty.coe.uh.edu/brobin/homepage/Educational-Uses-DS.pdf

Samuel, RJ and Zitun, AB (2007) Do teachers have adequate ICT resources and the right ICT skills in integrating ICT tools in the teaching and learning of English in Malaysian schools? *The Electronic Journal on Information Systems in Developing Countries* 29/2.

Saumell, V (2010) Life after course books. *Ken Wilson's blog.* Available online at: http://kenwilsonelt.wordpress.com/2010/06/01/guest-post-18-vicky-saumell-on-life-after-course-books/

Selwyn, N (2013) *Education in a digital world: Global perspectives on technology and education.* London: Routledge.

Slavin, RE (1989) Research on co-operative learning: An international perspective. *Scandinavian Journal of Educational Research* 33/4: 231–243.

Stannard, R (2006) The spelling mistake: Scene one, take one. *The Times Higher Education.* Available online at: www.timeshighereducation.co.uk/story.asp?storycode=207117

Stevens, V (2004) 'Webhead Communities: Writing Tasks Interleaved with Synchronous Online Communication and Web Page Development', in Leaver, BL and Willis, JG (eds) (2004).

Stockwell, G (2007) A review of technology choice for teaching language skills and areas in the CALL literature. *ReCALL* 19/2: 105–120. European Association for Computer Assisted Language Learning. Available online at: www.f.waseda.jp/gstock/Stockwell_ReCALL_2007.pdf

Swain, M (1985) 'Communicative competence: Some roles of comprehensible input and output in its development', in Gass, S and Madden, C (eds) *Input in second language acquisition.* Rowley, MA: Newbury House.

Tawel, A (2012) *Comments on blogpost: The Complete Educators Guide to Using Skype Effectively in the Classroom.* Available online at: http://theedublogger.com/2011/04/03/the-complete-educators-guide-to-using-skype-effectively-in-the-classroom/

Tella, A, Toyobo, OM, Adika, LO and Adeyinka, AA (2007) An assessment of secondary school teachers uses of ICT: implications for further development of ICT use in Nigerian secondary schools. *Turkish Online Journal of Educational Technology* 6/3. Available online at: www.tojet.net/articles/v6i3/631.pdf

Thomas, M (ed) (2009) *Handbook of research on Web 2.0 and second language learning.* Hershey, PA: IGI Global.

Thorne, SL and Black, RW (2007) Language and literacy development in computer-mediated contexts and communities. *Annual Review of Applied Linguistics* 27: 133–160.

Tıraşın, K (2011) *Cellphones in the classroom, first babysteps taken!* Available online at: http://coffeeaddict.edublogs.org/2011/06/23/cellphones-in-the-classroom-first-babysteps-taken

Tıraşın, K and Uğur, C (2012) *Smartphones in grade 8: hot or not.* Presentation given at IATEFL conference in Glasgow, UK. Available online at: http://iatefl.britishcouncil.org/2012/sessions/2012-03-22/mobile-phones-grade-8-hot-or-not

Trucano, M (2012) 'Information and communication technologies', in Petrinos, HA (ed) *Strengthening Education Quality in East Asia: System Assessment and Benchmarking for Education Results.* SABER/UNESCO/The World Bank. Available online at: http://doc.iiep.unesco.org/cgi-bin/wwwi32.exe/%5Bin=epidoc1.in%5D/?t2000=031000/(100)

UNESCO (1997) *International Standard Classification of Education (ISCED).* Available online at: www.unesco.org/education/information/nfsunesco/doc/isced_1997.htm

Vygotsky, LS (1978) *Mind in society: The development of higher psychology process.* Cambridge, MA: Harvard University Press. (Originally published in 1930.)

Technology and adult language teaching

3

Technology and adult language teaching

Diane Slaouti, Zeynep Onat-Stelma and Gary Motteram

This chapter situates its discussion in adult learner settings and draws on the experiences and beliefs of three practitioners, Susan, Vida and Ivana, who represent some of the specific contexts in which adult language learning takes place. We firstly introduce them to you through vignettes of practice, in the hope that you will start this chapter with a mind's eye picture of a specific instance of their teaching. As we then move on to reflect on the nature of the adult learner, the specific contexts of learning, and the interface between technology and language learning, our teachers will provide insights into how this is enacted in their particular settings.

Case Study 3.1: Susan

Susan is an ESOL teacher (English to Speakers of Other Languages) in a UK further education context. With a staff of six full-time teachers, her department caters for about 300 adult learners, between 18 and 50 years of age. Class sizes are relatively small with, on average, 12 learners, from beginner (A1) to advanced (C1), mainly from Eastern Europe and the Indian subcontinent, although this profile tends to vary as migrant populations also change.

A view of Susan's classroom

Susan has a two-hour class with her intermediate level group of ESOL learners, who are all sitting in front of individual laptops allocated for their use in class. Headsets and microphones are placed next to the laptops. There is an interactive whiteboard, linked to Susan's machine, and at the start of the lesson, the opening slide of a PowerPoint file is displayed on it. Susan explains the aim of the day's lesson, which is to develop learners' confidence in being able to use reported speech. She briefly recaps the distinction between reported and direct speech, tapping the board to move between PowerPoint slides. The learners then turn to their own laptops and Susan asks them to access her ESOL Level One course area in her VLE, Moodle. They find some review tasks, created using Hot Potatoes software, which allows them to practise reported speech forms. She walks around the room, picking up on anyone who seems to be faltering with any of the tasks, and then turns their attention back to the interactive whiteboard. She has located some pictures of the Borneo jungle through a Google images search, and these are now displayed to the group. She sets the scene for a report on a plane crash in the jungle ten years ago, from which there were survivors. She organises the learners into pairs and each chooses the role of either reporter or survivor. The interview activity is supported by role cards from the coursebook, *Cutting Edge* (CUP), which learners take a few minutes to look at, and is to be recorded using the audio application, Audacity. Susan reminds them how to use this, and pairs get to work on conducting their interviews in different corners of the room. Once finished, Susan explains that they now need to create a written report for their newspapers. Learners listen to their recordings intently, switching between Audacity and Word, correcting what they hear themselves say, talking about their written text, referring from time to time to their handheld dictionaries. Susan observes how their engagement is carried through to the final display of the texts. She's pleased with the lesson because, she comments, the learners did all the work! The simple addition of the digitally recorded interviews has given a familiar task a new dimension, drawing all of them into the different language and skills development stages; it has done a lot for their IT confidence too.

Case Study 3.2: Vida

A view of Vida's classroom

Vida teaches English to Sociology students in the Faculty of Social Sciences at a university in Slovenia. Language work largely takes an EAP/ESP direction. Her classes, frequently numbering 40–50, are made up of learners generally aged between 18 and 25. When they enter the university, many have completed examinations at intermediate (B1) level, but Vida describes them as quite a mixture from elementary (A2) to advanced level (B2/C1).

Vida's learners, studying English for sociology, have been busy working on problem-based learning (PBL) enquiries for nearly six weeks. They now sit around the classroom in their working groups, not physically constrained by the fixed furniture organised in rows from front to back. They are looking at an animated final presentation, which is the outcome of one of the enquiries. This has been created using Movie Maker (Microsoft), and is projected on a central screen from the single laptop that Vida has brought in. Each group presents on their topic: the smoking ban in Slovenia; learning styles; problems of waste; alternative medicine, amongst others. The fairly time-limited presentations in this lesson belie the amount of activity which has led to this point; much of that is to be seen in Vida's PBL wiki, in which each group has occupied their space, adding to the PBL content generated by others in her different classes. A skim through a framing timetable reveals the different stages of the enquiry: forming groups and assigning roles; agreeing ground rules, including taking responsibility and commitment to deadlines; developing skills such as how to lead and minute group meetings, writing research questions to focus their enquiry; researching in different media; generating a collaborative report and this final presentation to their peers; peer assessment. Teamwork has been the essence both within and outside the classroom setting and that teamwork is in plentiful evidence in a busy wiki that has been the locus of attention since the beginning of the project. It is now brimming with records of early decisions about roles (leader, secretary, timekeeper, reporter), responsibilities and topic, minutes of meetings, sources consulted, summaries, all seen in terms of final product and process through the wiki editing functions. The single computer and screen seems not to have limited that sense of teamwork in the classroom. Vida has variously used it during the weeks to orchestrate whole-class collaboration on specific skills development (e.g. presentation guidance); whole-class support as each group take turns in editing their wiki content, drawing on the advice of their teacher and colleagues; and as today, learning from peers as they bring their projects to a close.

Case Study 3.3: Ivana

Ivana has a varied teaching portfolio in a State university in the Czech Republic. In any one week she may find herself teaching Business English in the Faculty of Economics; helping develop the lexical confidence of her students in the Technical Faculties (machinery, textiles, mechatronics); teaching general English to either of these or to a further group of 'third age' learners, who are 50 and over, the oldest of whom is currently 89. Levels are equally varied, between elementary (A2) and advanced (C2).

A view of Ivana's classroom

Ivana is with her intermediate group (Level B2) of 22 learners who study English as part of their economics degrees. They sit behind ranks of tables with the teacher positioned in the left-hand corner of the room, where there is a computer linked to a data projector hanging from the ceiling, and a cassette player. On the walls around the room are mostly black and white printouts of photos depicting aspects of Irish tourism and culture ('although the shamrock needed to look a little bit green, so I coloured that', she explains), a map of Ireland, various vocabulary items, and definitions. Apart from the vocabulary cards, the resources have been downloaded and printed from Google image and definitions searches. Along with these visual realia, Ivana has gathered together a range of print and online resources for her lesson. She has sought out a YouTube clip of Irish music; Irish limericks written by children, from www.greatwriting.co.uk; a text on St Patrick's day from the British Council/CUP Learn English materials, www.britishcouncil.org/learnenglish-central-magazine-st-patrick.htm, which she had located through email contact from one of the publisher networks she subscribes to. Links to all of these are provided in a class Moodle space, although Ivana has produced and printed her own comprehension questions to accompany the St Patrick's Day text. The limericks are also copied with some adaptations as she observes that the originals either contained mistakes made by the young writers, or there were some words which she judged too difficult for her learners. Over a 90-minute period, learners move through various activities, sometimes sitting in pairs or groups, sometimes moving to the realia on the wall or to the computer as they need to view content or take centre stage. Two students begin by giving presentations on an economics-related topic as directed by their subject teacher, and peers and Ivana give advice on language and delivery. A grammar review using the task she has created and uploaded to Moodle, and viewed via the data projector is followed by a listening and response task from the coursebook, Business Objectives (OUP). The class then turns their attention to the realia on the classroom walls. The vocabulary, some of which features in the St Patrick's Day text, is rehearsed and learners move around matching definitions and pictures. Experiences and expectations of a holiday to Ireland are shared before the text is projected onto the screen. The learners, divided into two groups, receive different sets of questions.

Ivana points out the interactive annotations in the onscreen text that allow for key vocabulary to be checked against the Cambridge online dictionary. Learners then receive a limerick each, and with the help of a hard copy English-Czech dictionary or the Cambridge online dictionary linked from Moodle, which they can use as they wish, they work together to understand the content and structure, and then write their own limericks. In the background the YouTube clip of Irish music is playing. 'It adds authenticity to the lesson, and "touches" the musical intelligence in my students', Ivana enthuses. The lesson finishes with Ivana telling her learners she will post their limericks in Moodle for all to read, and agreeing which resources her learners would like to see left there for future practice.

The adult learner

In 1973 Malcolm Knowles published a seminal work exploring the term andragogy, defined simply as the 'art and science of helping adults learn' (Knowles, 1980: 43) and in his later publication (Knowles et al., 2011) as 'the science of understanding (theory) and supporting (practice) lifelong and lifewide education of adults,' a refinement that elevates the dimensions of theory and practice relevant to this discussion. This work identified some central premises of the adult learner that have gone on to influence both understandings of formal and informal learning, and of teaching practice in different areas. The first, and most defining, of these is that what adults bring to any learning context are individual experiences of life, of the world, and of prior learning. This understanding may indeed appear as a truism to readers who are possibly adult learners themselves, and was certainly not a new observation in 1973. In the most recently edited update on Knowles' original work, Knowles et al. (2011) take us back to Lindeman, writing in 1926, who, himself influenced by the thinking of John Dewey, argued that the starting point of adult learning is the learner and their reality:

> Every adult person finds himself in specific situations with respect to his work, his recreation, his family life, his community life – situations which call for adjustments [...] Subject matter is brought into the situation, is put to work, when needed.

(Lindeman, 1926 in Knowles et al., 2011: 36).

The identity of our adult language learners can be defined in relation to all of these domains, and across first and second language cultural settings (Belz, 2002), which we may not always either be aware of, or actively acknowledge. The role of experience in learning is not simply a point of reference, however. It is considered central by various adult educators and in itself suggests adult learning is an essentially problem-oriented endeavour that the experiential both informs, and at the same time is a focus of activity. Kolb (1984), whose contribution to understanding of the role of the experiential in learning is recognised, argues that it 'is the process whereby knowledge is created through the transformation of experience' and reflection is instrumental in that transformation (Schön, 1983; Boud et al., 1985). Adult learners profit from being able to relate material and tasks to prior and current experience, but also through opportunities for new, lived experiences through which they can reflect and act on implications for them as individuals (Tennant and Pogson, 1995). What is key is the fact that 'models of adult learning developed from within adult education move beyond examinations of learning as a decontextualised process to address questions relating to the meanings of, and motivations for, learning in people's lives' (Barton and Trusting, 2003: 32).

Deriving from this, adults may also be assumed to be goal-oriented in their language learning, and Mezirow (1997: 8) notes that 'often, adult learners' immediate focus is on practical, short-term objectives'. These may be to enter higher education through preparation for examinations such as IELTS or TOEFL; to access study in higher education through pre- or in-sessional EAP or ESP courses; for employment reasons where English is an international language of business communication; or to integrate into a new cultural setting through ESOL classes such as Susan's. Adults may also have less academic or workplace orientations such as leisure or travel.

We must be careful not to make too many assumptions that all adult language learners are equally purposeful and directed, however. Merriam (2001) describes how understanding of andragogy has modified over time to take better account of the contexts of adult learning, and the specific characteristics of the adult learner, and their own learning background. Motivations may indeed be varied. Some will be in situations such as those in which Ivana and Vida work, where English is a component of a university course, and for some of these learners, the goal may simply be to pass an exam imposed by an institution, though this focus is no less immediate than more intrinsically motivated objectives. There may, therefore, be both intrinsic and extrinsic impetuses, impacting on what happens in the language classroom and indeed, on how self-directed an adult learner is prepared to be. Learning to pass an exam may result in much less self-direction than in the adult looking to be able to study in an English-speaking country or attend an English-speaking conference. Expectations of learner and teacher roles are also key. As Cotterall (1995: 196–197) observes, 'all behaviour is governed by beliefs and experience'. In her exploration of factors impacting on adult learner readiness for autonomy, the role of the teacher is ranked highest with 'diagnosing difficulties, allocating time, establishing the purpose of activities' characterising many learners' perceptions. This, of course, has implications for teacher practice in general, and for the ways in which technology might be harnessed in different settings.

We must also remember that, on the whole, language learning is a relatively small part of multi-faceted adult lives. Although Ivana and Vida's university-based language learners may be in full-time education, such activity is squeezed across timetables to support main subject studies. Susan's ESOL learners are with her for a few more hours a week, but they are often people with families, a new social setting to negotiate and a challenging life beyond the classroom door. The 'social and cultural situatedness' (Kern, 2006: 186) of each of these scenarios is important. As a consequence, as Smith and Strong (2009: 2) suggest, adult learners 'usually require immediate value and relevance from their studies, and they often learn best when they are engaged in developing their own learning objectives'.

Adult learners may, therefore, have developed very strong perceptions of what works for them, and how they want to learn. With respect to integration of technology this can act as a powerful filter. Those preferences may have developed through positive or negative learning experiences; they may be culturally situated; they are grounds for negotiation to help the learner towards the most impactful learning. Oxford and Crookall (1989) review a number of studies into language learning strategy use amongst adult learners and exemplify by reporting on a study by Sutter (1987) with refugees learning Danish as a second language, whose initial strategy preferences they describe as being 'related to ethnic and personal biases'. They recount teachers negotiating new strategies to make the most of the social learning setting they found themselves in, for instance, 'students' desire to make word lists (their preferred strategy) was channelled into the creation of a dictionary, which was done co-operatively, a camouflaged social strategy that facilitated the preferred technique and was therefore non-threatening' (Oxford and Crookall, 1989: 413). More recently, Kennedy (2002: 430) explores cultural expectations in relation to the Chinese learner in Hong Kong and observes that whilst understanding prior learning can empower the language teacher, 'Hong Kong adult learners are receptive to new modes of learning and go on to adopt learning styles quite different from those they deployed in school'. He describes a stereotypical picture held by teachers of 'rote learning' preferences of the adult Hong Kong learner, not borne out in practice. Supported by research by Tang and Biggs (1996), who reported pragmatic use of schoolchildren's strategies relevant to the exams which drove their academic trajectory, Kennedy observes that this did not equate with a preferred learning style that carried over into adult learning; nor did it mean that adult learners would not establish more purposeful strategies in a new learning setting. These very situated studies serve to remind us that 'a learning approach must not be confused, as it often is, with the context-independent learning style' (Tang and Biggs, 1996: 165; in Kennedy, 2002: 438).

This brings us to a final premise of andragogy and that is the unique relationship between learner and teacher. In recognising the adult with all they bring to the learning context, he or she should 'feel accepted, respected, and supported' (Knowles, 1980: 47). Knowles talks of 'a spirit of mutuality between teachers and students as joint inquirers'. As our teachers explore technology in use with their learners, there is a strong sense of mutual engagement, responding to needs, seeking feedback on what works, and finding ways round apparent barriers.

Contexts of learning

To summarise, in the words of Burns (1995: 233):

> By adulthood people are self-directing. This is the concept that lies at the heart of andragogy ... andragogy is therefore student-centred, experience-based, problem-oriented and collaborative very much in the spirit of the humanist approach to learning and education ... the whole educational activity turns on the student.

These 'principles' of andragogy are useful reminders of what defines our adult learners, but how they play out for different learners in specific settings is various. As Merriam (2001: 6) points out, over time this resulted in 'andragogy being defined more by the learning situation than by the learner'. This chimes with our current understandings of the socio-cultural dimension of language learning and a pedagogy of particularity (Kumaravadivelu, 2001: 538) which proposes that for 'language pedagogy to be relevant, it must be sensitive to a particular group of teachers teaching a particular group of learners pursuing a particular set of goals within a particular institutional context embedded in a particular socio-cultural milieu'. This takes nothing away from an awareness of the adult learner and all that they bring to the learning table, but applies a layer of contextual sensitivity that helps us to understand the decisions our case teachers take in their use of technology.

Teachers of adult learners reading this chapter may find themselves in a higher or further education setting, a private language school which may be a local or international organisation, or a franchise; they may be in a business or industrial setting, dealing with learners in small groups or one-to-one teaching scenarios; they may be teaching outside a formal institutional setting from their homes or the homes of their learners. These settings are key drivers in many ways. Exploring technology use in formal adult learning, Mumtaz (2001) identifies how institutional perspectives on the role of technology in particular subject teaching are influential in teacher decision-making. Institutional drivers might mean that teachers find themselves able to be more or less autonomous in their decision-making around approach, materials and means, including use of technology.

This might be immediately observable in technology access, and our three cases illustrate a range. Variations may be explained by the type of institution in which a teacher works, often seen in differences between the public and privately-funded. Learners and teachers may be engaging with very high-tech environments, possibly described as technology-supported. Susan, for example, describes the institutional aspirations and government expectations surrounding ICT use for learning, and this is borne out in interactive whiteboards in her classrooms, relatively easy access to mobile recording devices, and the facility to download software such as Audacity, should she need it.

Susan describes an institution that believes that technology should be used for language teaching. It is perhaps a context which is characterised by Selwyn et al.'s (2006: 13) observation of the 'technologification' of adult learning in the UK further education setting, influenced by governmental pressures through the inspection systems (OFSTED), as technology use is looked for during their audits. As Susan says:

> If you're not using it, they want to know why. And there are targets that this Department has got to reach, this level of IT by such a year and the part-time courses have to be shown to be using the VLE for assessment purposes.

For Susan, the VLE is Moodle and she recognises that strong institutional ambitions to integrate technology have also influenced how she uses this with her part-time adult learners.

> Because we have to use the technology, it is changing the way that we teach. So we have to have a blended learning approach; they want to see us using it outside the class time as well as for homework, so I suppose it's changing the way we think in that respect. I set things via the VLE for people to do their homework.

Vida references her institution's commitment to the integration of technology into language teaching to the European Bologna reforms, and although she says the response has been mixed across state and private institutions in Slovenia, and across faculties in her own institution, she identifies how universities are responding to a vision of learner-driven technology use. On the ground, how the institution provides the infrastructure for such aspirations is developing. Although there are lab facilities, for example, Vida never uses these for her own language classes as they remain largely within the domain of courses such as Informatics. However, this does not stop Vida using limited resources in her classroom to set conditions for collaborative, problem-based learning, making the most of what a wiki offers.

Ivana describes an institution which talks positively about the use of technology, and also identifies how this does not mean wide-ranging or consistent access to facilities. On a weekly basis she finds herself moving between a room with a single computer, internet access and projection screen, and video playback for some classes; a second room with interactive whiteboard and projection, where she may use DVDs or CD ROMs with a beamer[3]; a regular classroom, where she uses a portable recorder and a blackboard. The 'mobility' of the teacher across settings may be a theme familiar to many teachers of adults. Like Susan and Vida, though, Ivana makes use of the 'virtual classroom' as a blended dimension bridging between in-class activity and the extended locus of learning which may be individual or group oriented.

The 'particularities' of the situation are important to the teacher as they pursue the goal of lesson planning. Lack of access to significant numbers of computers for language learning activities might, for example, be seen as constraining to ambitions to integrate technology. However, social tools such as wikis, and virtual learning environments such as Moodle allow our teachers to provide flexible access to their adult learners, whatever the physical constraints of the face-to-face learning context and whatever the restrictions in the available time. The specific use of these opportunities reflects not only the particularities of learner needs in the three contexts, but also the beliefs the three teachers hold about language learning and about the role technology can play for them and their adult learners.

Extending and distributing adult learning

So integration is a key theme, and beliefs about the relationship between what happens within and beyond the classroom setting suggest an increasingly seamless expansion of the context of learning. Tasks using specific tools may be demonstrated inside the classroom on single computers and projection; tasks may be started within the classroom for group or individual completion beyond; most make use of an online environment to provide the home base for this extended scenario.

The opportunities to extend contexts of learning afforded by technology allow Vida to make decisions about how she will take advantage of her face-to-face time with her learners. She has made conscious decisions to use technology in ways that allow her to apportion time to different activities in different learning spaces.

---

[3] Often referred to as an LCD projector.

Most important to her is to be able to attend to speaking skills work in a face-to-face setting, leaving the technology to mediate other language activities.

> My goal was to free up some time in class for the discussion in class, so my classes are much less grammar practice etc. They are much more dedicated to speaking so that I can have more time for speaking in class – face-to-face speaking. The technology allows me to get extra time for that.

Her webpages and blog provide out-of-class support for online reading and listening, grammar and vocabulary development; her wiki scaffolds collaborative learning; learners use various tools to prepare their work for presentation.

Ivana describes a rather more varied provision, which changes even between her 'Tuesday and Thursday classes'. She has set up a Moodle space for her classes and uses this 'on Thursdays' when she has one computer with projection. Her vignette describes one such class. She creates specific activities (e.g. language practice tasks and games), which learners can engage in around the screen. There is no access on Tuesday; she mainly uses DVD and the beamer technology, or takes along her own laptop, largely to do audio-based work. However, Ivana also uses Moodle to blend her teaching activities with available opportunities, whatever the classroom setting. Despite their busy academic timetable, she describes how her learners continue to use the Moodle content out of class time, mostly for independent rather than any collaborative work.

Teachers harnessing technology for adult learners: beliefs and decisions

Each teacher talks about technology allowing them to fill some particular 'needs gap'. This is variously described in terms of opportunities, for Ivana to establish a self-access resource, for Susan to provide for individualised or differentiated tasks, and for Vida to provide for learner-centred collaboration. There are many ways to respond to such perceived needs, and specific technology choice relates to context, understandings of the adult learner and to the teachers' own beliefs about language learning.

As her lesson vignette illustrates, central to Ivana's practice with technology is an eclectic approach to assembling and adapting resources, as she is able. Published materials are important to her. Identifying notable online materials from publishers, she is impressed by those that provide both flexibility and, in particular, the option to create interactive tasks:

> Resources for Business Objectives (OUP) and New English File (OUP), for example, provide a link to a place where the texts from the textbook can be changed into gapped exercises… For other books this is not provided and it is a pity.

When Ivana builds lessons around these varied resources, she draws on them rather like a coursebook, sequencing and orchestrating moves in plenary, pair and group focused activity. Although specific resources are described as filling gaps such as cultural knowledge or providing further targeted practice, what her learners find there has a comforting familiarity.

Ivana has a keen sense of the rich repository of resources that is available to her. Her aspirations for CD-ROM or web-delivered material are to provide differentiated, interactive tasks for groups of learners, but she adds, they need to provide a 'framework for practice'. This sense of 'control' is not described in any behaviourist paradigm, but emerges from an awareness of a sense of possible 'chaos' that trying to work with limitless resources can engender. In sharing weekly lesson accounts, Ivana describes how she uses Moodle to manage all of these resources for her learners both in-class and beyond. The teacher-created tasks based on resources from the internet, which we see in her vignette, serve in-class and directed homework activity which her learners need in their busy lives, but also build an ever-developing self-access resource. Her learners invariably log on to find new content on a daily basis, and are motivated by these opportunities for 'chunks of learning'. This is also a negotiated process. Interestingly, her vignette describes how she negotiates with her learners what will be left in Moodle for future reference and what can be 'taken down' to 'tidy up' the learning space.

Susan's use of technology is shaped by her understanding of her adult learners within an ESOL setting, negotiating formal language learning and life beyond the classroom. Her views on technology for language learning are clear:

> It's got to be appropriate and it's got to be relevant to my students, so it's not just a case of I like it. I like to use it at the right time.

Timeliness is an important notion. ESOL learners come from varied learning backgrounds and expectations of teacher role may be equally varied. Susan's vignette describes her using the interactive whiteboard to guide her learners through language review and practice, based on coursebook content, but she also talks about concerns to nurture more constructivist learning, that she believes needs to be gradually scaffolded as her learners move through levels of competence:

> I suppose that whole presentation and practice, those approaches, we don't really tend to focus on those using technology these days. There's a lot more self-discovery, we send them out to find things and then bring them back.

She frequently uses Powerpoint on the interactive whiteboard, as documented in her vignette. However, this is not described purely as a presentational device. It serves multiple roles:

> For structuring my class, they can work through it; feedback on any activities, so we are not having to write it on the board – quite fast feedback that way. Also a resource for those that are absent. The whole PowerPoint is printed off and if someone wasn't in class, I can hand them that. They've got the exercises, they've got the answers, they've got pretty much everything that was done if I structured my class around the use of it.

There is a sense of her using different technologies to give her learners a sense of direction, but she is mindful that tools such as PowerPoint and indeed the interactive whiteboard can tip the balance towards teacher-centred focus, and she emphasises the opportunities for learners to come to the board and interact with the content.

Within this picture, Susan is very aware of the nature of her learners, who come with so many different levels of both language and ICT skills. She has to provide opportunities for differentiation and scaffolding to help them map a path through their learning trajectories, and this scaffolding derives not just from her, but from their co-learners. Describing how she developed her approach to the listening task which figures in her vignette, she observes:

> The reported speech revision class was lots of fun and very productive. Using the headphone splitters allowed me to pair up weaker and stronger students making the activity meaningful to all of them. It also enhanced the learning experience as they had to discuss answers before selecting them on screen. Recording the discussion and saving it to the VLE allowed students to listen to themselves following the discussion and also provided the stimulus for a piece of writing using reported speech.

Like Ivana, providing motivating and clearly organised learning materials for her adult learners is central. Her perceptions of the Skills for Life materials, produced by the Department for Education and Science, around which she is to base her ESOL teaching, are 'so dry that they need supplementing'. She too refers to a collection of artefacts (digital and print) that can be re-purposed to cater for her specific learners, and terms these 'electronic resource packs'. She looks to the web for opportunities to download realia, as seen in her vignette, or find general texts and links to support resources such as online dictionaries, which learners use frequently. Specific practice content comes from publishers and organisations she judges provide for the needs of the ESOL learner: One Stop English (www.onestopenglish.com/), BBC Learning (www.bbc.co.uk/learning/), BBC Skills Wise (www.bbc.co.uk/skillswise/), A4esl (http://a4esl.org/), manythings.org (www.manythings.org/). Within her electronic resource pack, she creates a lot of her own materials, including language exercises using Hot Potatoes, which are delivered via the VLE.

Susan is also aware of the need to act as custodian of such learning materials, organising pathways so that technology does not get in the way of learning, especially for more personalised, independent access. This attention to scaffolding clear learning events is also witnessed in her rationale for choosing, creating and using specific materials and tools. In Moodle, she appreciates the simplicity of the interface for her learners; on some published materials she observes:

> [...] if you don't design your own, some of them are very cluttered and there's too much going on and so they kind of get lost as soon as they get on and don't follow it too easily I don't think.

Vida is very aware of the English for Specific Purposes context in which her learners need to use their language. This requires her not only to provide opportunities for them to develop the familiarity with specific language to deal with content, but also to put that language to use in the types of enquiry-oriented activity through which the subject is taught. Vida's resource pack involves her compiling materials relevant to her specific learners in a book format: English for Sociology Students 1 and 2. These materials consist of tasks assembled around authentic texts that she has collected. The various units provide vocabulary, grammar and language skills practice.

Vida supplements these with further online texts and, very frequently, with podcasts/vodcasts. She never uses published CD/DVD materials mainly because of a lack of such materials in the specific subject area of sociology; online resources allow her to plug those gaps and she lists examples: recorded interviews and transcripts with famous sociologists, politicians etc. at Berkeley University, http://globetrotter.berkeley.edu/conversations/; vodcasts of talks on various themes from TED – Ideas Worth Spreading, www.ted.com/; online concordancers e.g. www.webcorp.org.uk/; spreadsheets from Social Trends, http://data.gov.uk/dataset/social_trends

Mindful of how her learners will need to be able to apply their language in research-oriented activity, but also of the challenge of dealing with large classes, Vida has developed her use of a wiki as a home base for collaborative, problem-based learning. Moreover, with this being seen as a natural locus of collaborative activity by her learners away from the classroom confines, the single computer and projection within the classroom are no longer seen as constraining; each serves its purpose in the macro picture. Computer and projection becomes a management tool for in-class presentation and discussion; the wiki helps her realise her beliefs about language learning as a social constructivist endeavour. There is a happy marriage between the affordances of the tool and her aspirations.

> [...] it offers me the possibility of more immediate feedback on their progress and more communication with the students; group members can participate better; groups are much more motivated to create better products; knowledge sharing among the students is better; the students are more responsible for their group's success.

Within the classroom, the single computer and projection play a particular role for Vida and her learners. It is not a device for teacher direction; it sits there centre stage as a tool for learner presentations, internet searches and vocabulary work with online dictionaries. Like Susan, Vida also has particular views of PowerPoint, seeing this less positively in a classroom in which learner-centred activity is prime.

> I still prefer to use the blackboard because if I had all of my lesson on the PowerPoint then it is just them listening, but I prefer to ask them to get the key words out of them and then write them on the board. I am still the teacher who uses the blackboard because I want them to participate.

Vida looks to uses of technology which allow her learners to take a lead. She also identifies, even in talk about learner presentations, the importance of the 'visual', that is, encouraging learners to interpret in more than flat, text-based PowerPoint slides. Similarly of note is the use of Moviemaker for learners' enquiry outcomes described in her vignette:

> I try to do a lot of presentations so the groups every time have a small piece of homework which they can present in class instead of me talking. I say, for next time this group summarises it [a reading text], prepares the visual, prepares difficult work, definitions, whatever, so it is them acting like teachers, and some are really great. With some groups it is worse, but it is them all the time in front of the class and me sitting down. Even with debates sometimes I have classes that

are not good at debating. If I realise that, then I have a group preparing debate questions in advance and then leading the discussion with the visual.

This view of language learning as a social practice means she makes it her priority to ensure that, given the potential contextual constraints of large classes, restricted class contact time, and relatively restricted access to technology, her learners are active and have opportunities to interact in English.

Reaching into the adult's world: authenticity and autonomy

So what we see is teacher practice reflecting what we have characterised as general understanding of the adult learner, but the particularities of both learner and context help us to appreciate what preoccupies teachers and how they use technology in specific ways and towards perhaps slightly different ends. There are, nevertheless, some shared constants. Most evident is the thread of independent learning, which is clearly woven through these accounts of technology decision making. The resourceful activity around materials creation and collation, which all three of our case study teachers engage in, appears to characterise their way of working with their adult learners whether in a university or ESOL setting. Decisions about technology use constantly revolve around what happens within classrooms and what can be provided for more self-directed learning opportunities. There is a sense of the bank of digital artefacts 'killing more than one bird with one stone' so to speak; but this multi-context thinking is part and parcel of their appreciation of their adult learners' needs and motivations. The virtual learning spaces which serve this purpose may be within institutionally-supported tools such as Susan's or developed by the teacher on a more individual basis as in the cases of Vida and Ivana; they host records of classroom learning and extended tasks that provide for the flexibility that the learners look for; creating tasks with software such as Hot Potatoes is almost a normalised part of their repertoire. However, it is not simply a matter of teacher-generated tasks. All use technology to make ties with the adult's world. Ivana is particularly adamant about access to the real world of her adult learners through the texts she finds online.

If I can use the wealth of texts on the internet, it will also be done in a way I would never be able to replicate ... in their real life, in their business, in their career, whatever, they must be exposed to things they can really meet in their professional and private lives. Just with one textbook of course you cannot do it.

Vida's collection of learning material and her facilitation of problem based learning around themes determined by her adult learners echoes Ivana's concern for relevance. Without internet access and the realisation of the affordances of the wiki, this would prove difficult to respond to. In turn, this opening of the doors to the adult's world of reference is accompanied by a concern to provide them with the necessary toolkits to make their language learning transformative. Authenticity and autonomy go hand in hand.

Understanding of learner readiness for autonomy has been well researched (Benson et al., 2011; Cotterall, 1995), and in exploring the nature of 'autonomy', Littlewood (1996: 428) identifies ability and willingness as two key conditions for learners to be able to act independently. He explains:

Ability depends on possessing both knowledge about the alternatives from which choices have to be made and the necessary skills for carrying out whatever choices seem most appropriate. Willingness depends on having both the motivation and the confidence to take responsibility for the choices required.

Throughout these teacher accounts, there is plenty of evidence of the choices that technology facilitates, but also of teacher awareness of the need to guide their learners. There is an interesting question about the skills dimension. The educational landscape of lifelong learning is very different from when Knowles first explored the nature of adult learning (1973). Susan reflects on the increasing demands made on her UK-based ESOL learners' ICT skills and their lack of experience in this respect. Susan believes that internet literacy, online communication skills and ICT skills are an important part of language teaching, and that learners do need her to facilitate opportunities both within and beyond the classroom to develop their confidence in these areas. Susan makes sure to open email accounts for all of her learners in the beginning of the year, and to give them her email address saying they can contact her anytime, encouraging them to email each other as well.

> *It is really important that they can use the computer so ICT skills are really important there. I suppose it is in today's context – you are expected to communicate with people by emailing, for example, and it is important they can get hold of me in that way.*

Those literacies are not just defined by societal drivers, but educational ones too. In the context of second language learning as part of a skills for life agenda, Susan's institution sets out its own stall in terms of expectations, and she identifies developing ICT confidence as part of her role.

> *I teach Level One and their exam is on a computer. They've only got one hour to do 40 questions so it doesn't leave a lot of time for thought about the English if you're trying to master how to get to the next question, how to go back.*

Developing ICT confidence, then, opens up new opportunities, which teacher and adult learner can explore together. All three teachers are resourceful in this objective, but this line of thinking is particularly exemplified by Susan, as she considers how blogs offer support for purposeful reflection that turns an institutional requirement for target setting and independent learning programmes into a more personal engagement from her learners.

> *[...] we have target setting with them and independent learning programmes to fill in, you say to them at the end of the term, so what did you do this term, how do you feel, what have you got better on. They just go oh yeh, it's okay I'm better. So if we write something at the end of each week, they can reflect on what they've learned that week – what they didn't like, how they didn't progress with something. It goes straight onto the blog.*

The adult ESOL learner, therefore, needs to develop ICT skills because they have to be able to operate in the ESOL world beyond the institution's doors; they need ICT skills to be learners within it; developing skills brings gains in both dimensions, resulting in more autonomous exploration of technologies which transcend these two settings. This is integral to Susan's understanding of the contexts of language use which her adults populate, to the extent that, as her vignette identifies, her final judgement of the success of her lesson is in relation to these drivers.

What do adult learners expect of technology?

One of the principles of adult learning identified at the start of this chapter was recognising that adults will bring not only expectations, but beliefs and learning preferences to the classroom. These act as a filter to teachers' own decision-making, and may be evident in the confidence with which teachers use technology in class or the affective responses (Horowitz 1995, 1999) they have to its use.

There is plenty of evidence to suggest that the relationship between learner expectations and teacher example is strong. Vida is using technology to expand learning opportunities, to facilitate learning at different times and through different tools. Working with young adults in a university setting, she is aware of the mobile technologies her learners use, and juxtaposes this with her belief that they do not then expect to come to class and be lectured 'in an old-fashioned way'. Vida's problem-based learning activities take place largely outside of her classroom setting; learners make use of her wiki space and she encourages the use of any mobile technology that groups may independently have access to. They are similarly encouraged to present their group collaborations to the class using multimedia, the tool used by learners being Movie Maker, which she describes as being generally available to them, again outside the classroom, on their own laptops or computers. Her learners seem to respond to her attempts to provide for flexible learning with enthusiasm, and to the teacher–learner relationship that this seems to open up. The example she cites specifically is the use of a forum discussion, which she implements 'over the weekend', and she reports her learners' comments: 'wow we would love more, we would like other teachers to do that'.

Ivana voices a strong belief about the sort of technology-supported activities that motivate her learners. She feels that the interactive types of tasks that she creates using Hot Potatoes are received most positively. Similarly, she identifies learners' lack of enthusiasm for more static presentational approaches, and PowerPoint is again a source of comment:

> I can put PowerPoint presentations where I summarise various things for writing, they have some models of giving presentations, so yes it's like lecturing in the computer but they don't like it that much.

Her attention to her learners' 'musical intelligence' (Gardner, 1983) is noted in her commentary on her vignette. The variety of technology-facilitated support for her learners and negotiation with them as to what she provides through Moodle is evidence of the mutual engagement that lies behind her approach.

Again Susan's learners serve to remind us that technology use may not be experienced in the same way by all learners. This she attributes in her own setting to various reasons depending on the group or individual. Learners come from a wide range of home contexts, with a range of experience and levels of confidence with ICT. Some feel that it should be a natural part of their language learning experience. Many have, for example, bought themselves handheld dictionaries. However, she identifies her lower level learners and some from specific countries as not 'quite understanding the use of IT idea'; her Bangladeshi learners, for example, 'are not too *au fait* with computer usage'. She also suggests that some of her older learners are both less expectant of, and less interested in, technology use.

Concluding remarks

This final reminder brings us back to our starting points of not only an understanding of what characterises the adult learner, but also of a 'pedagogy of particularity' (Kumaravadivelu, 2001). Three different teachers of adult second language learners may have provided very different accounts of the 'possible and practical' (Kumaravadivelu, 2001). This chapter has only briefly referred to the implications of mobile technologies; none of these teachers at this point in time, and with these groups of learners, were working with computer mediated communications as a means of opening up access to interactions with other speakers of English beyond the immediate cultural context; none found themselves negotiating the opportunities that computer cluster access might have afforded. What they do provide is narratives that illustrate the dimensions of the particular in the adult education settings which are home to these teachers and their learners.

Knowles' original work on andragogy (1973) was based largely on a contrast with school experience, characterised by teacher directedness and a focus on subject learning (to which Knowles assigned the label of pedagogy). The picture that the concept of andragogy provided us with was of:

■ the adult learner as moving towards independence and the teacher's role as one which scaffolds a transition to self-direction

■ the adult learner's life experience as a resource and a point of reference for learner-centred activity

■ the adult learner's readiness to learn and awareness of themselves as learners

■ the learner's orientation to learning, that is the adult learner knows why he/she is learning and the goals they aim for.

In presenting these accounts of how technology finds its place in adult learning contexts, these principles and indeed their socio-cultural caveats variously come to the fore in different decision making. It is also a fact that these accounts represent a snapshot in time; there is no doubt the specifics of technology use will have already evolved in these teachers' practice – signs of that evolution were already evident in our conversations with them. However, the dynamics between teacher, learner, technology and context means that already the particularity of another group of adult learners may have provided new insights into the possible and practical (Kumaravadivelu, 2001). We are grateful to our teachers for inviting us at this particular moment in time, and for sharing their professional understanding.

References

Barton, D and Trusting, K (2003) *Models of adult learning: a literature review.* London: National Research and Development Centre for Adult Literacy and Numeracy, Institute of Education, University of London.

Belz, JA (2002) 'Identity, deficiency, and first language use in foreign language education', in Blyth, C (ed) *The Sociolinguistics of the foreign language classroom: Contributions of the native, non-native, and near-native speaker.* Boston, MA: Heinle & Heinle.

Benson, P, Grabe, W and Stoller, FL (2011) *Teaching and researching autonomy in language learning 2nd Edition.* London: Pearson Education.

Boud, D, Keogh, R and Walker, D (eds) (1985) *Reflection: Turning experience into learning.* London: Kogan Page.

Burns, R (1995) *The adult learner at work.* Sydney: Business and Professional Publishing.

Cotterall, S (1995) Readiness for autonomy: investigating learner beliefs. *System,* 23/2: 195–205.

Gardner, H (1983) *Frames of mind.* New York: Basic Books Inc.

Horowitz, EK (1995) Student affective reactions and the teaching and learning of foreign languages. *International Journal of Educational Research* 23/7: 573–579.

Horowitz, EK (1999) Cultural and situational influences on foreign language learners' beliefs about language learning: a review of BALLI studies. *System* 27: 557–576.

Kennedy, P (2002) Learning cultures and learning styles: myth-understandings about adult (Hong Kong) Chinese learners. *International Journal of Lifelong Education* 21/5: 430–445.

Kern, R (2006) Perspectives on technology in learning and teaching languages. *TESOL Quarterly* 40/1: 183–210.

Knowles, M (1973) *The adult learner: A neglected species.* Houston, TX: Gulf Publishing Company.

Knowles, M (1980) *The modern practice of adult education: From pedagogy to andragogy.* New York: Cambridge Adult Education Company.

Knowles, M, Holton, E and Swanson, R (2011) *The adult learner: A neglected species.* Seventh Edition, Oxford: UK.

Kolb, D (1984) *Experiential learning: Experience as the source of learning and development.* New Jersey: Prentice Hall.

Kumaravadivelu, B (2001) Toward a postmethod pedagogy. *TESOL Quarterly* 35: 537–560.

Lindeman, EC (1926) *The meaning of adult education*. New York: New Republic.

Littlewood, W (1996) Autonomy: an anatomy and a framework. *System* 24/4: 427–435.

Merriam, S (2001) Andragogy and self-directed learning: Pillars of adult learning theory. *New Directions for Adult and Continuing Education* 89: 3–13.

Mezirow, J (1997) Transformative learning. *New directions for Adult and Continuing Education* 74: 5–12.

Mumtaz, S (2001) Factors affecting teachers' use of information and communications technology: a review of the literature. *Journal of Information Technology for Teacher Education* 9/3: 319–341.

Oxford, R and Crookall, D (1989) Research on language learning strategies: Methods, findings and instructional issues. *Modern Language Journal* 73/4: 404–419.

Schön, D (1983) *The reflective practitioner: How professionals think in action*. New York: Basic Books.

Selwyn, N, Gorard, S and Furlong, J (2006) *Adult learning in the digital age: Information technology and the learning society*. London: Routledge.

Smith, AFV and Strong, G (eds) (2009) *Adult learners: Context and innovation*. Alexandria, Virginia: TESOL Publications.

Sutter, W (1987) *Learning styles in adult refugees in North Jutland*. Denmark: County of North Jutland.

Tang, C and Biggs, J (1996) 'Hong Kong students cope with assessment', in Watkins, D and Biggs, J (eds) *The Chinese learner*. University of Hong Kong: Comparative Education Research Centre.

Tennant, M and Pogson, P (1995) *Learning and change in the adult years: A developmental perspective*. San Francisco: Jossey-Bass.

Technology-integrated English for Specific Purposes lessons: real-life language, tasks, and tools for professionals

4

Technology-integrated English for Specific Purposes lessons: real-life language, tasks, and tools for professionals

Nergiz Kern

Introduction

English for Specific Purposes (ESP), including Business English (BE), has a long history and has become increasingly popular since the 1960s (Anthony, 1997). Universities now offer MAs in ESP courses; there are ESP and BE journals; and special interest groups like the IATEFL or TESOL ESP SIGs (Anthony, 1997) and BE SIGs. Many language schools offer ESP and BE courses, and increasing numbers of more and more specialised ESP coursebooks, for subjects such as aviation, medicine, and legal English, or BE books such as English for email, are published. There are also conferences dedicated to teaching BE and ESP (www.esp-conference.de/).

Before describing how technology is used in ESP, I am going to spend some time talking about ESP in general terms.

What is ESP?

If we leave compulsory education aside, people have always learned a language out of a special need and for a special purpose. This could be the need to communicate with someone who does not speak a shared language about something 'specific', for example, a tourist who needs to ask someone for directions, a hobbyist who wants to find out more about his favourite subject on the internet, a business person who needs to attend meetings with international partners, or a technician who needs to order parts from a catalogue that is only available in one specific language.

So, what do we mean exactly when we say English for Specific Purposes then? What is the difference between a general English course and an ESP course? Interestingly, despite being long established, this has always been debated, even in a recent IATEFL-TESOL discussion, held in February 2012, and the definitions of ESP have not only changed over time but different definitions have existed side by side (Smoak, 2003). In the beginning, teachers often thought that in ESP courses, teaching specific vocabulary was their task. However, in many situations adult professionals know the technical terms related to their field much better than the teacher, who often does not know the field-specific terminology (Smoak, 2003). What learners need is to learn how to use those words in sentences, how to understand authentic texts with certain field-specific expressions, or how to communicate effectively in typical situations that arise in their jobs. This is why the analysis of needs, discourse genre, and linguistic corpora has become so important (Dudley-Evans and Johns, 1991; Hewings, 2002) in ESP.

However, it is still the case that a lot of the language adult ESP learners need will not be much different from general English, and indeed, the line between both is often blurred (Anthony, 1997). First, it was emphasised that in ESP needs analysis was of paramount importance. However, being influenced by ESP, even in general English courses, a needs analysis is carried out now more and more, especially with the shift to a more learner-centred approach in teaching.

Despite this fact and the ongoing discussions, it is generally understood and accepted that there is a difference between the two. Anthony (1997: online) mentions that 'some people described ESP as simply being the teaching of English for any purpose that could be specified. Others, however, were more precise, describing it as the teaching of English used in academic studies or the teaching of English for vocational or professional purposes.' In 1991, Dudley-Evans and Johns said 'ESP requires the careful research and design of pedagogical materials and activities for an identifiable group of adult learners within a specific learning context' (1991: 298). Context, situational practice, cross-cultural issues, authenticity of communication and materials, and needs analysis are terms that come up in various definitions of ESP (Grosse and Voigt, 1991; Dudley-Evans and St John, 1998).

Dudley-Evans and St John (1998) offer an extended and flexible definition based on Streven's (1988 in Dudley-Evans and St John, 1998: 3):

Absolute characteristics
- ESP is defined to meet specific needs of the learners
- ESP makes use of underlying methodology and activities of the discipline it serves
- ESP is centred on the language (grammar, lexis, register), study skills, discourse and genre appropriate for these activities.

Variable characteristics
- ESP may be related to, or designed for, specific disciplines
- ESP may use, in specific teaching situations, a different methodology from that of general English
- ESP is likely to be designed for adult learners, either at a tertiary level institution or in a professional work situation; it could, however, be for learners at secondary school level
- ESP is generally designed for intermediate or advanced students; most ESP courses assume some basic knowledge of the language systems.

(Dudley-Evans and St John, 1998: 4–5)

This definition can serve as a framework that can encompass various ESP contexts (Arnó, Soler and Rueda, 2006a).

Variations in definitions have also to do with the different needs of learners in their workplace. A large airline company, for example, offers English lessons to their technicians. However, after looking more closely at what they needed, it turned out that most of the technicians only needed to know the English words for the parts of an airplane. In fact, the internal training material for new technicians was a mix of the L1 for the grammar and all the non-technical words, and only the technical words were in English, for example: *Carriers shaft'*ın üzerinde iki tane *planet gear* vardir. In another department, however, technicians need to understand more complex English texts when reading original manuals supplied by various aircraft components producers. These employees need to learn English grammar, sentence structure, etc., as well as the technical terms. This also shows why needs analysis is so essential in ESP.

Over time, some areas of ESP have come to be seen as separate, such as EAP and Business English. In fact, this manifests itself even in this book, where there is a separate chapter for EAP and even these areas have split up further. There is, for instance, ESAP (English for Specific Academic Purposes) such as English for Medical Students, English for Science and Technology, and English for Law. Also, Business English has split into more specific areas such as English for Human Resources, English for Banking, English for Secretaries. So, it seems that the 'S' in ESP has become more and more specific over time (Hewings, 2002), which leads Dudley-Evans and Johns (1991: 336) to remark that 'there is a dilemma about how specific the business and vocational English courses should be...'.

Having discussed what ESP means, we can now look at how technology is used in ESP and BE classes, and how this relates to the definitions of ESP set out above.

Technology use in ESP

A look at the programme of an ESP conference in 2011 shows that several sessions were about how to use certain technologies in ESP lessons. Does this show a new trend of more technology use in ESP, or has technology always been integrated in ESP courses?

A brief history of technology use in ESP

Just as in general English language teaching and learning, technology in its various forms has long been used in ESP, whether in the form of a tape recorder or sophisticated digital technology. But maybe its impact on ESP has been more profound (Arnó, Soler and Rueda, 2006a). ESP teachers have always used available tools to devise materials and create situations relevant to their students' needs (Arnó-Macià, 2012).

However, technology's role in language learning in general, and in ESP in particular, has changed over time and significantly so in recent years (Arnó, Soler and Rueda, 2006a). Not only has the view of learning changed with time, from the behaviourist to communicative to an integrative view (Warschauer and Healey, 1998), but technology has also evolved and become more ubiquitous in everyday life, and particularly in the professional world. Both of these have affected how technology is employed in ESP lessons.

In the past, teachers had to book computer rooms or language labs to go with their learners and allow them to use CALL software with mostly drill-type exercises (Arnó, Soler and Rueda, 2006a). Today, technology has become integrated into the classroom physically and pedagogically rather than being an add on. Computers particularly have come to be seen and used as a tool to accomplish certain tasks or to communicate (Warschauer and Healey, 1998; Warschauer and Kern, 2000). Therefore, Garrett (2009: 719) defines CALL now as 'the full integration of technology into language learning' with its three elements of theory, pedagogy, and technology playing an equally important role.

Although technology has always played a role in ESP (Arnó-Macià, 2012), the internet has had a particularly strong impact. As ESP puts emphasis on the needs of learners, and authentic materials and tasks, IT has become a very suitable tool for ESP (Arnó, Soler and Rueda, 2006a), specifically, the 'second wave of online language learning' (Kern, Ware, and Warschauer, 2004: 243), which Arnó-Macià (2012: 91) describes as going 'beyond language learning by focusing on culture and social discourses' and allowing ESP learners to collaborate and engage in authentic communication in their professional discourse community, to access up-to-date information relevant to their profession, and to publish their ideas, which can all give them a sense of empowerment as learners. This is why Warschauer and Kern (2000) termed teaching using IT as 'networked-based language teaching'.

In the business world in particular, and generally in professional life, the internet has taken centre stage and allows, in an increasingly globalised world, fast and efficient communication and collaboration, information generation, exchange, and management. The professional world today would in most cases not be possible without information technology. This places a challenge on teachers who need to prepare their ESP students to 'deal with global communicative practices online, in all their complexity' (White, 2007: 325).

As learners' needs and authentic tasks are paramount in business English and other ESP courses, many language teachers have integrated the same kinds of technology into their courses which their learners use in their profession, whether it is the word processor and email, the internet as a source for authentic material and place for authentic communication, virtual conferencing platforms, simulation software, or, in recent years, mobile technologies.

Benefits of technology use in ESP

While each type of technology has its own specific advantages, it is worth listing some of the general benefits of using it in ESP.

Some benefits of technology in language learning are the same for ESP learners as for general English learners. For example, finding native speakers as learning or communication partners or reading or watching the news in the target language for those who do not have easy access to these locally. In lessons, teachers can bring the outside world into the classroom, provide authentic contexts in which English is used, expose students to different varieties and accents of English, and give students listening practice.

But, whereas in general English lessons even the teachers themselves can be a valuable resource for listening, speaking and authentic language use, in many cases technology, whether, for example, in the form of videos or on the internet, is the only means for ESP students to access the specific language they need in order to communicate appropriately. Butler-Pascoe (2009: 1) states that it is the 'hybrid nature of ESP', having to teach both the language and the 'field-specific content' that makes it challenging for teachers, who often do not have the field-specific knowledge to teach. Although it is not usually the case that teachers also have to teach the content, especially when teaching adult professionals, they do need to teach the field-specific language, which they might not always know, and which changes and develops over time.

When teaching professionals, the needs also go beyond the language itself; they also require the use of authentic tasks, tools, and context (Bremner, 2010; Evans, 2012).

According to Butler-Pascoe (2009: 2), 'at least three primary models exist for delivering ESP instruction:

1. ESP taught by English teachers using field-specific content.
2. Field-specific courses taught by teachers in the disciplines using English as the language of instruction.
3. A collaborative model in which both English and field-specific teachers have joint input into the development and/or teaching of the course'

and 'innovative uses of today's technology' can play an important role in all three. Interestingly, Butler-Pascoe (2009) mentions that, besides being used for teaching and learning ESP, the same technologies can also be used to help ESP teachers communicate with each other and their students.

Butler-Pascoe (2009: 2–3) lists 14 advantages of technology for ESP, which she later describes in more detail:

1. Provides interaction and communicative activities representative of specific professional or academic environments.
2. Fosters understanding of the socio-cultural aspects of the language as practised in various fields and professions.
3. Provides comprehensible field-specific input and facilitates student production.
4. Provides sheltering strategies for language development and content-specific understanding (modelling, bridging to students' background experiences, contextualising, metacognitive activities, etc.).

5. Uses task-based and inquiry-based strategies reflective of tasks in discipline-specific settings and situations.

6. Uses authentic materials from specific disciplines and occupations.

7. Supplies authentic audiences, including outside experts in specific fields.

8. Supports cognitive abilities and critical thinking skills required in the disciplines.

9. Uses collaborative learning.

10. Facilitates focused practice for the development of reading, writing, listening, and speaking skills across the curriculum and disciplines.

11. Is student-centred and addresses specific needs of students.

12. Uses multiple modalities to support different learning styles.

13. Meets affective needs of students: motivation, self-esteem, and autonomy.

14. Provides appropriate feedback and assessment of content knowledge and English skills.

Technologies for ESP

There are many different technologies that are successfully used in ESP courses from the traditional tape recorder or CD player, to interactive whiteboards, ICT, Web 2.0 tools, mobile technologies and 3D virtual environments. It is impossible to list them all. Therefore, in this section, I will look at some more widely used ones in greater detail and will show practical and concrete examples of how they are used by teachers in different ESP courses around the world.

Skype/online conferencing tools

There are many online voice-over internet protocol (VoIP) services that allow users to make telephone or video calls and conduct group conferences using their computer, and Skype is one of the better known and is widely used (Mullen et al., 2009). In its basic form, the application is freely downloadable and calls made between computers are without charge. Audio and video conferences can be made between participants, however, free video calls are restricted to two participants. The new version of Skype also allows screen sharing, which means that the teacher or students can show Word documents, slide presentations, or websites on their screen to the other participants in a Skype session, to talk about them or explain something.

There are free and paid add-ons and services and third-party applications that can extend Skype's functionality such as whiteboards and software that allow the recording of voice or video conversations on Skype. Text chat can be used concurrently with voice and video and is recorded automatically. Skype can also be integrated into Moodle, a free open-source learning management system (Godwin-Jones, 2005).

Skype is used in many different ways for formal and informal language learning and teaching. A search on the Skype community platform shows how many language courses, language chat groups or conversation clubs there are. Many teachers also offer online courses via Skype, which are often individually bookable lessons.

There is also a special social media language course and materials integrating Skype called English Out There (http://englishoutthere.com/), which can be used by online teachers or as self-study material by learners. Wisniewska (2010) mentions the use of Skype in one-to-one language lessons in her book *Learning One-to-One*.

Other teachers invite guest speakers via Skype into their classrooms thus breaking down distance barriers. I have, for example, been invited to talk with students at a language school in Morocco, on several occasions. Skype is also used for tandem language learning either on a one-to-one basis or arranged by teachers for whole classes to bring them together with classes in other countries or regions in order to practise the target languages (Godwin-Jones, 2005; Elia, 2006; Mullen et al., 2009; Eröz-Tuğa and Sadler, 2009). Besides the obvious advantages of practising the target language in authentic communication with a native speaker, tandem language learning can help learners become more autonomous (Elia, 2006).

Mullen et al. (2009: 101), who emphasise 'a task-based approach based on the principles of tandem learning', stress the fact that although the familiarity with the tandem concept might make learners and teachers think that they can use the same principles as face-to-face or asynchronous email tandem, this would be a mistake because Skype is a real-time or synchronous communication tool and activities would need to be different. Hampel and Hauck (2006: 3) also emphasise that 'it is not sufficient to see the new learning spaces' such as the internet, video conferencing tools, or email 'as replica[tion]s of conventional face-to-face settings.'

The convenience of learning from a distance from the comfort of one's home or from any location where one happens to be, in the case of frequent travellers, and having access to teachers and native speakers around the world are some reasons for the popularity of Skype for language learning. Other reasons might be the mostly free service, availability for major computer platforms (Windows, Mac, Linux, etc.), the reliability of the service, the relatively good quality of audio and video if used with a broadband connection, and also its ease of use. Many language learners are also already familiar with the tool from their professional work and use it to communicate with colleagues or business partners.

However, just because a particular technology is widely used does not mean it will automatically enhance language learning. Its particular affordances that lend themselves for language learning need to be considered and appropriate tasks need to be devised, in order to be able to make effective use of it (Levy, 2009). Skype, like any other technology, is just a tool, and it needs to be used in a pedagogically sound way to have a 'value for language learning' (Levy, 2009: 775). For example, when students do tandem-learning activities, giving learners tasks to do (Mullen et al., 2009) or asking them to keep a learning journal with reflections on the exchanges or creating a portfolio (Elia, 2006) can help enhance the learning of such exchanges.

Some teachers integrate Skype into their course in a more structured way as part of a blended learning solution, as in the first case study in this chapter contributed by Cornelia Kreis-Meyer, the head of a language school in Germany.

Case Study 4.1: English for politicians

The students

In this course, the student is a German politician in his mid-fifties who was at B1 level in his speaking skills when he started the course and has reached B2 level after two years. He is a very 'confident, assertive and extremely eloquent speaker' of German and is also confident when speaking English despite grammar or vocabulary mistakes.

He decided he needed to improve his spoken English skills, particularly in terms of 'sufficient speed and language accuracy' in order to be able to communicate 'without ambiguity and stress for the listener' in situations when he 'explains his political position on topical issues; express his own ideas; to discuss problems at a high conceptual level; to react to questions by reporters' or take part in international meetings and interviews.

Some of the meetings are teleconferences and interviews are conducted on the telephone or other virtual conferencing tools, which are then streamed on television.

The course

The course is a blend of 30 minutes online and 90 minutes face-to-face instruction per month, and is paid for by the government.

One teacher conducts the Skype lesson and another teacher the face-to-face sessions so that the student is exposed to two different accents (US and British English) and different teaching approaches.

The blend of online and face-to-face sessions was chosen to give him practice in both modes of communication in which he needs to speak English.

Materials and technology used

Internet news channels like CNN or the BBC and the English online version of the German political magazine *Der Spiegel* are used to provide authentic content. The student determines the topics, 'which always revolve around topical political issues.'

Types of activities the technologies (and materials) are used for, and their relevance for the learner

Skype, with and without camera, is used to simulate telephone or video interviews and teleconferences. The text chat function is used as a protocol to record corrections and feedback by the teacher, which are made at the same time as the students is, for example, giving a statement, and which is then used to discuss the session afterwards with the learner. At other times, this function is used to give written prompts when the student is searching for words while speaking and thus simulates a teleprompter.

In both situations, the tool allows the correcting, commenting, and prompting to happen without interrupting the student's speaking flow orally, which can be regarded as one of the affordances of text chat, and an advantage over offline face-to-face teaching, where the teacher would either have to interrupt the student or provide delayed feedback.

However, seeing the teacher write corrections in text chat could become a distraction and it might even hamper fluency when the student tries to read the comments and at the same continue speaking. This can 'impose a lot of load on learners' (Willis and Willis, 2007: 138) and make it difficult to deal with the feedback. The student might also be tempted to stop, go back, and correct himself, taking on board the teacher's correction. Whether this is positive or negative might depend a lot on how confident the student is, what the exact purpose of the activity is (fluency or accuracy), and what kind of process for feedback the learner and teacher agreed on. In any case, it is an affordance that needs to be evaluated carefully in terms of pedagogy.

One way of allowing for a distraction-free speech is to record the Skype session. For example, in this case, the teacher sometimes asks the politician to give one-minute statements as a reply to a controversial question and records the audio with an application called 'Sound Studio'. After the statement, the teacher and student listen to the recording and discuss it.

Skype is also used in this course to simulate phone interviews. In this case, the politician provides the teacher with a set of questions about a chosen topic. The teacher takes on the role of the interviewer and asks the questions, which the politician answers. Like above, feedback and prompts are either provided immediately via text chat or noted down to discuss with the student afterwards.

Usability and constraints of the technology
Skype is very intuitive and easy to use and does not normally require any training. The Skype services used in this course are free. It does, however, require a fast internet connection, especially when video is used and the audio and video quality, which is normally very good, can vary considerably at certain times when the service is used by many people at the same time.

Because the student is a government official, his lesson takes place in high-security surroundings. So, any tool that requires online access needs to pass through a firewall. With Skype this was not an issue, possibly because it is widely used for interviews and online conferences; thus, it did not need to be installed specifically for the course.

Attitudes of students and institution towards the technology
The last point is important for another reason. Being a very busy politician who only has exactly 120 minutes per month allocated for the English course and not being particularly technology savvy, the student understands the need for using technology, especially because he needs to be familiar with some digital technologies professionally as well, but would not be prepared to spend time learning how to use sophisticated e-learning tools. As mentioned above, he was already familiar with Skype, and it is an easy-to-use tool that does not require any training in general.

This point cannot be underestimated when deciding which tool(s) to use in a course. Teachers might believe in the effectiveness of a particular tool for language learning or teaching purposes but it is of paramount importance to consider the benefits and the time it takes for students (and teachers) to learn to use the tools.

At the institution that provides the course for the politician, they provide a lot of one-to-one executive training in several languages. According to the head of the school, who fully supports the use of digital technologies, their trainers are very willing to use Skype for its ease of use and Skype is the only tool that their students readily accept, especially because they also use it at work and because they can participate in the lessons even when they are abroad. The tool has become 'normalised' (Bax, 2003) for the learner and they do not need to learn how to use it.

Although I agree with Levy (2009), who suggests that training learners is essential when using certain technologies for educational purposes, even if the learner is familiar with them from other contexts, if a tool is used in a very similar way to how a professional uses it at work, such training could be done in a very short time so as to make it acceptable for the learner, who, as is the case with the politician, does not want to, or cannot spend time learning about tools.

The internet

Technology, especially the internet with its abundance of authentic material (texts, audio, videos, etc.) and information on many topics, the tools and possibilities for communication, and platforms that allow sharing of ideas and knowledge, is particularly important in ESP.

One way in which ICT has changed how languages are learned is that it allows learners to immerse themselves in the target language and community easily, which, in the past, was only possible by more or less extended stays in the country where the target language was spoken (Warschauer, 2006), and which only a relatively small number of more affluent students could afford. But even with visits, it was very difficult for ESP learners with a very narrow focus on specialised language to find appropriate opportunities to meet their language needs. Most immersion programmes are for general English, with some offering learning opportunities and internships for Business English students. With the widespread use of ICT, most ESP students can now find language materials for their needs, interact with their professional community, or with other learners in their field online (Arnó, Soler and Rueda, 2006a). The internet and the various tools that are available there can also help learners to become more autonomous and allow them to monitor their learning (Zhong, 2008).

With this mediation of technology in learning, what comes to the fore is that the learners' task is no longer to acquire a body of encyclopaedic knowledge that must be internalised, but rather to decide on what needs to be learned, how the input relates meaningfully to each individual's needs, and how the learning experience is shaped and adapted over time, within a constructivist view of learning. This use of the internet as a learning resource is especially appropriate in a Language(s) for Specific

Purposes (LSP) context, given that it is in LSP settings where the students' roles as experts of a discipline are more apparent (Arnó, Soler and Rueda, 2006b: 253).

Theoretical frameworks like constructivism and socio-cultural theory give useful insights into learning processes and these are translated into approaches that can integrate online tasks, for example, task, problem, or content-based learning, and we find these referred to in ESP course design (Hampel, 2006; Luzón-Marco and Gonzàlez-Pueyo, 2006; Palalas, 2011; Arnó-Macià, 2012).

Many English teachers now use the internet in their courses, set online homework, and use it to find materials and ideas for their lessons, even if only occasionally. Some have become online teachers. Others also use it for their own professional development as a 'virtual staffroom' to connect with colleagues around the word, share ideas, participate in webinars or conferences, or write and read blogs (see discussions of PLNs in Chapter 3).

This extended staffroom is particularly important for ESP teachers, whose multiple roles, for example as teacher, materials designer, collaborator, assessor, and researcher have expanded and evolved through IT, allowing collaborations with field-specific experts and other colleagues around the world, and giving them more easy access to an abundance of multimedia materials for even the most specialised of fields in order to design materials and courses that meet their learners' needs (Arnó-Macià, 2012: 90). Today's technology makes it further possible for teachers to create more sophisticated and professional looking (multimedia) materials and online or blended courses.

In the following sections, I will write in more detail about the three main areas that the internet is used for in ESP, namely as a source for authentic, specialised material, a place for authentic communication, and a collection of tools that allow for the sharing of ideas, knowledge, and student- or teacher-created materials. These uses will be illustrated with concrete examples from case studies.

The internet: a source for authentic materials

ESP teachers often find themselves in the role of materials collector and designer to a greater or lesser degree (Krajka, 2003; Arnó-Macià, 2012). Sometimes, there are coursebooks available, especially in more common ESP courses such as Business English or general technical English, however, ESP students often have more varied and very specific needs (Krajka, 2003). In addition, the language and tasks in coursebooks do not always reflect those in real life, such as the language, contents and use of email communication in Business English (Evans, 2012), so that these coursebooks need supplementing. For very specific ESP courses or needs, such as English for 'European studies, biotechnology, philosophy, library science' (Krajka, 2003: 2), there are no coursebooks at all or they are very expensive, and teachers have to create the material for a complete course. In such cases, and in courses of which the teacher is not a content expert at all, the availability of online material is invaluable.

When I was asked to teach aviation maintenance English, for instance, I was faced with three main challenges: I did not know much about the field other than the knowledge any other lay person would have; most aviation coursebooks were for pilots and tower crew but not for technicians, and the third challenge was that the students, being from a vocational high school, also did not yet have much field-specific knowledge and had a relatively low level of English.

I did bring a keen interest in technology to the course, which is essential when teaching such an ESP course. But the internet was, for me, indispensable when preparing and teaching this course, especially as it was a low-budget course, and it would not have been possible to buy any commercial training videos, for example. Another course I had to develop from scratch, because no coursebook fitted their needs, was for city planners.

In such cases, teachers have always collected materials that were produced for other purposes, like company newsletters, technical manuals, reports, etc. But these are not always easy to come by, especially when it comes to more specific terminology and the particular needs of students.

With the availability of a wealth of information and materials on all kinds of topics and in various forms on the internet, finding relevant and up-to-date material has become much easier. Besides company websites, there are websites with user-generated content such as How Stuff Works (www.howstuffworks.com) or E-How (www.ehow.co.uk), where lay people or professionals can share videos and text showing and describing how certain things are done (from repairing an airplane, to blogging, to how to give a presentation), and websites dedicated to certain professions or fields of knowledge where teachers or learners can read, watch, or download materials.

However, Garrett (2009) warns that the mere use of authentic web-based resources does not represent CALL and that for a true integration of technology into the lessons, developing authentic tasks to go with the authentic material is of paramount importance. Depending on the level of expertise of the learner, students can also be asked to decide on content and create materials, thus, taking on responsibility for their learning, becoming more autonomous (Krajka, 2003) by using all their learning skills and developing web literacies (Krajka and Grudzinska, 2002).

In the Taxi English course which I developed and taught (Kern, 2011), the learners, the taxi drivers with years of experience in their job, provided most of the content. Contributing to the course in such a profound way gives learners, particularly adults, a sense of achievement and empowerment. Adult learners can often find themselves in this awkward situation of being a learner again, which can make them feel vulnerable. By bringing their expertise into the course, this can be overcome more easily. In the first case study we saw a similar situation in which the learner, the politician, is an expert in his field and knows exactly what the topic of a lesson should be and which online sources (news websites, etc.) to use; he even provides the questions he wants to be asked. The teacher is there as a communication partner, model speaker of the target language, and a guide; and provides language and feedback exactly when, and where, it is needed.

Other advantages of using web-based materials and involving the student in co-creating the course are that students will be more exposed to the target language, which can help them develop better language skills. Additionally, they will learn how to deal with authentic materials in order to make use of them. They will also learn skills that might be useful professionally, such as 'extracting information, analysing websites, producing summaries or reports' (Krajka, 2003: 3). By using the internet in such a way, students will acquire digital literacy skills besides learning the target language. These are reasons why Krajka (2003) suggests using web-based coursebook supplements.

In an ever-faster changing world, whether in technology or business, up-to-date information is very important. Coursebooks take several years to be published. By then, the information, vocabulary, or expressions contained in the chosen texts is out-dated and as a result has much less face validity. The internet can close this gap, when teachers or learners complement their coursebook with online reading material. Askari-Arani (2004) reports on a research study on an English for Medical Purposes course, in which traditional textbook and internet articles were used. The results showed that the course with the internet articles was more successful. A possible reason could be that they included up-to-date information and topics, which made them more relevant, interesting and thus more motivating for the learners (Askari-Arani, 2004).

Sometimes, however, it is very difficult and time-consuming to find exactly the kind of material a teacher needs for a certain level or context and to prepare lessons based on these. This is where websites like Macmillan's www.onestopenglish.com or http://breakingnewsenglish.com come into play, and which can be seen as a middle way between following a coursebook or entirely creating one's own materials. They can help teachers make use of website resources without having to spend hours searching for materials and designing tasks for them. They also allow teachers to download a limited number of units or pages from coursebooks.

A similar service is provided by http://English360.com, which allows teachers to create a course using digital versions of published materials from Cambridge and adding their own from the internet (for example, videos, audio), and giving learners and teachers tools to arrange these, take quizzes, etc., similar to a learning management system. These services show how traditional publishers are trying to adapt to the new technologies and cater to the new needs of teachers and learners. Almost all newly published books or new editions of well-known coursebooks have an online component, which is more or less integrated with the book.

Learner autonomy

Students can also use the internet for self-study purposes without the need for a teacher. Often learners will ask their teachers which websites they would recommend which they could use to improve their English. The internet, with its hyperlinked structure allowing learners to choose the material and which direction to go and to do this at their own pace, is in line with constructivist learning theory and enables learners to become autonomous (Luzón-Marco, 2002), which is one of the skills students need to develop today (Felix, 2005).

However, without the guidance of a teacher, only the most motivated and perhaps those who already have a higher level of English will be able to make good use of the resources available in order to improve their language skills. Many students, and maybe particularly those who would need the extra practice, however, can feel lost or overwhelmed by the amount of material available and can become discouraged by this. Others might not know how to make use of the resources. This is similar to the situation in which students use some technology proficiently every day for entertainment purposes or their work, but when it comes to using the same technology for language learning, they do not always know how. Levy (2009: 779) points out that the 'default position of users is different from that of learners'. The same is true for the internet. Students need training in how to approach online texts with hyperlinks, for example. They need training in developing critical literacy skills (Vie, 2008 in Arnó-Macià, 2012: 99) and evaluating websites, and help in appreciating different genres of writing.

Technology itself does not bring about autonomy but with the appropriate support, guidance, training, and scaffolding, it can help learners to gradually become autonomous (Luzón-Marco, 2002; Arnó-Macià, 2012).

One example of how technology can be integrated into a course and learners gradually trained to deal with authentic materials and tasks in the target language is the English for Urban Planners course website (http://englishforcityplanners. nergizkern.com [Best City]), which is the online part of a blended course. The students, who are city planners, need to do online research about urban planning for their work, but they did not know how to approach English texts that were often beyond their level of English. On the website, they are guided step by step through tasks that help them to understand the reading passage. Additionally, it includes links to relevant websites, where they can find more texts of interest to them and try out the same approaches on their own.

Another example for scaffolding online learning is to use WebQuests, which Luzón-Marco (2002) believes provide suitable content-based activities for ESP classes in which learning the target language and learning discipline-related content and skills are integrated. According to him, such activities are based on a constructivist and communicative approach, which help students with communicative competency, critical reading, synthesising, and problem-solving skills.

A place for authentic communication

Teachers often have students engage in role plays in the classroom to simulate target settings in which they will need to use certain language. This is because teachers and even learners often do not have (easy) access to the target setting so they have to create an imaginative scenario and environment. Today, the internet is the target setting for many ESP learners. The internet is not only being used to help students learn English by accessing authentic materials or chatting with native speakers, but it has become one of the environments where professionals meet, communicate, collaborate and work. Although this is of concern for general English learners and teachers as well, it is of particular interest and importance for ESP.

By using such internet and communication technologies to collaborate internationally and communicate with fellow students around the world, and engage in genuine conversations with experts in their field, teachers and learners can 'bridge the gap between the LSP classroom and workplace demands' (Arnó-Macià, 2012: 100) or as Bremner (2010: 121) puts it, between the 'textbook and the workplace'. In order for this to happen effectively, however, teachers need to understand the characteristics of internet communication so that they can help their ESP students to deal with specific aspects or features of this type of communication and environment (Murray, 1988) such as 'cyber genres' (Shepherd and Watters, 1998: 1), intercultural aspects of communication (Arnó-Macià, 2012), and multimodal communication (Hampel and Hauck, 2006; Bremner, 2010).

Because many ESP learners already use the internet to network with other professionals to share discipline-specific information and take part in specialised forums, ESP teachers started using relatively new technologies such as social networking and Web 2.0 tools with their students often before many general English teachers did because of the centrality of students' needs in ESP (Arnó-Macià, 2012). These technologies allow students to immerse themselves in their professional communities online and give teachers the means to create materials and lessons that can guide students in this, and simulate target situations much more realistically in the actual setting they normally take place in, using the same or similar tools they already use or will use for work (Arnó-Macià, 2012). In other words, the internet is authentic not only because of the authenticity of the language that can be found there but also authentic as a place, which is very important in the situated learning approach according to which the socio-cultural setting has an influence on the learning and its outcome (Lave, 1991; Hampel, 2006; Mayes and De Freitas, 2007; Bremner, 2010; Arnó-Macià, 2012). The more the learning situation and activities resemble the students real-life situation and tasks, the more the students will be motivated to learn, and the more relevant the learning will be.

An English language course can be situated on two levels. What do I mean by this? For example, the teacher can show a video in which a scene is shown in which a typical situation is depicted in which the target language is used. What is shown can be an authentic situation, a situation or context in which the students in an ESP course will find themselves. Similarly, a teacher could take students to such a place or, if this is not possible, in a simulated place in a 3D virtual environment. This is the first level.

The second level is when the students, who are, for instance, taken into a 3D world, actually have to use 3D virtual worlds in their professional lives. Some companies use such virtual environments for business meetings or employee training. Another example is when students participate in a discussion forum online to practise language used in such forums and if they actually use or will have to use such forums at work. In this case the technology is not only used to simulate a situation or an environment but is actually the context or environment in which the learners will have to use English in their professional lives.

We can see this happening in all three case studies. For example, students learning English for Advertising, should they go on to study advertising and work in this field, they will have to use similar kinds of technologies as used in the blended course project described in Case Study 4.3. The politician in Case Study 4.1 will be in situations where he will give interviews on Skype or similar tools. The same is true for the Business English course in Case Study 4.2, as business people nowadays often participate in online conferences using virtual meeting rooms.

In the Business English case study we will see a practical example of how Mercedes Viola, a Business English teacher in Uruguay, integrates various real-life communication tools or meeting 'locations' into the language course to simulate real professional situations in which the learners need to use English.

Case Study 4.2: Business English

The students
In this particular course, there are three students aged 40 to 55, who are managers in a 'learning organisation' which has its focus on 'knowledge production and management' and which provides its services to international customers. The company is working on transforming its work environment into a 'powerful learning environment.' Given the organisation's focus, the managers participating in the course need to 'generate new knowledge' by 'exchanging' and 'enriching' existing knowledge. This takes place primarily in English.

The learners, being busy managers, it is important for the teacher to develop activities 'that help them make the most of the time they can devote to English, to enjoy the experience,' and 'to get positive outcomes.' The learners' motivation is higher when the activities and the content are relevant to their lives. Being familiar with the content additionally helps them to focus more on details.

The context
The course is a blend of a face-to-face component, which takes place at the organisation, and an online component. It is not compulsory but employees are encouraged to participate.

Materials and technology used
The majority of the audio and written texts are authentic materials from the organisation itself. A mix of technologies such as an educational platform, Skype, email, and virtual conferencing rooms are used. The internet is also used to introduce the students to tools such as online dictionaries.

Types of activities the technologies (and materials) are used for and their relevance for the learner
The activities and technology are based on the real-life needs of the learners and are used to simulate situations in which they have to use English. For example, if the managers need to give presentations in English, they prepare and give one in the lesson, which is recorded in order to be watched together later to give feedback on language use and other presentation skills.

Conference call simulations are held using Skype, as this is the tool which is used by the company for the same purpose. The procedure is similar to the one in Case Study 4.1. Feedback is provided while listening to the recording.

To simulate webinars and online meetings, the same virtual room is used which the students use for work. To practise email writing and do other types of activities, the educational platform is used.

Students are also shown what kind of tools are available to them online (for example, dictionaries) and how they can use them, in order to help them become more autonomous learners.

Usability and constraints of the technology
Most of the tools, services and platforms that are used in this course ask for an account creation at the beginning and signing in whenever they are used. The online educational platform asks for a fee per student per month. Teachers can either use ready-made material made available on the platform or create their own. Most of the other tools do not charge any fees.

The managers participating in this course are relatively adept at using the technologies in this course because they use technology at work and some of the tools are the same as they use at work.

Firewalls can sometimes be an issue, which is why technologies which are used by the organisation are chosen whenever possible. Permission from the IT department had to be sought to install Skype and some other tools.

Attitudes of students and institution towards the technology
As the way the technology is used in class is very similar to how it is used by the students at work, and as they, therefore, understand the purpose and see how it can help them with their real-life tasks, they accept using it.

Having said that, these particular learners do 'value human interaction' and would therefore not want a fully online course. The online component is used to 'reinforce' what was learned in class and to simulate work situations in which they have to operate in English on the internet.

Most teachers at the language institution are ready to learn how to use technology in class, and even the more hesitant ones have had some experience with using it for teaching and learning purposes.

A collection of tools
Besides offering a wealth of authentic materials and being a place where communication takes place, the internet also provides us with an ever growing range of tools for such tasks as communication, sharing, networking, designing and creating materials, and publishing, from the very simple to the most sophisticated. Some only exist for a short time, while others become 'staple tools', widely known and used.

Examples of tools that have become established are publishing tools like blogging platforms: WordPress and Blogger, for example, or podcasting services like Podomatic; platforms that serve as repositories and sharing environments for videos, slides, and images such as Flickr, YouTube, Vimeo, and Slideshare; collaborative knowledge collection, writing, and publishing tools such as wikis; learning management systems such as Moodle; social networking tools such as Twitter and Facebook, or the alternative for educational use, Edmodo. There are many alternative tools in the aforementioned categories and hundreds if not thousands for many other purposes, which cannot all be listed here. Only a handful of these tools were created specifically for educational purposes but educators around the world have been creatively reappropriating many of these tools for their and their learners' purposes.

Online games are gaining popularity among language teachers and learners (Godwin-Jones, 2005, Thorne, 2008), and there are wikis, blogs (e.g. http://games2teach. wordpress.com), and books (Mawer and Stanley, 2011; Sykes et al., 2012; Reinders, 2012) that explain how they can be used in a pedagogically sound way. Games have always been used in language classes, however, recently the concept of gamification or game-based learning has been used to justify using online games or game-like tools and environments for learning (and other) purposes. It can be defined as making use of gaming techniques and features, such as awarding points or creating competition. The aim is to make learning more engaging, fun, and thus motivating (Sørensen and Meyer, 2007; Mawer and Stanley, 2011).

Less widely used but slowly becoming established in certain ESP fields are 3D virtual worlds such as Second Life, which though not originally designed with educators in mind, are used by educators for simulating the real world to train people in various professions such as nurses, border guards, midwives, etc. These same 'places' can be used for role plays with ESP students (Godwin-Jones, 2005) and real interactions with other people (Thorne, 2008). These worlds are also social places where learners can meet people from other countries, make friends and actually do things together almost like in real life. Based on such simulations in virtual environments and video games, 'serious games' are developed for language learning and teaching (Godwin-Jones, 2005: 20; Sørensen and Meyer, 2007).

In the third case study, we will see how Ayden Yeh, an English teacher at a private college in southern Taiwan uses an elaborate combination of online and offline tools in her English for Advertising course to help students achieve the multiple aims of the course.

Case Study 4.3: English for Advertising

The students
The course participants are aged between 25 and over 30 and there are around 32 on each course. The level of English of the students is quite good because they have been studying English since primary school. They are all professionals with daytime jobs and, therefore, studying at college is a demanding task. They usually choose this course because it has relevance to their professions (e.g. business administration, marketing and sales, and international trading).

The context
English for Advertising is a blended 18-week (one semester) elective course students in their third year can take for two credits.

The course has three main aims:

1. to familiarise students with basic advertising concepts

2. to allow students to implement in practice what they have learned, by producing print, radio, and television commercials; and by doing so:

3. to improve their English language skills.

As can be seen, this is a content and language integrated learning course (CLIL), which is typical for many ESP courses.

Materials and technology used
The following Web 2.0 tools are used:
Yahoo! Groups, a blog, PowerPoint, Slideshare (a platform for publishing presentations), GoogleDocs, document archiving service (e.g. thinkfree.com), online video servers (e.g. Blip.tv, YouTube).

Offline tools:
Digital audio and video recorders, media player, editing software such as Windows MovieMaker, other types of multimedia tools.

Types of activities the technologies (and materials) are used for and their relevance for the learner
Yahoo! Groups is an online discussion platform that can be accessed online or via email and is used as an online learning platform for discussions and general course communication, and to archive files such as learning materials and course syllabi. At the same time, it helps build rapport among students and between them and the teacher.

The class blog serves as a publishing platform to present students' work to a wider audience and as a portfolio. Additionally, it is used by the teacher as a place to publish certain learning materials which students use in or outside the classroom.

Some student or teacher-created materials like images, PowerPoint slides, or videos need to be uploaded to a special service before they can be embedded in a blog. For this purpose, Slideshare.com, GoogleDocs, and Blip.tv or YouTube are used.

By connecting the Yahoo! Group email address with the blog, students get automatic notifications when there is a new blog publication.

'Web 2.0 tools provide a virtual extension of the classroom where students can learn and showcase their creativity to the rest of the world.'[4]

The digital media and tools used offline on the computer are used to create radio and television commercials. Transferring and sharing files is made easy because of the digital format. Because of this, and the relatively inexpensive and readily available

---

[4] The quotations in this section are from the teachers interviewed for this case study.

tools, digital audio and video 'have a great impact on language learning, particularly in enhancing students' oral and communicative competence by producing authentic language in the form of digitally recorded materials.'

Producing commercials is a task that demands good collaboration among students in order to be successfully accomplished, which helps the students to learn through interacting with each other.

'The task process begins with pre-task activities where students participate in lectures and discussions of advertising samples. It is also during this time that language and learning objectives, task guidelines, requirements, and criteria for assessments are given to students. In the second stage, students brainstorm, plan, and gather sufficient information to help them pin down their topic and task strategy. The next step is to implement the creative execution. In this stage students engage in copywriting, preparing the storyboard (for television), producing the advertisement, and writing their report paper (...). The third stage is the presentation, where they present their final projects, and the final stage is the assessment, where students are evaluated based on the quality of their presentation, report paper, and the collaborative execution of their project (...). Throughout the process, students use the English language to learn the content while learning how to use it to communicate/express their ideas.'

In order to work together efficiently and produce a commercial, the students had to engage in effective communication, which took place in English. This helped them practise the target language and thus meet the language aim of the course.

Course and technology evaluation
'Task assessment is done using the students' report paper, audio/video commercial materials, a scoring rubric given during the workshop, and notes taken during the presentations. The feedback I provide is based on the criteria stipulated on the scoring rubric and how successfully the students met the task requirements (both technical and language skills) and the overall quality of their commercials.'

Usability and constraints of the technology

Compared to the other case studies, especially the first one, this course employs a wide range of online and offline tools. This means that students need some training in using them, although, being young professionals, they might be familiar with at least some of them. Given the duration of the course, and the aims of the course, which include learning how to produce advertisements, a short technical training workshop seems justifiable and acceptable for the students.

Attitudes of students and institution towards the technology

The students had to write a report based on seven questions, one of which was about the technology used in the course. According to some of the comments, the students thought that it was 'fun to learn something new ... to be able to create a short film by using IT' and 'easy to handle'. Another student commented that 'by practising to be a good voice over, we can enhance our fluency of speaking. By writing scripts for TV and radio commercials, we can enhance our writing skills and creativeness.'

There was no collaboration with other colleagues and 'support from colleagues is hard to find'. As it is not a research project, the course is not supported by the institution either.

Mobile learning

Mobile technologies have not been integrated in any of the case studies explicitly, although they might have been used by the students to access online course materials, the internet and podcasts, but they are worth mentioning briefly here as they are more and more widespread and very relevant for many ESP and Business English students, who often need as much flexibility as possible in their courses.

The technology is readily available for no extra cost and ESP learners use them daily in their professional lives, mostly in the form of mobile or smartphones and iPods, but also in the form of tablet PCs such as the iPad, which means they do not need much training in how to use the technology itself. In addition, many business students will have a mobile phone plan, often paid for by their employer, that allows them to access the internet or send short messages without incurring any extra costs.

Many ESP or Business English students are frequent travellers. With modern smartphones, they can use downtime, such as time at the airport, to go through learning material, listen to a podcast, leave a comment on a forum discussion, or reply to an email from their tutor (for example, with feedback on a task).

There are more and more specific language tools available for learners, who can use these tools to practise grammar, note down and review vocabulary, look up words, etc. However, particularly for ESP students, the more interesting uses of mobile technology will be, as above, 1) for simulations of real work situations and 2) for accessing learning material, podcasts, and internet resources, wherever students happen to be and whenever they want to. Most importantly, however, mobile technology allows for a situated learning approach because learning can take place in the student's actual work environment. In the Taxi English course mentioned above, I created mini podcasts as a summary of our face-to-face lessons to give extra listening practice, which the taxi drivers could listen to during downtime while waiting for the next passenger. This means they were in their work place, at the taxi rank or in their taxis, where the conversations recorded in the podcasts actually take place.

As with any other technology, mobile technologies are most effective when they are integrated into a course rather than used haphazardly, so that students understand their value and see the relevance to their course (Edirisingha, Salmon and Fothergill, 2007; Kukulska-Hulma and Sharpless, 2009; Palalas, 2011).

Blended learning – integrating technology

In all three case studies in this chapter, the courses are designed taking a blended learning approach. There is a mix of face-to-face and online learning and of synchronous (e.g. Skype, video conferencing rooms) and asynchronous (e.g. discussion groups, blogs, learning management systems) communication tools.

According to research into ESP blended learning, careful planning and integration of online and face-to-face components are important (Arnó-Macià, 2012). Garrison and Kanuka (2004) assert that a careful blend of asynchronous and synchronous communication tools and integration of other tools used in a course can enhance learning.

In ESP courses, blended learning has been adopted early as it can be particularly appropriate for Business English or ESP learners because it gives them flexibility in where and when they learn (Arnó-Macià, 2012). At the same time, it allows teachers to create highly specialised courses, which would be difficult to arrange in a face-to-face class due to the low number of students (Garrett, 2009). Teachers can also offer self-access materials online, or supplement the coursebook with extra authentic materials that are more relevant to their students (Krajka, 2003), thus being more responsive to their needs (Garrett, 2009). The concept of responsiveness can also relate to the course design, the tools, methodologies and activities used (Tudor, 1996 in White, 2007: 322) and what kind of blend is chosen. It focuses on various 'aspects of individual learners' such as their learning styles and strategies, interests, and their contributions (White, 2007: 322).

In other words, in the ESP context, teachers need to take a flexible approach, which is also regarded as one of the features of education in the third millennium (Felix, 2005). Collis and Moonen (2002) list five dimensions of flexibility: programme, study material, location, forms of communication, and types of interaction. Blended learning can allow teachers to be flexible in all five of these dimensions.

Besides the benefits mentioned so far, blended courses can additionally help learners in developing 'autonomy, out-of-class learning, self-assessment, individualization' (Trinder, 2006: 192), and learning or enhancing their electronic literacy skills (Arnó-Macià, 2012).

In the three cases, several benefits of a blended approach can be seen. In the first case, it allows for flexibility in location. In Case Study 4.2, Viola argues that 'blended learning/teaching has proved more successful than just f2f or just online'. She adds that 'it has the advantage of human contact and interaction; and technology provides tools to encourage autonomous learning. Most importantly, it helps simulate work-related situations.' Yeh points out that 'the integration of digital media and Web 2.0 tools into a traditional face-to-face platform creates an optimal learning environment for language learning.'

Drawbacks

Blended learning can also have some disadvantages such as the need to invest in more resources (e.g. financial, human, technical) (Garrison and Kanuka, 2004;

Littlejohn, 2004). The English for Advertising course shows how complex such a blend can sometimes be. It can be time-consuming to create such courses, and teachers need to have some technical knowledge and training, and have access to particular technologies.

It is essential for institutions and teachers to consider these and other issues before setting up a technology-integrated blended course and to find ways to make it sustainable (Garrison and Kanuka, 2004; Littlejohn, 2004).

Challenges of technology use in ESP

Teachers and institutions that integrate technology into their ESP courses can face multiple other challenges (Felix, 2005; Krajka, 2003; White, 2007) such as:

- issues of accessibility, availability and reliability of the technology
- the need for one-off and ongoing teacher and learner training
- varying levels of tech-savviness of teachers and learners
- time and resources needed to create technology-integrated courses
- the need for new ways of managing classes in which technology is used, including how to deal with technical problems during lessons
- having to adapt to the changing roles of teachers as well as learners, particularly in online courses, etc.

These issues need to be thought through carefully to enable a smooth and successful integration of technology and ensure that teachers as well as students will accept the use of the technology as a valuable addition to their ESP course, rather than a distraction from the real purpose, which is learning the target language.

Conclusion

Whether they like technology or not, ESP teachers today cannot afford not to integrate technology into their courses, because technology plays an essential role in their learners' everyday professional lives, in which they need digital and electronic literacy skills to communicate internationally across cultural borders using different media, and to become autonomous learners who can keep up with the fast-paced professional world.

Teachers who like technology and feel comfortable using it, will keep up with the latest developments and often readily adopt and experiment with various technologies in their teaching, whether offline or online. Sometimes, they are criticised by more techno-critical educators for unnecessarily using technology without having a proof for their effectiveness in helping students learn better or faster. Kohn and Hoffstaedter (2008 in Levy, 2009: 779) describe this as the 'caravan effect', metaphorically comparing technophiles to travellers who stop briefly to drink from a waterhole, by which they mean the latest technology, and then move on to the next waterhole, and so on.

ESP teachers might be less prone to this because they generally focus more on their learners' needs and are more aware of the limited time and busy schedules they have. Even if they were not, their students would most probably be reluctant to use technologies they would see as a waste of time or too difficult to use. Therefore, ESP teachers will mostly practise what Chapelle (2003: 9) suggests: a 'critical, technologically-informed pragmatism.' In ESP, as we can see from the case studies, the reason for using technology is not only or always because it makes learning the language more effective or efficient, but also because it can offer tools that simulate real life work situations, while giving students the opportunity to acquire and practise essential 21st century professional skills.

References

Anthony, L (1997) English for Specific Purposes: What does it mean? Why is it different? *On-CUE* 5/3: 9–10. Available online at: www.antlab.sci.waseda.ac.jp/abstracts/ESParticle.html

Arnó, E, Soler, A and Rueda, C (2006a) 'The Role of Information Technology in Languages for Specific Purposes: Some Central Issues', in Arnó, E, Soler, A and Rueda, C (eds) *Information Technology in Languages for Specific Purposes: Issues and Prospects.* New York: Springer, 3–18.

Arnó, E, Soler, A and Rueda, C (2006b) 'Information Technology in LSP: Prospects on a Brave New World', in Arnó, E, Soler, A and Rueda, C (eds) *Information Technology in Languages for Specific Purposes: Issues and Prospects.* New York: Springer, 247–261.

Arnó-Macià, E (2012) The Role of Technology in Teaching Languages for Specific Purposes Courses. *The Modern Language Journal* 96/Focus Issue: 89–104.

Askari-Arani, J (2004) Internet-based Medical Articles in EMP. *ESP World Journal* 3/2. Available online at: http://espworld.7p.com/Articles_8/Medical_A%20.htm

Bax, S (2003) The End of CLT: A Context Approach to Language Teaching. *ELT Journal* 57/3: 278–287.

Bremner, S (2010) Collaborative writing: Bridging the gap between the textbook and the workplace. *English for Specific Purposes* 29: 121–132.

Butler-Pascoe, ME (2009) English for Specific Purposes (ESP), Innovation, and Technology. *English Education and ESP* 1–15.

Chapelle, CA (2003) *English language teaching and technology.* Amsterdam: Benjamins.

Collis, B and Moonen, J (2002) Flexible Learning in a Digital World. *Open Learning: The Journal of Open and Distance Learning* 17/3: 217–230.

Dudley-Evans, T and Johns, AM (1991) English for Specific Purposes: International in Scope, Specific in Purpose. *TESOL Quarterly* 25/2: 297–314.

Dudley-Evans, T and St John, MJ (1998) *Developments in ESP. A multi-disciplinary approach.* Cambridge: Cambridge University Press.

Edirisingha, P, Salmon, G and Fothergill, J (2007) 'Profcasting – a Pilot Study and Guidance for Integrating Podcasts in a Blended Learning Environment', in Bernath, U and Sangrà, A (eds) *Research on Competence Development in Online Distance Education and E-learning.* Oldenburg: BIS-Verlag, 127–137.

Elia, A (2006) Language Learning in Tandem via Skype. *The Reading Matrix* 6/3: 269–280.

Eröz-Tuğa, B and Sadler, R (2009) Comparing six video chat tools: A critical evaluation by language teachers. *Computers & Education* 53: 787–798.

Evans, S (2012) Designing email tasks for the Business English classroom: Implications from a study of Hong Kong's key industries. *English for Specific Purposes* 31: 202–212.

Felix, U (2005) E-learning Pedagogy in the Third Millennium: The Need for Combining Social and Cognitive Constructivist Approaches. *ReCALL* 17/1: 85–100.

Garrett, N (2009) Computer-Assisted Language Learning Trends and Issues Revisited: Integrating Innovation. *The Modern Language Journal* 93/Supplement s1: 719–740.

Garrison, DR and Kanuka, H (2004) Blended Learning: Uncovering its transformative potential in higher education. *The Internet and Higher Education* 7: 95–105.

Godwin-Jones, R (2005) Emerging Technologies Skype and Podcasting: Disruptive Technologies for Language Learning. *Language Learning & Technology* 9/3: 9–12.

Grosse, CU and Voigt, GM (1991) The Evolution of Languages for Specific Purposes in the United States. *Modern Language Journal* 75/2: 181–195.

Hampel, R (2006) Rethinking Task Design for the Digital Age: A Framework for Language Teaching and Learning in a Synchronous Online Environment. *ReCALL* 18/1: 105–121.

Hampel, R and Hauck, M (2006) Computer-mediated Language Learning: Making Meaning in Multimodal Virtual Learning Spaces. *The JALT CALL Journal* 2/2: 3–18.

Hewings, M (2002) A History of ESP. *ESP World Journal* 1/3. Available online at: www.esp-world.info/Articles_3/Hewings_paper.htm

Kern, N (2011) Tools for Taxi Drivers. *English Teaching Professional* 77: 56–58.

Kern, R, Ware, P and Warschauer, M (2004) Crossing frontiers: New directions in online pedagogy and research. *Annual Review of Applied Linguistics* 24: 243–260. Available online at: http://dx.doi.org/10.1017/S0267190504000091

Kohn, K and Hoffstaedter, P (2008) *Authenticated language learning with do-it-yourself corpora.* Paper presented at the 13th International CALL Conference, August – September 2008, Antwerp, Belgium.

Krajka, J and Grudzinska, Z (2002) Using the Internet in the Language Classroom to Foster Learner Independence – Ideal and Reality. *IATEFL Poland Teacher Development and Autonomous Learning SIG Newsletter* 7/May 2002: 9–16. Available online at: http://iatefl.org.pl/sigs/tdal/n7krajka.htm

Krajka, J (2003) ESP on the Web – A Proposal for a Web-based Coursebook Supplement. *ESP World Journal* 2/2. Available online at: http://esp-world.7p.com/articles_5/ESP%20ON%20THE%20WWW_2.htm

Kukulska-Hulme, A and Sharples, M (2009) Mobile and contextual learning. *Research in Learning Technology* 17/3: 159–160.

Lave, J (1991) 'Situating Learning in Communities of Practice', in Resnick, LB, Levine, JM and Teasley, SD (eds) *Perspectives on Socially Shared Cognition.* Washington, DC: American Psychological Association, 63–82.

Levy, M (2009) Technologies in Use for Second Language Learning. *The Modern Language Journal* 93/Supplement s1: 769–782.

Littlejohn, A (2004) *Reusing online resources: a sustainable approach to e-learning.* Routledge.

Luzón-Marco, MJ (2002) Internet Content-based Activities for English for Specific Purposes. *English Teaching Forum* 40/3. Available online at: http://eca.state.gov/forum/vols/vol40/no3/p20.htm

Luzón-Marco, MJ and Gonzàlez-Pueyo, MI (2006) 'Using the Internet to Promote Autonomous Learning in ESP', in Arnó, E, Soler, A and Rueda, C (eds), *Information Technology in Languages for Specific Purposes: Issues and Prospects.* New York: Springer, 177–190.

Mawer, K and Stanley, G (2011) *Digital Play: Computer Games and Language Aims.* Surrey: Delta Publishing.

Mayes, T and de Freitas, S (2007) 'Learning and E-Learning: the role of theory', in Beetham, H and Sharpe, R (eds), *Rethinking Pedagogy for a digital age.* Routledge, 13–25.

Mullen, T, Appel, C and Shanklin, T (2009) 'Skypebased Tandem Language Learning and Web 2.0', in Thomas, M (ed) *Handbook of research on Web 2.0 and Second Language Learning.* Hershey, PA: Igi Global. J, 101–118.

Murray, DE (1988) Computer-Mediated Communication: Implications for ESP. *English for Specific Purposes* 7: 2–18.

Palalas, A (2011) ESP for Busy College Students: Is the Blend of In-class, Online & Mobile Learning the Answer? *The IALLT Journal* 41/1: 108–136.

Reinders, R (ed) (2012) *Digital Games in Language Learning and Teaching.* Palgrave Macmillan.

Shepherd, M and Watters, CR (1998) *The Evolution of Cybergenres.* Proceedings of the Thirty-First Annual Hawaii International Conference on System Sciences (HICSS' 98) 2: 97–109.

Smoak, R (2003) What is English for Specific Purposes? *English Teaching Forum* 41/2: 22–27.

Sørensen, BH and Meyer, B (2007) *Serious Games in Language Learning and Teaching – A Theoretical Perspective.* Digital Games Research Association (DIGRA). Available online at: www.digra.org/dl/db/07312.23426.pdf

Sykes, J, Reinhard, J, Liskin-Gasparro, JE and Lacorte, M (2012) *Language at Play: Digital Games in Second and Foreign Language Teaching and Learning.* Prentice Hall.

Thorne, SL (2008) 'Transcultural Communication in Open Internet Environments and Massively Multiplayer Online Games', in Magnan, S (ed) *Mediating Discourse Online.* Amsterdam: John Benjamins, 305–327.

Trinder, R (2006) 'Integration of E-learning into a Tertiary Educational Context', in Arnó, E, Soler, A and Rueda, C (eds) *Information Technology in Languages for Specific Purposes: Issues and Prospects.* New York: Springer, 191–210.

Vie, S (2008) 'Digital divide 2.0'. Computers and Composition, 25, 9–23, in Arnó, E, Soler, A and Rueda, C (eds) *Information Technology in Languages for Specific Purposes: Issues and Prospects.* New York: Springer, 99.

Warschauer, M and Healey, D (1998) Computers and language learning: An overview. *Language Teaching* 31: 57–71.

Warschauer, M and Kern, R (eds) (2000) *Network-based language teaching: Concepts and practice.* New York: Cambridge University Press.

Warschauer, M (2006) Foreword, in Arnó, E, Soler, A and Rueda, C (eds) *Information Technology in Languages for Specific Purposes: Issues and Prospects.* New York: Springer, 191–210.

White, C (2007) Focus on the language learner in an era of globalization: Tensions, positions and practices in technology-mediated language teaching. *Language Teaching* 40/4: 321–326.

Willis, D and Willis, J (2007) *Doing Task-Based Teaching.* Oxford University Press.

Wisniewska, I (2010) *Learning One-to-One.* Cambridge University Press.

Zhong, Y (2008) A Study of Autonomy English Learning on the Internet. *English Language Teaching* 1/2. Available online at: www.ccsenet.org/journal/index.php/elt/article/view/467/477

English for Academic Purposes

5

English for Academic Purposes

Jody Gilbert

Introduction

English for Academic Purposes (EAP) is generally considered one of two branches within the larger field of English for Specific Purposes (ESP), the other branch being English for Occupational Purposes (Hamp-Lyons, 2011; Hyland and Hamp-Lyons, 2002; Flowerdew and Peacock, 2001). EAP is identifiable by its focus on teaching English with the primary goal of preparing non-native speaking (NNS) learners for academic study and research in English-medium courses and institutions. Although EAP teaching can and does occur at many levels of academic study, it is traditionally associated with study at university or college level, (Hyland and Hamp-Lyons, 2002), in post-secondary or higher education institutions (HEIs). According to Strevens (1988, cited in Flowerdew and Peacock, 2001) key characteristics of ESP/EAP are as follows: design which is intended to meet specific learner needs; teaching content (themes/topics) related to specific disciplines; a focus on discipline-specific language use; teaching English with a specific purpose, in contrast with 'general English.'

EAP programmes can be found throughout the world, but are especially prevalent at tertiary institutions in the English speaking countries of UK, USA, Canada, Australia, and New Zealand. Normally, international students who wish to take degree programmes in these countries must meet institutionally-determined language proficiency requirements before commencing their studies. There are usually several ways to do this, but the two most common routes are submission of a satisfactory English language proficiency exam score (for example, TOEFL, IELTS) or completion of a recognised EAP preparatory programme. In some cases, students must achieve a satisfactory proficiency exam score in addition to completing a designated EAP programme. Most institutions will provide EAP programming in-house, although more universities in the UK, Australia, and Canada are now choosing to outsource their programmes to private schools in so-called 'pathways' programmes.

Students can enrol in EAP courses before they study in university content courses, or concurrently with content study. In the UK this is referred to as *pre-sessional* and *in-sessional* programming. North American institutions describe these courses as *sheltered* and *adjunct* courses. Sheltered, or pre-sessional courses, are more often meant to prepare students for general academic study, whereas in-session courses may well focus on specific disciplines, with the intention of having the EAP faculty work more closely with the content faculty to deal with the specific language demands of a certain subject (Thompson, 2005).

EAP programmes and courses are typically intensive. Student contact hours in pre-sessional programmes can reach upwards of 25 hours per week. Teachers can find themselves under institutional pressure to move students through the courses and into full undergraduate studies, as EAP programmes in English-speaking countries are often seen as 'feeder' programmes which can serve to boost international undergraduate enrolment.

In post-secondary institutions where English is not the medium of content course instruction, English language courses are normally more general purpose. Students take these courses for a wide range of reasons: out of general interest, to fulfil a degree requirement, or with the goal of overseas travel or study. However, it is increasingly common for non-English medium post-secondary institutions to offer academic content courses which are taught in English. In these institutions, responsive English language programmes may adjust their curriculum and teaching to account for this need, and the teaching may take on more of an EAP flavour by focusing on typical academic tasks and appropriate language use for academic contexts.

Specificity and dual purposes in EAP

Preparing non-native speakers (NNS) for the demands of academic study in an English language environment requires a dual focus of helping students to develop both the language competency and study skills which will help them to succeed. Hyland and Hamp-Lyons (2002) refer to this duality as 'general English' and 'study skills,' which includes tasks such as listening to lectures, giving presentations, and academic writing. This approach can be called English for General Academic Purposes (EGAP), aimed at preparing students for general academic studies across disciplines. In cases where more specific needs are identified, either because EAP learners are grouped by their chosen academic discipline or taking in-session/ adjunct EAP along with content courses, the teaching approach may be more focused and developed based on conventions of discipline-specific language use. This approach is known as English for Specific Academic Purposes (ESAP), and is built on an '...understanding of the cognitive, social and linguistic demands of specific academic disciplines' (Hyland and Hamp-Lyons, 2002: 2). Both the general and more discipline-specific approaches to EAP teaching raise important issues in curriculum design, especially relating to the proficiency levels of students. Flowerdew and Peacock (2001) discuss specificity in terms of *narrow* and *wide-angle* approaches and outline several theoretical arguments regarding the appropriate blend of discipline-specific and general or 'core' English language in EAP programmes, especially at the lower proficiency levels.

Needs analysis

EAP teaching grew from a practical need to prepare NNSs for academic study in English-medium courses. As English emerged as the predominant world language for business, communication, and scholarly work, the demand for English language support grew as more overseas students enrolled in academic degree programmes in English-speaking countries. In response to a growing international student population in the UK in the 1950s and 1960s, universities began to offer short ad hoc language courses to support NNS in their studies (Jordan, 2002). It soon became apparent that general English teaching would not adequately prepare these students for academic study. Theorists in ELT methodology were recognising that the traditional linguistically-driven teaching methods aimed at learning a general English would not adequately prepare NNS to use language effectively in discipline-specific academic contexts. As Flowerdew and Peacock (2001: 11) write, 'What was needed was an approach to language teaching which was based on descriptions of the language as it was used in the specific target situations.' Programmes became more formal and were developed based on analysis of student needs and practical uses of academic language in target contexts. This focus on the practical remains a key driver in EAP from curriculum design to classroom teaching, as programmes and instructors grapple with the continually shifting needs of students and other changes in the contexts in which they teach.

In the field of ELT, it is considered best practice to include some level of needs analysis in course design (see Dudley-Evans and St John, 1998; West, 1997) to help address practical needs of students. In target environments, EAP students can be expected to undertake academic tasks such as listening to lectures and note-taking, writing academic essays, preparing and delivering presentations, and participating in group discussions. Approaches to needs analysis vary by context, and data can be collected through testing, questionnaires, interviews, focus groups, and direct observation of post-secondary classroom lectures or activities. Formal needs analysis studies in EAP have yielded valuable information for teachers and course designers. Many of these investigations have focused on specific skill areas, such as Horowitz (1986) who identifies a mismatch between the typical writing tasks assigned by EAP instructors and the writing tasks actually required by university professors, or Ferris (1998), who found large discrepancies in expectations between content instructors and EAP students in listening and speaking tasks.

Technology and EAP

Current needs analysis in EAP reveals that, along with linguistic demands, many academic tasks involve the use of technology. Students and faculty are expected to produce word-processed reports and documents, create digital slides to enhance presentations, use email to communicate and collaborate, access and participate in online learning platforms, and conduct research using online electronic databases and the internet. This expectation is still growing, and forward-thinking EAP practitioners realise it makes good sense for students to develop technology-related knowledge and skills as part of their EAP study. As Jarvis (2008: 2) writes, '[f]or today's NNS students ... being able to operate efficiently, effectively, and appropriately in academic contexts has an additional element, and that is being able to do so in an electronic environment. Such environments have, of course, become a prevalent feature at many higher education institutions (HEIs) across the globe.' From a needs-based perspective, the use of technology to support academic study can be viewed as part of the study skills side of EAP. In their purposeful efforts to prepare students for the academic contexts they will enter, EAP teachers are integrating a variety of technologies into learning experiences which support language learning. Many of these learning experiences also mirror current uses of technology in target post-secondary learning environments.

Hamp-Lyons and Hyland (2005: 1) argue that context and purpose are '...what drives the teaching and research' in EAP, distinguishing it from more general approaches to English language teaching. Each type of technology use in EAP teaching described in this chapter is rooted in learner needs as recognised by researchers and classroom instructors, and the classroom illustrations of technology use are inextricably linked to the EAP teaching contexts they are embedded in. First discussed is the use of technology to help EAP learners build accurate linguistic knowledge through concordancing. Next, the need for learners to develop critical e-literacy skills is examined, and examples of hands-on webpage searching and evaluation experiences are presented. Following this is an example of how a simple class wiki can help EAP learners share and build the important cultural knowledge needed to more fully participate as members of the wider communities in which they live. Finally, web-based learning management systems (LMS) are explored, and an example shows how flexible learning opportunities can be provided where learners see limited class time in intensive programmes.

Concordancing and corpus analysis: developing linguistic knowledge

Introduction

In a general overview of EAP, Hamp-Lyons (2011: 96) writes that '[o]ne valuable development for the EAP classroom has been the use of corpora and concordances, through computer systems, to allow EAP students to conduct their own mini research projects ... providing students with hands-on exercise in figuring out how language works'.

Language corpora are collections of spoken or written text, created for the purposes of linguistic analysis or description. Specially designed software along with digitised corpora can provide a linguistic resource that allows researchers, materials developers, classroom teachers, and language learners to closely examine English as it is actually written and spoken in a range of contexts. This use of corpus-related technology to investigate language is often associated with EAP, given EAP's needs-focused interest in the authentic uses of academic language. Hamp-Lyons (2011) adds that the compilation and exploitation of digitised academic corpora have led to important advances in EAP, especially in the area of genre analysis for the purposes of materials development. Further, concordancing tools allow for both instructors and students to investigate lexical and grammatical patterns of academic language as it is actually used in written and spoken forms.

What is concordancing?

Concordancers are software programmes which allow users to search thousands, and in some cases millions, of words of a corpus for in-context occurrences of particular morphemes, words, or phrases. A typical search returns a series of text lines, aligned to allow for user analysis of how the inputted text (keyword in context, or KWIC) is used in the context of genuine written or spoken text. Figure 5.1 shows an extract from a concordance search for decline, built from an academic corpus.

Figure 5.1: Concordance output of decline – Brown Corpus

Studies of the growth and	DECLINE	of children's fears indicate that fears du
stantially by the current	DECLINE	in business activity, we have been able to
esident, said, 'A drastic	DECLINE	in freight loading due principally to the
educed output, industrial	DECLINE,	widespread unemployment'. But the solutio
an intermediate or major	DECLINE,	usually while the bottom is being formed
nd unexpected movement	DECLINE	during the preschool years, but that fears
will produce a prolonged	DECLINE	of interest rates? My answer is in the neg
o explain the April sales	DECLINE	as a reaction from a surge of consumer buy
ommuter railroad service	DECLINE,	and have failed to offer a helping hand.
ring the year and should	DECLINE	in coming months. Thus we enter 1961 in a
there would be a similar	DECLINE	in the market values of other automotive a
ear, but I look for some	DECLINE	in radios from the high rate in 1961 to mo
ping out and facing some	DECLINE.	In earlier business cycles, when this occ
have. The causes of the	DECLINE	of the commuter railroads are many and c
blight account for the	DECLINE	of central city churches. Central cities r
a long period after the	DECLINE	of his procreativity. Some recent writings
olyphosphates spelled the	DECLINE	of soap usage when the synergism between
1957. Nowhere has this	DECLINE	been more painfully evident than in the Ne
ize of London, started to	DECLINE.	The Afghans invaded; the Safavids fell fr
11,744. This year-to-year	DECLINE	for Dallas County closely follows the nati

Generated from: www.lextutor.ca/concordancers/concord_e.html

Concordancing software allows for quick extraction of multiple occurrences of the keyword (input) in context from a designated corpus. By analysing the series of concordance lines in Figure 5.1, a user can form hypotheses about the lexical and grammatical properties of the keyword *decline*. For example, *decline* occurs in contexts related to business and economics, *decline* occurs in both noun and verb slots, and *decline* can be followed by the prepositions *in* and *of*.

Concordancing in the classroom

Flowerdew (1996) proposes that concordancing has the potential to support language learning in several important ways, and can be undertaken by both teachers and learners. For teachers, concordancing can offer input for materials development and classroom teaching, and provide a source of lexico-grammatical information about naturally occurring language. For learners, concordancing can provide opportunities for inductive learning, a resource for error analysis and correction, and opportunities for 'serendipity learning' (Johns, 1988, cited in Flowerdew, 1996).

Early explorations of teaching with concordancers most often involved EAP specialist research and materials development rather than direct use of concordancers by classroom teachers and learners, due to limited access to the required technology. Issues of access have eased greatly, with a range of corpora and concordancing software now freely available online. Although the pedagogical advantages of corpus-based teaching are theorised by many proponents, actual classroom use in EAP appears quite limited (Thompson, 2005, Stevens 1996), and longitudinal empirical studies are rare (Yoon, 2011). Thompson (2005: 16) states, '…there is a widespread lack of knowledge among EAP teachers about the principles of corpus creation, the criteria for evaluating the data that is obtained from corpus searches, and the potential uses of concordancing both in the classroom and in materials development'.

One way that concordancing software can be used by EAP teachers is to develop teaching materials. For example, Thurnstun and Candlin (1998) used a concordancing programme for vocabulary learning materials in EAP, targeting selected items from the University Word List. These items were grouped by rhetorical function (for example, stating a topic; referring to research; reporting research) and then presented to students on paper in a 'chain' of teacher-guided vocabulary learning tasks. An academic corpus provided multiple opportunities for students to investigate a single item in the context of authentic academic language, and practise the skill of guessing unknown vocabulary from context. The tasks required students to analyse the concordance lines, and included true/false questions, gap-fills, and improvised writing using target vocabulary. Student feedback on the tasks was highly positive, and the authors also note that the investigation of target vocabulary using concordances not only helps them to develop the ability to guess the meanings of unknown words from context, but also enriches students' knowledge of collocation and grammatical structures in the context of authentic language. The authors observe that '[c]oncordancing allows a materials developer enormous possibilities for the creation of such exercises from authentic texts' (273). Similar exercises to those suggested by Thurstun and Candlin are appearing in commercially produced ESL textbooks, especially in 'guessing vocabulary in context' and collocation-type exercises.

Thompson (2005) discusses the use of corpora to produce frequency-based wordlists which can provide a useful basis for teacher and programme materials development. Vocabulary profiling of digitised text can help EAP students target the most important vocabulary items in the context of reading texts for vocabulary learning, based on frequency of use. One web-accessible example of this is 'Web-VP' or 'VocabProfile' (available online at: www.lextutor.ca/vp/eng/) which provides a vocabulary profile of any digitised text as inputted by the user. As stated on the website, 'VocabProfile will tell you how many words the text contains from the following four frequency levels: 1) the list of the most frequent 1,000 word families, 2) the second 1,000, 3) the Academic Word List, and 4) words that do not appear on the other lists.'

It is widely acknowledged that much of the work in concordancing for language learning is rooted in the early investigations of Tim Johns, who used concordancing in his teaching of postgraduate ESL students for several years (see Johns, 1991).

Johns coined the term 'data-driven learning' (DDL) to describe his idea that learners could actively research naturally occurring language through concordancing, intuiting rules and patterns of language for themselves rather than first being told what those rules and patterns are, and then attempting to construct meaningful text. Johns (1991: online) explains that DDL represents a unique approach to inductive language teaching in so far as it puts '...the learners own discovery of grammar at the centre of language-learning'.

Lee and Swales (2006) report on a corpus-based EAP experimental course in which six doctoral students at the University of Michigan took part in a series of activities designed to introduce them to concordancing tools and their potential applications in building lexico-grammatical knowledge of academic English. The students also created a corpus of their own writing for comparison with a corpus of academic writing, as well as a specialised corpora from samples in their own field of specialisation as models for further comparison. Students presented findings from their corpus work at the conclusion of the course. Post-course interviews indicated that the participants were highly positive about the experience, some describing the DDL approach as 'empowering' and noting that the tools enabled autonomous exploration and analysis of discipline-specific native speaker language. According to the researchers, most students in the course purchased their own copies of the concordancing programme, allowing them to use the concordancing tool outside of the classroom and in their future studies.

In another classroom study, Charles (2007) describes a pilot project in an advanced EAP writing course in which graduate level students used concordancing to analyse rhetorical functions such as 'defending your own research' and 'criticizing research of others.' The project required detailed concordance searches and careful analysis in order to reveal patterns in the use of rhetorical functions at the discourse level. Student feedback on the project was highly positive.

Yoon (2011: 131) provides a summary of some of the current thinking around potential benefits of learner concordancing with a focus on EAP writing skills development. He writes that concordancing can offer 'rich exposure to the most common and typical language forms and patterns that they are likely to encounter outside the classroom', and provide opportunities for students to work with 'real language' instead of language which has been designed specifically for language learning purposes. Yoon (2011) explains further that concordancing can allow students to see how words function in different contexts and genres, provide opportunities to investigate lexical and grammatical patterns in language, and the potential to develop this linguistic knowledge inductively and autonomously. Rather than the teacher or a text presenting students with direct explanations of word meanings or grammatical patterns, students can analyse language through concordancing, and arrive at their own discoveries about how naturally occurring language is commonly used. From his review of 12 studies on learner concordancing, Yoon (2011: 138) concludes that 'learner concordancing can be a viable research and reference tool for enhancing the linguistic aspects of L2 writing and increasing learner autonomy'. At the same time Yoon notes that there is no clear evidence that learner concordancing is any type of 'miracle cure' for L2 learners. Flowerdew

(1996: 99) also cautions against over-application, stating, 'Instead of concordancing being promoted as a panacea, able to solve all teaching and learning problems, considered evaluative studies will allow concordancing to be incorporated appropriately into the teacher's battery of reference and teaching resources as the useful additional teaching and learning tool that it undoubtedly is.' To date, it appears that 'a perhaps overenthusiastic concordancing literature' (Flowerdew, 1996: 99) has not resulted in widespread use of concordancing in language classrooms.

For teachers who do want to bring concordancing into their classrooms, a solid understanding of the concept behind DDL and knowledge of how to effectively conduct corpus investigations and accurately interpret concordancing results are essential. As Stevens (1996: 4) writes, 'Concordancers are certainly not tools that computer novices can be turned loose on without proper preparation beforehand.' Flowerdew (1996) stresses the need for learner training, and Yoon's (2011) review of studies of corpus use in EAP writing concludes that explicit learner preparation and ample practice is required if students are to use concordancing effectively. The activity often requires both learners and teachers to develop new technical skills in order to use concordancing programmes effectively. Bringing concordancing into the language classroom can also require a re-examination of some fundamental beliefs about language learning and teaching for both teachers and learners, such as the traditional roles of teacher and learner and DDL's emphasis on linguistic knowledge in the era of communicative teaching approaches.

Case Study 5.1: Concordancing in the classroom

Andy teaches EAP at a small, primarily undergraduate university in Canada. He has undertaken graduate studies in TESOL, and has been teaching in the programme for nine years. Andy uses a variety of technology in his teaching, and first learned about concordancing at a regional TESOL conference during his second year of teaching in the EAP programme.

At the university, EAP instruction takes place in a modularised programme, consisting of grammar, reading, communication, and writing courses, each at three levels of proficiency: Intermediate, High Intermediate, and Advanced. In the 65-hour Advanced Grammar course, a key goal is for students to improve grammatical accuracy in their writing. This is often cited as a critical goal for EAP writers and supports the aims of the other courses in the programme, especially the writing course.

The curriculum provided for the Advanced Grammar course is organised around specific structures and patterns to be taught such as noun clauses, adjective clauses, passive voice, and gerunds/infinitives. Teachers are generally given freedom to adjust the curriculum depending on learner needs, and use methods they feel most comfortable with. One of Andy's priorities when teaching the Advanced Grammar course has been to find ways to more actively engage learners in a course which is traditionally form-focused and textbook-driven. In an effort to shift the emphasis away from textbook-based practice exercises and encourage students to take a more active role in their learning, Andy has introduced a variety of tasks which are aimed at facilitating student-initiated explorations of English grammar. One of these tasks involves the use of a web-based concordancing programme (www.lextutor.ca). Corpus Concordance English (www.lextutor.ca/concordancers/concord_e.html) allows users to input keyword(s) and search around 20 different corpora for occurrences in context. The programme offers additional features such as customisable output configurations and collocation searches. Once concordances are generated, users are able to follow any hyperlinked KWIC to see the larger context that the concordance line has been extracted from.

Andy takes his Advanced Grammar students to the computer lab each week for technology-enhanced language learning activities such as collaborative text reconstruction, quizzes, video response assignments, and WebQuests. Technology infrastructure at the university is excellent, and instructors have access to network drives, computers and digital projectors, and up-to-date computer labs. Over the semester, students spend approximately six hours on concordancing activities in the computer lab. This includes introductory activities and explanations, pair work, and individual work. Andy introduces the class to concordancing in a computer lab, about halfway through the course. He first discusses concepts such as corpora and concordance lines, and the possibility of focusing on language use in academic contexts by searching academic corpora. As Andy does this, he displays live examples from www.lextutor.ca using the digital projector in the computer lab. He then encourages students to follow his examples at their own computers, to become familiar with the website and various functions in the concordancing programme. In order to further stimulate curiosity and interest, Andy purposefully chooses structures which exemplify the variation in language and defy some of the more traditional grammar textbook 'rules'. For example, a search of 'could to' demonstrates that it is possible for the modal 'could' to be followed by 'to', as in, 'he did all he COULD TO make it a good report'.

At this point, Andy explains that the purpose of the activity is to provide the opportunity for students to learn about grammar in a different way, through exploration and research, using the concordancer as a tool to analyse 'real' academic language. He provides students with worksheets to guide discovery learning experiences for structures that are most conducive to concordancing work, such as gerunds/infinitives, word forms, and verb+particle patterns.

An excerpt for a gerunds/infinitives investigation is provided below. Andy displays searches for the first two or three words and discusses the results with the class before allowing students to begin working in pairs or individually. Andy finds this is important, because students need guidance if they are to interpret the concordancing results properly. Some searches turn up few or no results, and students need to be reminded of the limitations of such results in order to avoid inappropriate conclusions about the particular structures they are investigating.

Figure 5.2: A concordancing activity

This is a list of 2K level and AWL level words which can be followed by gerunds/ infinitives. Being familiar with how these common words are used in writing will help you find and correct errors in your own writing. In other words, you should know these patterns very well!

Rather than simply looking up the patterns in a reference text, try using lextutor to discover them. This activity can help you to learn because you must actively search for the information.

For each word:

1. Guess whether the word is followed by a preposition + gerund (or other) or followed by an infinitive, or both. Remember, many of these words can be followed by other kinds of nouns as well.

2. Find concordances for the word in lextutor. If you cannot find examples, simply leave the word for later and continue.

Recommended settings for corpus concordance:

Keyword: 'contains'

Corpus: 'Brown + BNC Written (2+m)'

WORD	MY GUESS	EVIDENCE
2K		
accustomed	accustomed with doing?	**ACCUSTOMED** to studying
advise	advise him to leave?	**ADVISE** us to act
		ADVISE the network to get
afford		
afraid		

Web-based research: the internet as information source in EAP courses

Proficiency in reading and competency in research are basic requirements for students in HEI programmes, and the widespread availability of internet access on post-secondary campuses means much of this activity takes place in electronic environments. Studies show that the internet has been the preferred research tool for post-secondary students in the US and UK for several years. For example, Jones (2002) surveyed 2,054 post-secondary students at 27 different US colleges. The study found that 73 per cent of respondents reported using the internet more than the library for information searching, and only nine per cent used the internet less than the physical library. In a pilot survey, Slaouti (2002: 107) found 'evidence of widespread usage' of the internet for academic study among 786 students at the University of Manchester. Ten years later, indications are that student internet use for research purposes has only increased, as libraries continue to expand their digital repositories and work towards integration of internet search engines such as Google Scholar into their databases (Helms-Park et al., 2007).

According to Stapleton (2003, 2005a), study-related internet use by EAP students most often involves information searches. It has become quite normal for EAP students to use web-based information as content for course assignments such as research essays and presentations, and they will very likely continue to do so in their academic careers. In light of this, a more detailed theoretical background is presented below, focusing on the set of complex skills and literacies which are required if students are to make effective use of the internet to support academic study.

Today, most EAP students arrive to the classroom as 'digital natives' (Prensky, 2001: online) and they can appear technically proficient at using computers and mobile devices for many functions, including internet searches. However, technical computer skills are quite different from the skills required to conduct efficient web searches, read and navigate digital text and hypertext effectively, and determine the validity and reliability of web-based information. There is a distinction to be made between electronic literacy, or e-literacy, and computer literacy, which is a 'very limited view of computer-related education ... referring to only the most basic forms of computer operation' (Warschauer, 2003: 111).

Jarvis (2009: 51) writes, 'The notion of equipping learners for academic study raises specific challenges of e-literacy skills for non-native speakers (NNS) of English and it is by no means clear whether EAP providers are rising to this challenge'. In an earlier paper, based on a survey of computer use at HEIs in the UK, Jarvis (2004: 126) raises this concern:

> ...[UK university] providers are focused exclusively on computers for language work ... it is surprising to note the confidence that providers have in the perceived understanding that EFL students are competent in the use of computers in their academic studies... Providers of EAP might ask the following questions... Do students really know how to access and evaluate relevant WWW sites? And how to paraphrase, quote and appropriately reference material from the WWW?

Shetzer and Warschauer (2000: 2) propose a framework for electronic literacy which attempts to account for the complex and continuously evolving nature of online communication, or 'how people use computers to interpret and express meaning'. Lamy and Hampel (2007) prefer the term multiliteracies (The New London Group, 2000), which includes a critical awareness of the implications of the social construction of meaning on the internet arising from different cultural and linguistic perspectives.

Leu et al. (2004) describe literacies arising from rapid change in the internet and ICT as *deictic*; the meanings of those literacies are time-dependent. This idea is reflected by Coiro et al. (2008: 5):

Literacy is no longer a static construct from the standpoint of its defining technology for the past 500 years; it has now come to mean a rapid and continuous process of change in the ways in which we read, write, view, listen, compose, and communicate information. Thus, literacy acquisition may be defined not by acquiring the ability to take advantage of the literacy potential inherent in any single, static, technology of literacy (e.g., traditional print technology) but rather by a larger mindset and the ability to continuously adapt to the new literacies required by the new technologies that rapidly and continuously spread on the internet.

There is a strong consensus that, compared to gathering information from reading traditional print text, researching and reading online involves different processes of comprehension (Coiro 2003; Leu et al. 2004), requires the development of new literacy skills, and demands a critical approach to evaluating web content (Stapleton 2003, 2005a, 2005b; Slaouti, 2002; Shetzer and Warschauer, 2000; Anderson, 2003).

Understanding researching on the web

Researching on the web can be a significant challenge for EAP students because they must do so with a critical mindset and make quick judgements about reliability while confronting a deluge of information (Warschauer, 2003; Stapleton, 2003). In consideration of the nature of reading and researching online, '...it makes little sense' explains Warschauer (2003: 114) 'to discuss critical literacy as a separate or special construct; rather, critical literacy is an essential element of reading in the online era'.

The filtering mechanisms which allow access to information through libraries are very different from those on the internet. In successive papers, Stapleton (2003; 2005a; 2005b) stresses that before web-based sources were available, students mainly used sources which were relatively reliable and credible since they were published and available in libraries. Library sources have undergone standardised screening processes before reaching the student, but this is not the case on the internet, where any user can post content. This lack of centralised control or any type of filter has led to both a proliferation of information on the web, and huge variability in the quality of its content, leaving the user solely responsible for determining the degree of credibility of any given web source (Stapleton, 2003; Dalton and Proctor, 2008; Warschauer, 2003).

According to Stapleton (2003), research is showing that L2 learners may lack the critical thinking skills to make effective judgements about the credibility and quality of information on the internet. Although the concept of critical thinking is not clearly defined among practitioners, and the concept itself may suffer from some ethnocentric bias (Atkinson, 1997), there is still a need for EAP students to develop autonomous strategies for determining the credibility of web-based information if they hope to be effective learners and collaborators in academic communities. In his case study of L2 composing processes, Stapleton (2010: 304) writes, 'substandard approaches to sourcing appear widespread among students ... indicating a need for basic researching skills build in both as part of the taught curriculum and as the feedback'.

Providing opportunities for student internet use in EAP courses offers several potential benefits. The internet represents an opportunity for students 'to handle a real-world tool' (Slaouti, 2002: 111), a rich research source, an opportunity to develop autonomous and lifelong learning skills (Shetzer and Warschauer, 2000; Kasper, 2000), and quick access to authentic materials (Brandl, 2002).

In the EAP classroom, e-literacy skills can be developed through internet-based projects and activities. Ramachandran (2004: 82) provides a detailed account of two projects in her EAP classroom. One activity is a WebQuest (see http://webquest. org/), which she describes as '...a project-based learning activity that is often used to integrate the internet into instructional activities across disciplines'. Ramachandran makes several recommendations regarding WebQuest tasks in the EAP classroom: tasks must be carefully designed to suit the interests and language levels of the students; background information and introductory activities should be provided; a description of the process should be given at the outset; instructor guidance should be provided throughout the activity. The second activity was the writing of a research paper, which involved searching the internet for topic-relevant information and determining the reliability of web-based sources. Ramachandran (2004: 84) comments that as a result of the project, '...students' choices of resources were informed, and they became more aware of the pitfalls to avoid later when embarking on a research project in a university course'. She also remarks that students built collaborative skills through the research paper project, and serendipitously learned about citation building software available, both online and as a feature of word processing programs.

Jarvis (2009: 52) describes a classroom EGAP project designed to help students develop 'the necessary language and electronic literacy skills so that they might successfully function in English in an academic environment'. Tasks in the group project include submission of a report and an oral presentation. Groups undertake web-based research on their chosen topics of interest, write draft reports, consider feedback from classmates and instructors by sharing and collaborating on drafts posted on the course website, and deliver a presentation based on the final paper.

Luzon-Marco (2010) also provides a description of how WebQuests 'webtasks' might be used to develop e-literacy skills in learners as well as autonomy. Students in an ESAP course (Technical English for Chemical Engineering) complete a series of web tasks aimed at familiarising them with the specialised discourse of their discipline. Students choose their own specific issues of investigation under the broad topic of 'environmental issues.' Some example issues are discussed, and a pre-designed online 'Resources Section' provides links to a range of web-based information sources from government webpages, blogs, and wikis, helping students to get started. The 'Resources Section' also includes a series of questioning activities designed to 'help students reflect on the nature of internet resources' (p. 37). Students then begin to search out web-based resources which are relevant to their chosen issues. Linguistic, technical, and other web-research support is provided as students gather web-based information in order to write a report on their chosen issue, and present the report orally.

Online learning environments: collaboration and project-based learning

Developments in SLA research, shifting perspectives on CALL, and innovations in web-based technology are influencing the current thinking around the potential uses and roles of web-based technology in language teaching. In a review of empirical studies of online technologies in language teaching, Wang and Vasquez (2012: 413) claim that SLA research 'has been experiencing a paradigm shift: ... from a cognitive orientation to a social orientation, from classroom contexts to naturalistic settings, and from L2 learning to L2 use... Interestingly, this shift in SLA research seems to be in alignment with many of the fundamental attributes of Web 2.0 technology (such as ease of participation, communication, information sharing, and collaboration)'.

Miller et al. (2012: 184) write that technology such as Web 2.0 is well-suited to project-based learning (PBL) approaches in EAP '...because students can be encouraged to draw on a range of technological tools in order to research, present and share their projects'. Miller et al. (2012) describe an EAP course project which involved student use of a course weblog along with video production and sharing software. Groups of students worked collaboratively to plan, film, and share short science documentaries through video and Web 2.0. According to the authors, participants found the experience engaging and highly positive, and felt that their language skills improved through working on the project. In another example, Kessler et. al (2012) discuss how Google Docs can support a collaborative writing project among advanced proficiency EAP students. The study investigated the details of how students write collaboratively in using online word processing, and focused on the types and accuracy of changes made by writers, and the levels of participation within collaborative groups. As a result of their investigation and earlier studies, Kessler et al. recommend that practitioners take a flexible approach to writing pedagogy in order to take full advantage of new technologies for writing, as students 'engage in the writing process in new and unexpected ways' (p. 104).

In a review of research on Web 2.0 technology for language teaching, Wang and Vasquez (2012) found that wikis have been the second most commonly researched Web 2.0 tools. Little documentation on the use of wikis in EAP teaching exists. However, the ease of use and diverse functionality of wikis make this technology a popular initial choice for EAP teachers who are looking for a web-based platform to support course projects and activities.

Case Study 5.2: Using a wiki to provide additional cultural support to EAP learners

Beth teaches in an ESL programme at a comprehensive, primarily undergraduate, university in Canada. The university enrols around 13,000 students, with approximately 90 per cent studying in undergraduate courses, and an international student population of around six per cent. Historically, nearly all ESL students go on to study undergraduate courses at the university as completion of the programme provides them with their language requirements for entry into degree programmes.

Because of this link with the university, the programme has a strong EAP focus. Students are generally recent high school graduates, although some may have taken one or two years of post-secondary education.

Chinese students make up a large portion of the ESL population, and Saudi Arabian Cultural Bureau (SACB) sponsored students comprise around one third of the total programme enrolment. Over the past two years, the ESL programme has seen significant growth, enrolling upwards of 400 students per semester. This has resulted in some challenges, including a lack of instructors and classroom space along with organisational and administrative complications.

The programme offers semesters of 12 weeks, three times per year. The curriculum is intense and it is not unusual for students to leave their studies in the upper levels to take the IELTS or TOEFL exam in an attempt to meet the ELP requirements without completing the ESL programme at the university. ESL classes are taught at six levels and are organised into two types: core and skill. Instruction in core courses takes place for 15 hours each week. The skills are integrated, and each core course uses a theme-based text. A significant effort has been made to develop resources to supplement the texts in the core courses.

Skills course instruction takes place for six hours each week. Students have the option to choose either an oral/aural communication skills focus on speaking and listening, or a writing and grammar skills course. Students planning to gain admission to undergraduate studies at the university complete Level 050 and complete the 050 skills class in writing and literature.

Informal research indicates that students who complete the ESL programme generally fare better in undergraduate studies than those entering studies based on satisfactory TOEFL or IELTS exam scores only. There also seems to be better retention of the ESL programme's students in the university's credit programmes compared to exam entry track students.

Beth has been a teacher in the programme for eight years and she has taught all levels. Beth's educational background includes a Master's degree in English, as well as certificate training in TESOL, and a recently completed diploma in TESOL. In her final project for the diploma programme, Beth learned about wikis through her project supervisor.

Beth's final project was built around her interest in the links between cultural integration and achievement in language learning. This interest was sparked by some informal observations of student English competence in social settings. For example, while out for an end of semester dinner with the Level 050 (advanced) students, Beth was surprised to discover that some of the students seemed uncomfortable with basic communicative functions such as asking a waiter for a drink or sending back food which was not prepared properly. She felt that although the intensive language courses were preparing students for academic tasks such as presentation and essay writing, many students still lacked the ability to use language effectively in everyday social situations. Beth's observations were that many students live on campus and stick with their own cultural groups, and despite high levels of academic language knowledge, many students lacked the ability to use language effectively in socio-cultural contexts outside of the ESL classroom.

Recognising this need, Beth set about searching for solutions. From both informal observations and her investigations of published research, Beth knew that students who had more integrated experiences in homestay families or through volunteering opportunities, tend to have much more success adjusting culturally, and this adjustment has a positive influence on their academic success. For the large group of students who lived on campus and had more ghettoized experiences, she considered common approaches such as peer programmes with Canadian native-speaker volunteers, or producing a handbook which could be used by current and prospective students to learn more about some of the cross-cultural differences they might face in the local community. However, Beth was most interested in taking the perspective of the students as a starting point, and basing her approach on their own experiences. She planned to survey her students on paper, asking about the biggest perceived differences between their home country cultures and Canadian culture, in common categories such as transportation, greetings, and mealtimes. During the planning process, she encountered several logistical issues. At that time, her supervisor suggested moving the project online, using a wiki.

Beth had no experience with wikis, and limited experience with educational technology in general. Following her supervisor's suggestion, Beth moved her project to an online wiki, allowing more students to access it at any time, and adding potential for the project to grow. By sharing one wiki account, students could have the opportunity to express their views on Canada anonymously, and feel good about writing on the internet to a wider audience, an opportunity which they do not have very often in the programme. Beth could also respond to student input and post links to further information, and there was potential for other teachers in the programme to participate as well. Although the project was not the single solution to the problem of limited cultural integration, Beth felt that students could use the wiki to learn more about cultural differences either before they arrived or while they were studying. She hoped students would see the wiki as an interesting and an engaging way to learn.

Beth discovered the wiki was easy to create and was impressed by the technology. She used the wikispaces platform (www.wikispaces.com) and found that by exploring the wiki tool, she learned what she could potentially do and how the wiki could be used by her students. Ideas for the wiki developed quickly. Beth began by creating a single page containing a survey of the various cultural topics, and then expanded the wiki by creating a page for each country. During computer lab classroom time, Beth introduced the wiki to her students and the students were very interested in the idea. She approached the ESL programme lead and offered to provide seminars on using the wiki to other classes. The idea was supported by administration and feedback from other instructors on the seminars and use of the wiki was very positive.

Beth finds that the wiki work is most productive when she has students in the lab, although a few students have posted comments outside of regular class time. She also finds that as the wiki evolves, student input is becoming more interesting and varied. Beth plans to continue using the wiki in her teaching, and explore more ways to use wikis with her students.

In her initial thinking, Beth was hoping that students would find the wiki valuable enough to provide regular input, and she wanted it to be used by as many students as possible and open it up to students beyond the ESL programme she teaches in. She would like the wiki to be more active and have more time to spend working on it with her students, but the instructional time is very limited due to the intense nature of the programme. Beth hopes to continue developing and expanding the wiki in the future.

Learning management systems: additional opportunities to engage in learning

Most HEIs which operate EAP programmes also support at least one version of a web-based learning management system (LMS) designed to support teaching and learning at the institution. These systems are also referred to as course management systems (CMS), or virtual learning environments (VLEs). In most cases, EAP instructors at the institution will also have access to this system, which can host a range of online resources and tools such as tutorials, language skills activities, quizzes, message boards, wikis, and blogs, all within one central online space.

An LMS allows teachers-as-designers to quickly build a course website as a complementary self-access resource to enhance face-to-face instruction, as a virtual classroom space in blended or hybrid approaches wherein some face-to-face instruction is replaced by online work, or as an entirely online distance learning course. Basic administration and development of these resources does not require advanced technical skills or any knowledge of programming languages, and institutions will often have specific resources dedicated to the training and support of faculty in at least one LMS. Today, the two most common systems in use at HEIs are Blackboard and Moodle (Godwin-Jones, 2012).

As technology has advanced, the number of commercially available LMS has grown substantially and the choices are still expanding as deployment of these systems is at an all-time high at HEIs. For example, in the US post-secondary system, 99 per cent of the 927 institutions surveyed in 2008 supported at least one LMS (Arroway and Sharma, 2009). In 2010, Moodle was the most popular official LMS at Canadian universities, supported at about 40 per cent of institutions, while Blackboard retained about 19 per cent of the market share (Contact North, 2012). EAP students in these contexts should thus expect to use an LMS in their academic courses, and it follows that some specialised technical skills and competencies in specific modes of online communication are needed if EAP students hope to fully participate in undergraduate learning.

For the face-to-face EAP instructor in a post-secondary context, an institutionally sanctioned LMS can offer a convenient and relatively stable online platform to complement course activities. As with any content course, an LMS can serve many practical functions for the face-to-face EAP instructor. Although some of these functions may have little direct consequence for language development, they should not be dismissed as they can support an organised, flexible, and transparent approach to overall language course design and instruction. Popular systems such as Blackboard and Moodle include the following functions:

1. Serve as an up-to-date information hub for course participants, with scheduling, announcements, and private individual access to course grades and feedback. The LMS can be adjusted to reflect any unplanned changes to course scheduling or the syllabus, and participants can be notified immediately through a messaging system.

2. Fulfil the traditional class website function of repository for course materials for student self-access. In web-enabled classrooms with digital projectors, audio-visuals and written materials such as short exercises or questions can be posted on the LMS and also displayed on a projection screen for the class. This provides students with convenient access to the same set of materials and resources that the instructor displays in class, allowing students to review and/or preview class material online.

3. Operate as a central online learning space, providing access to a range of activities which have the potential to support language development. Skills-focused activities such as tutorials, quizzes, and listening comprehension exercises can be created beforehand and released for student access as needed. A typical LMS will also offer a further set of Web 2.0 tools related by their capacity to facilitate communication, sharing of information, and collaboration, such as message boards, instant messaging, blogs, and wikis. It is normally up to classroom teachers to determine which blend of tools to use, based on what language learning affordances each tool offers, and how these tools might provide pedagogical advantages in specific teaching contexts.

Within the context of increasing LMS use in post-secondary courses, EAP's strong focus on language use in target situations provides a solid rationale for integrating some LMS work into EAP courses. The majority of information on LMS use in ELT comes mostly from EFL perspectives in contexts where the medium of content course instruction at the institution is not English. For the most part, the information is descriptive and exploratory, focused on the practical aspects of LMS integration with language teaching, applications of certain tools within an LMS, some of the ways that teachers and ELT departments are using these tools, and reports of student perceptions and attitudes. Writers are currently exploring several areas of LMS use which may have implications for EAP contexts. These areas include reports of learner feedback on LMS integration (Liou and Chang, 2005), impacts of LMS use on learner autonomy (Dang and Robertson, 2010), blended vs fully distance approaches (Harker and Koutsantoni, 2005), and LMS applications for EFL writing (Wu, 2008).

Case Study 5.3: Using an LMS in the EAP classroom

Sarah co-ordinates and teaches on the English programme for business and economics students at a German university. She began her career teaching EGAP for entry-level college students in Germany, and gained experience teaching Business English in higher and further (adult) education institutions and in private companies. About ten years ago, Sarah joined a university-funded project to develop an online resource for business students at German universities. Although her main job was to create content for the site, Sarah grew interested in CALL through her work on the project, and she enrolled in an Educational Technology and TESOL MA programme as a result. Around this time, the university language centre, which was responsible for the project, implemented Moodle and Sarah began using the LMS to create EAP and ESP blended learning and distance learning courses, drawing on the insights she was gaining from her MA studies. She also facilitated online intercultural exchanges for the language centre using a range of other tools, including wikis and blogs.

At the university Sarah teaches at, studies in other languages are generally not a requirement in degree programmes. However, students enrolled in the Business and Economics Programme study English as well as Chinese, Spanish or French in order to meet degree requirements, constituting about 25 per cent of the degree courses at both bachelor and master levels. The programme sees around 400 new students each year at the bachelor level, and around 60 at the master's.

In the bachelor degree, students receive four hours of classroom instruction each week, focusing on grammar revision and vocabulary development. Grammar content is taught separately following a largely form-focused curriculum, while films and articles from mostly US and UK journals, such as Business Week and the Economist, are the vehicle for vocabulary development. At the end of the first year, students must sit a final examination which includes a grammar section as well as an essay section based on the texts they have read throughout the year.

In the second year, students continue with four hours of English instruction each week, but the focus shifts towards oral fluency and writing for business. The last required English course focuses on advanced oral fluency and is usually taken at the end of year three.

During the first year, all other degree programme courses are taught in German. In the second and third years, students have options to choose English-medium content courses, in which English content may range from reading requirements only, to courses being taught and assessed entirely in English. English-taught content course offerings are increasing at the university, as is the case at many European universities, in an effort to promote mobility for both staff and students. However, students on these courses do not usually receive additional course-specific language support.

Sarah sees the students she teaches on the Business and Economics degree programme burdened by heavy workloads and study stress, and many seem to focus on completing the English courses as efficiently as possible. There is little time in their busy lives for more intense academic undertakings such as autonomous reflective learning. Much of the activity in the courses is driven by the semester or year-end examinations, and the teaching sometimes becomes largely focused on preparation for these exams under the significant time constraints.

Sarah has recently assumed the role of Co-ordinator of English, and has identified many opportunities for development in the language programme. Her main concern with the current situation is that, although students are gaining exposure to general academic and business/economics language through course activities, they do not get enough practice in the language or skills specific to their content course studies. At the same time, time constraints will not allow for additional course hours for this support.

Initial departmental meetings have focused on building a common understanding of curricular goals, and the differences between teaching general and academic English, and English for Business and Economics. Further, writing has been identified as an important area in need of development, and a vehicle through which students could have their academic writing skills assessed. In some English-medium content courses in the second and third years of study, professors require students to display their understanding through writing in summative assessments. However, the professors in these courses traditionally do not provide much feedback or emphasis on English language use in their assessments, focusing instead on content only. To help participants on these courses, it was decided that first-year and second-year students would spend more time developing academic writing skills and exploring in detail the distinctions between the choice of vocabulary and writing style of the more journalistic articles they usually read compared to English 'academic writing style' for their subject.

To support students both in expanding their academic and specific vocabulary and in developing academic and business-related writing skills, Sarah began looking at how the integration of a web-based Moodle learning environment might facilitate the introduction of more specifically targeted language learning activities. In terms of vocabulary development, Sarah has started to work with colleagues to bring the topics addressed in language courses more in line with the Business and Economics content courses and then to identify key vocabulary items. Sarah wants to work towards using Moodle as a central space for gathering vocabulary in glossaries and developing self-access vocabulary learning activities with the quiz function. She has introduced several Moodle-based activities into her own courses on a pilot basis. Although working on Moodle is optional and students do not receive course credit, they have responded well to the pilot activities, with the majority (around 80 per cent) of Sarah's first-year students opting to use the resources in Moodle to help with vocabulary learning, instead of the more traditional paper-based exercises and quizzes that are still available. Online activity reports show that students are using the Moodle vocabulary quizzes regularly, with many re-taking each quiz multiple times to review their learning during the course and before the examination.

In terms of writing skills, Sarah intends to develop self-access writing tutorials in Moodle to support students in the specific writing skills they need throughout their studies, from first-year essays to seminar papers and dissertations. This plan is in the early stages and requires more consultation with content teachers, which has proven to be a challenge as there is traditionally very little time or opportunity for communication between the English instructors and content faculty at the university. However, initial Moodle-based activities have already been set up to guide first-year academic essay-writing.

Sarah is also piloting Moodle for its potential to support collaborative and reflective work within a problem-based learning approach. In this approach, third-year students work in groups to develop a project around an area of global business interest, directly linked to a required content course. The process involves articulating a problem, formulating a hypothesis, brainstorming ideas, researching, and producing presentations and reports on the group's work. Teams of four students meet to discuss the project, record meeting minutes, go back to working on their own contributions, and meet again. This work cycle continues, eventually leading to a presentation and paper describing the findings. Students use the wiki tool in Moodle to document the project progress, posting minutes from their meetings and collaboratively developing and submitting their presentations and papers. At various points during the course, students submit their reflections on learning using the Moodle journal activity. In practice, Sarah has observed that most of the project collaboration and editing takes place offline rather than in the Moodle wiki, so that the wiki only shows the end results rather than the process of learning. This may be related to the frustration students have expressed with technical aspects of the Moodle wiki tool, so Sarah is considering alternative wiki sites for collaboration. This is not an ideal solution since it means students will need to log in to a different website outside of Moodle, and Sarah is looking for other possible solutions. Journal reflections on learning, however, have proved surprisingly successful, with students articulating their learning needs, problems and personal sense of learning in a single tool, enabling Sarah to respond to the individual comments easily, as well as providing a useful source of information for needs analysis.

As more English-medium content courses are offered, in the faculty in particular, and at the university in general, Sarah sees an increasing need for student language support, especially in the areas of specialised vocabulary and academic writing. Time constraints mean that students require flexible self-access to this support, and Moodle has demonstrated the potential to provide this. Sarah sees the vocabulary work through Moodle as 'a way in' to begin introducing students and colleagues to the potential benefits of an online learning platform, with a wider vision of establishing Moodle-based learning resources for English for Business and Economics across the curriculum. Further development of the resource itself will require increased technical support for Moodle to address instability issues and closer collaboration among colleagues to build an effective resource for students.

Conclusion

This chapter has provided an overview of some of the ways technology is being used in EAP teaching practice. Technology has become a normal part of the learning experience in post-secondary contexts, and EAP teachers are accounting for this in the activities they design. While some technologies, such as concordancing, are directly aimed at supporting language acquisition, others are more often used to develop study skills and provide opportunities for language use in typical academic tasks. Integration of tools such as the internet for web-based research, various Web 2.0 platforms, and LMSs can encourage students to use language purposefully and collaboratively in technologically-mediated learning environments.

Many contextual factors influence the EAP teacher's decision and ability to use technology. The most obvious and often cited of these is time. The intensive nature of EAP courses and institutional demands to 'get through' the curriculum with learners means that instructors can have difficulty finding the time needed to judiciously investigate and integrate technology in their teaching. One approach is to integrate technology with programming during the process of curriculum design, rather than leaving technology as an 'add-on' to the curriculum. This involves more fundamental discussions of EAP programme values and teacher beliefs surrounding the role and relevance of technology in the academic lives of EAP students. On the other hand, limitations on classroom time can serve as motivation for teachers to use technology, leading instructors to develop self-access online study materials, which allow students more flexibility in choosing how and when to study.

Each of the instructors in the classroom illustrations has taken part in professional development and academic TESOL studies, and it has been through these activities that their interest in using technology for language teaching has developed. The role of teacher education and professional development is widely recognised as a key to effective integration of technology in language teaching.

Further, teacher and learner access to reliable and updated technology is essential, especially when introducing more complex activities such as learner concordancing. Networked computer labs with digital projectors allow teachers to provide hands-on experience and technical support for learners as new technologies are introduced in the EAP classroom.

It has often been stated in the CALL literature that technology is not a method, and that technology itself does not improve teaching and learning; rather, it is how technology is used that can lead to learning. Although the classroom cases in this chapter do not offer direct evidence of learning resulting from technology use in EAP, they do provide some insight into how technology is viewed by practising teachers, and how technology is being integrated into some of today's EAP teaching contexts. The particular technologies discussed in the cases are quite well known and not especially remarkable in the field of ELT. However, the practices of the teachers are truly innovative for their particular contexts. This perspective on innovation places less emphasis on the technology itself, and more emphasis on teacher practice. In each situation, the teacher's approach to technology integration is rooted in learning needs emerging from the immediate teaching context, rather than an arbitrary teacher-centred decision to simply use a new technology in the classroom. This approach allows the teachers to maintain a focus on pedagogical goals and the learner needs which inform these goals, as they explore how to effectively integrate technology into their teaching practice and maximise the learning opportunities for their students.

References

Anderson, NJ (2003) Scrolling, Clicking, and Reading English: Online Reading Strategies in a Second/Foreign Language. *The Reading Matrix* 3/3. Available online at: www.readingmatrix.com/articles/anderson/article.pdf

Arroway, P and Sharma, B (2009) *EDUCAUSE Core Data Service Fiscal Year 2008 Summary Report*. Available online at: http://net.educause.edu/ir/library/pdf/PUB8006.pdf

Atkinson, D (1997) A Critical Approach to Critical Thinking in TESOL. *TESOL Quarterly* 31/1: 71–94.

Brandl, K (2002) Integrating Internet-Based Reading Materials into the Foreign Language Curriculum: From Teacher-to Student-Centered Approaches. *Language Learning & Technology* 6/3. Available online at: http://llt.msu.edu/vol6num3/brandl/default.html

Charles, M (2007) Reconciling top-down and bottom-up approaches to graduate writing: Using a corpus to teach rhetorical functions. *Journal of English for Academic Purposes* 6/4: 289–302.

Coiro, J (2003) Reading Comprehension on the Internet: Expanding Our Understanding of Reading Comprehension to Encompass New Literacies. *The Reading Teacher* 56/6. Available online at: www.readingonline.org/electronic/elec_index.asp?href=/electronic/rt/2-03_column/index.html

Coiro, J, Knobel, M, Lankshear, C and Leu, DJ (2008) 'Central Issues in New Literacies and New Literacies Research', in Coiro et al. (eds) *Handbook of Research on New Literacies*. NewYork: Lawrence Erlbaum Associates, 1–21.

Contact North (2012) *Online Learning in Canada: At a Tipping Point, A Cross-Country Check-Up 2012*. Available online at: www.contactnorth.ca/online-learning-canada

Dalton, B, and Proctor, P (2008) 'The Changing Landscape of Text and Comprehension in the Age of New Literacies', in Coiro et al. (eds) *Handbook of Research on New Literacies*. New York: Lawrence Erlbaum Associates, 297–324.

Dang, TT and Robertson, M (2010) Impacts of Learning Management System on Learner Autonomy in EFL Learning. *International Education Studies* 3/3. Available online at: www.ccsenet.org/journal/index.php/ies/article/view/5399

Dudley-Evans, T and St John, MJ (1998) *Developments in English for Specific Purposes*. Cambridge: Cambridge University Press.

Ferris, D (1998) Students' Views of Academic Aural/Oral Skills: A Comparative Needs Analysis. *TESOL Quarterly* 32/2: 289–316.

Flowerdew, J (1996) 'Concordancing in Language Learning', in Pennington, M (ed) *The Power of CALL*: Houston: Athelstan, 87–113.

Flowerdew, J and Peacock, M (2001) 'Issues in English for Academic Purposes', in Flowerdew, J and Peacock, M (eds) *Research Perspectives on English for Academic Purposes*. Cambridge: Cambridge University Press, 8–24.

Godwin-Jones, R (2012) Challenging Hegemonies in Online Learning. *Language Learning & Technology* 16/2. Available online at: http://llt.msu.edu/issues/june2012/emerging.pdf

Hamp-Lyons, L (2011) 'English for Academic Purposes', in Hinkel, E (ed) *Handbook of Research in Second Language Teaching and Learning, Volume 2.* New York: Routledge, 89–105.

Hamp-Lyons, L and Hyland, K (2005) Editorial for 4/1: Some further thoughts on EAP and JEAP. *Journal of English for Academic Purposes* 4/1: 1–4.

Harker, M and Koutsantoni, R (2005) Can it be as effective? Distance versus blended learning in a web-based EAP programme. *ReCALL* 17/2: 197–216.

Helms-Park, R, Radia, P and Stapleton, P (2007) A preliminary assessment of Google Scholar as a source of EAP students' research materials. *The Internet and Higher Education* 10/1: 65–76.

Horowitz, D (1986) What Professors Actually Require: Academic Tasks for the ESL Classroom. *TESOL Quarterly* 20/3: 442–462.

Hyland, K and Hamp-Lyons, L (2002) EAP: issues and directions. *Journal of English for Academic Purposes* 1/1: 1–12.

Jarvis, H (2004) Investigating the classroom applications of computers on EFL courses at Higher Education Institutions in UK. *Journal of English for Academic Purposes* 3/2: 111–137.

Jarvis, H (2008) Electronic literacy reading skills and the challenges for English for Academic Purposes. *CALL-EJ Online* 10/1. Available online at: http://callej.org/journal/10-1/jarvis.html

Jarvis, H (2009) Computers in EAP: Change, Issues, and Challenges. *Modern English Teacher* 18/2. Available online at: http://usir.salford.ac.uk/11266/1/METHJ2009.pdf

Johns, T (1988) 'Whence and whither classroom concordancing', in Bongaerts, T et al. (eds) *Computer Applications in Language Learning.* Foris, Dordrecht, 9–33.

Johns, T (1991) *Should You Be Persuaded – Two Samples of Data-Driven Learning Materials.* Available online at: http://wordsmithtools.net/wordsmith/ corpus_linguistics_links/Tim%20Johns%20and%20DDL.pdf

Jones, S (2002) *The Internet Goes to College: How students are living in the future with today's technology.* Available online at: www.pewinternet.org/Reports/2002/The-Internet-Goes-to-College.aspx

Jordan, RR (2002) The growth of EAP in Britain. *Journal of English for Academic Purposes* 1/1: 69–78.

Kasper, L (2000) *Content-Based College ESL Instruction.* Mahwah: Lawrence Earlbaum Associates.

Kessler, G, Bikowski, D and Boggs, J (2012) Collaborative writing among second language learners in academic web-based projects. *Language Learning and Technology* 16/1: 91–109. Available online at: http://llt.msu.edu/issues/february2012/kesslerbikowskiboggs.pdf

Lamy, M and Hampel, R (2007) *Online Communication in Language Learning and Teaching.* New York: Palgrave Macmillan.

Lee, D and Swales, J (2006) A corpus-based EAP course for NNS doctoral students: Moving from available specialised corpora to self-compiled corpora. *English for Specific Purposes* 25: 56–75.

Leu, DJ, Kinzer, CK, Coiro, JL and Cammack, DW (2004) *Toward a Theory of New Literacies Emerging From the Internet and Other Information and Communication Technologies.* Available online at: www.readingonline.org/newliteracies/lit_index.asp?HREF=/newliteracies/leu

Liou, HC and Chang, JS (2005) *Two E-learning Projects for Quality of Higher Education in Taiwan ROC: Corpus-Based General and Academic English Learning Environments.* Paper presented at The Third AEARU Workshop on Network Education, 5 December 2005, Seoul National University. Available online at: http://candle.fl.nthu.edu.tw/newcandle/chi/publi/ Liou_AERU_2005.pdf

Luzon-Marco, M (2010) Webtasks for Learning Professional and Academic English: Adapting the Webquest Model. *Computer Resources for Language Learning* 3: 29–44.

Miller, L, Hafner, CA and Ng Kwai Fun, C (2012) Project-Based Learning in a Technologically Enhanced Learning Environment for Second Language Learners: students' perceptions. *E-Learning and Digital Media* 9/2: 183–195.

New London Group, The (2000) 'A pedagogy of Multiliteracies designing social futures', in Cope, B and Kalantzis, M (eds) *Multiliteracies: Literacy learning and the design of social futures.* New York: Routledge, 9–38.

Prensky, M (2001) Digital Natives, Digital Immigrants Part 2: Do they really think differently? *On the Horizon* 9/6. Available online at: www.marcprensky.com/writing/Prensky%20-%20Digital%20Natives,%20Digital%20Immigrants%20-%20Part2.pdf

Ramachandran, S (2004) Integrating New Technologies into Language Teaching: Two Activities for an EAP Classroom. *TESL Canada Journal* 22/1: 79–89.

Shetzer, H and Warschauer, M (2000) *An Electronic Literacy Approach to Network-Based Language Teaching.* Available online at: http://books.google.co.uk/books?id=wFH56QxG2uwC&pg=PA171&lpg=PA171&dq=An+electronic+Literacy+Approach+to+Network-Based+Language+Teaching&source=bl&ots=EIDKegYN7O&sig=f6Ryo3UfyMl81W_s5OTtEgIONJo&hl=en&sa=X&ei=OmanUcu9LorYsgbX6oDoDw&ved=0CDgQ6AEwAQ#v=onepage&q=An%20electronic%20Literacy%20Approach%20to%20Network-Based%20Language%20Teaching&f=false

Slaouti, D (2002) The World Wide Web for academic purposes: old study skills for new? *English for Specific Purposes* 21/2: 105–124.

Stapleton, P (2003) Assessing the quality and bias of web-based sources: implications for academic writing. *Journal of English for Academic Purposes* 2/3: 229–245.

Stapleton, P (2005a) Using the Web as a Research Source: Implications for L2 Academic Writing. *The Modern Language Journal* 89/2: 177–189.

Stapleton, P (2005b) Evaluating web-sources: Internet literacy and L2 academic writing. *ELT Journal* 59/2: 135–143.

Stapleton, P (2010) Writing in an electronic age: A case study of L2 composing processes. *Journal of English for Academic Purposes* 13/2: 295–307.

Stevens, V (1996) Concordancing with Language Learners: Why? When? What? *CAELL Journal* 6/2. Available online at: www.vancestevens.com/papers/archive/concordance1996.htm

Strevens, P (1988) 'ESP after twenty years: A re-appraisal' in Tickoo, M (ed) *ESP: State of the Art.* Singapore: SEAMEO Regional Language Centre: 1–13.

Thompson, P (2005) 'Assessing the contributions of corpora to EAP practice', in Kantaridou, Z, Papadopoulou, I and Mahili, I (eds) *Motivation in Learning Language for Specific and Academic Purposes.* Available online at: http://scholar.google.co.uk/scholar_url?hl=en&q=http://www.reading.ac.uk/internal/appling/thompson_macedonia.pdf&sa=X&scisig=AAGBfm2y0N39aND6TnX5R2jXGC0N50Ch1g&oi=scholarr&ei=Ds2lUY_hC4jOOb7TgFA&ved=0CC0QgAMoADAA

Thurnstun, J and Candlin, N (1998) Concordancing and the Teaching of the Vocabulary of Academic English. *English for Specific Purposes* 17/3: 267–280.

Tickoo, M (ed) (1988) *ESP: State of the Art.* Singapore: SEAMEO Regional Language Centre: 1–13.

Wang, S and Vasquez, C (2012) Web 2.0 and Second Language Learning: What Does the Research Tell Us? *CALICO Journal* 29/3: 412–430.

Warschauer, M (2003). *Technology and Social Inclusion: Rethinking the Digital Divide.* MIT Press: Cambridge.

West, R (1997) 'Needs analysis: state of the art', in Howard, R and Brown, G (eds) *Teacher Education for LSP.* Clevedon: Multilingual Matters Ltd, 68–79.

Wu, WS (2008) The application of Moodle on an EFL collegiate writing environment. *Journal of Education and Foreign Languages and Literature* 7. Available online at: http://web.chu.edu.tw/~wswu/publications/papers/journals/06.pdf

Yoon, C (2011) Concordancing in L2 writing class: An overview of research and issues. *Journal of English for Academic Purposes* 10/3: 130–139.

A practice-based exploration of technology enhanced assessment for English language teaching

6

A practice-based exploration of technology enhanced assessment for English language teaching

Russell Stannard and Anthony 'Skip' Basiel

Introduction

In this chapter of the book we take a practice-based look at how technology can be used in assessing English language teaching (ELT). We begin with a brief overview of the changes that have taken place in the area of assessment over the last 50 years. A common thread running through these changes is our starting proposition that over the last half century we have developed a greater understanding of how we might help someone to learn a language and these changes need to be reflected in the way we assess. Fundamentally, we hold the view that the ability to communicate and do things with language should lie at the heart of language learning. We need to develop certain skills in learners and these skills will help to make our language learners better communicators and 'users' of the language. It is therefore these skills that we need to focus on assessing. Some of these skills are global and associated with a general performance in using and working with the language and some of them are quite specific. They all need to be assessed if we are to effectively evaluate a student's overall language ability.

> The dominant view in the field continues to be that language ability consists of a number of interrelated areas, such as grammatical knowledge, textual knowledge, and pragmatic knowledge and that these areas of language knowledge are managed by a set of metacognitive strategies that also determine how language ability is realised.

(Bachman, online)

However, not only has our understanding of what skills and knowledge we need to be effective language users changed, and hence what we assess, but the way we assess has also changed. This is because our understanding of what assessment is and how to assess effectively has also developed. This changing in our understanding of the nature of assessment covers topics like who does the assessment, where it happens, who uses the assessment and when it happens. We understand that many different stakeholders may want to use the information gathered from assessments. We no longer take the narrow view that they are just for students and teachers. We also understand that a simple mark or score does not fully represent a real picture of a student's language ability. Even the goals of assessment have changed. It isn't about simply evaluating a student's level. Assessment has a role to play in motivation, self-reflection and washback (we will talk more about the terminology in the next section). In fact, good assessment can even provide opportunities for learning:

> In our view the main purpose of language testing is to provide opportunities for learning both for the students who are being tested and for the professionals who are administering the tests.

(Tomlinson, 1995: 39)

Technology is another area that is having a direct impact on language assessment. Technology can offer affordances that provide new ways of assessing. We can now assess and evaluate students in ways that simply were not available to us even ten years ago. We can video our students interacting in groups or even working on a monologue or story. We can get our students to record podcasts and audio files. We can get them to develop their written work in blogs and wikis. There is an abundance of tools that can be used in assessment and these broaden the types of assessment tasks we can create as well as offer quicker and easier ways to distribute them.

So assessment has changed. It has changed because firstly the skills and content of any modern language course have changed and because what we understand about the nature of assessment has also changed. It has also changed because of the impact of technology and the affordances that it offers, but that is still not the full picture. There are other 'drivers' that are also influencing both the way we teach and learn a language, and the way we assess it. Many of these have their roots in the changes that are taking place in mainstream education and not just language education. We know that the move towards a more communicative view of language learning began to emerge in the 1960s but the changes did not stop there. Over the next 50 years a whole range of ideas in mainstream education began to impact on language learning and on assessment too. For example, the importance of autonomous learning, learning based around tasks and real situations, the ideas around constructivism, the role self-reflection and peer reflection can play in learning, and the issue of motivation to name just a few (Stoynoff, 2012). We need to consider the influence of all these areas if we are to develop a clear picture of why assessment has changed and how we might effectively assess in the 21st Century language class.

This chapter is therefore in two parts. The first presents the key factors that have influenced the way assessment has changed. It breaks down the influences into four areas which in reality often merge. Firstly, the changes in language teaching; secondly, the changes in our understanding of assessment; thirdly, the impact technology has had; and finally, other drivers from mainstream education that have also influenced our views on assessment. The chapter includes a series of short case studies which provide real examples of the types of assessments that teachers are currently experimenting with using ICT. It is hoped that the practical examples set in the real lives of teachers in their contexts will offer you some useful ideas for adaptation for your own assessment practices.

Assessment

Assessment is a very broad term that can cover formal exams and tests, both external and internal, which are structured and built into the fabric of the academic year, as well as more informal types of assessment that teachers undertake as a part of their day-to-day practice. We recognise that tests and exams set both internally and externally by organisations such as UCLES have changed in major ways over the past 50 years; however, most teachers have little say in the exams offered by an institution since exams are generally set at institutional level or run by external exam bodies. Our focus, then, is on the types of assessments that the teacher can set while teaching a course. These are often less formal and may not even be part of the official evaluation of a student but because the teacher has control over these and has a much clearer idea of learners' needs at any point in a course of study, it is our view that these types of assessments have an important impact on a student's learning.

We provide a series of mini case studies or snapshots throughout this chapter. We spoke to a total of about 20 teachers and drew from some of their examples, as well as our own. Some interesting points emerged from the discussions that we had and it is worth pointing these out right from the start. We believe that this will help paint a much more real picture of what teachers are doing and perhaps provide encouragement to those teachers who are potentially reticent or worried about incorporating ICT into the assessment they do:

- e-assessment is still in its infancy and it is almost always experimental.

- Teachers often start with a tool that helps to broaden the skills base of their assessments. For example, they might introduce videoing a pair work activity or getting the students to keep a blog. Often the motivation is to broaden what they are assessing.

- The process tends to be developmental. Changing assessment procedures can be quite complex, so teachers might start by introducing a technology into their assessment to broaden the base, then later they might look at improving the evaluation criteria that goes with the assessment and later still they might look at the feedback they are providing. So, for example, they might start by getting their students to blog. Once they feel they have got the blog task right, they might start to look at the assessment criteria for the blog and then perhaps the feedback they are providing. The process is generally done in stages with the focus shifting as the teachers get more confident.

- The first steps are very important. As with the use of ICT in all domains, the initial first move into the area of ICT is crucial. Once teachers build their confidence they tend to become more experimental and make use of a greater number of tools.

We hope that through the 'snapshots' of real-life practice we can build towards a set of e-assessment design principles. We really hope that once you have read this chapter you might have a clearer understanding of why assessment is changing and some ideas about how to introduce assessments that include an ICT component.

Terminology

Before we look at why assessment has changed, we want to cover some of the terminology associated with assessment. We deal with a number of terms like summative, formative, portfolios, washback, peer evaluation, self-evaluation and reflection, but before we start it is worth just contextualising where assessment sits in the learning cycle.

The learning cycle

Figure 6.1 shows the learning cycle (Biggs, 1999). We can see from this diagram that first we need to think about our learning objectives and goals. We have already identified that what we expect to achieve in language classrooms and via assessment has changed significantly over the last 50 years, and continues to change. We need to create assessments that help us evaluate and understand whether our learning outcomes are being achieved. But we also recognise that the assessment itself may help us in achieving some of our goals (like, for example, better motivation, autonomy, or more collaboration amongst learners). The assessments we set up can be very varied in both the skills they focus on, but also the way they are executed. They may be grammar tests, readings, blogging, podcast recordings, group work writing, for example. The assessments might be individual, pair, or group-based. The evaluation and feedback of the assessments is also important. The feedback could be provided by other students, it could even be practised by the students themselves and so encourage self-assessment (sometimes referred to as ipsative assessment). What emerges from this process is a picture of the students' development and a better understanding of whether the content of the course is achieving its outcomes. In light of what we learn about learners' performance during the learning cycle (Figure 6.1), changes may need to be made to the content of the course.

Figure 6.1: The learning cycle

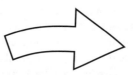

4. Re-align objectives and goals in light of the feedback from assessments.

1. Learning objectives and goals that reflect our current thinking about learning a language.

3. Use measurements to provide feedback and inform stakeholders of progress.

2. Set up assessments that reflect these goals and objectives linked to ICT tools.

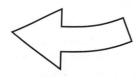

Let us say, for example, that the teacher is focusing on writing. The objective is to make the students more fluent in their writing and to get them to focus on the process of writing, as well as the end product. Various activities are set up in the class to support this, including the students writing regular blog posts after their ELT classes. As part of the assessment, students are asked to do a free writing exercise where each week they reflect on the following things:

1. What have you learned this week? What topics have you covered?

2. What things were new to you: grammar, lexis, ideas, content?

3. What specific vocabulary have you learned and can remember?

4. What haven't you understood from this week? What things do you need to do additional work on, or revise?

5. How do you feel about your general progress this week? How well have you worked? What factors influenced how much you worked?

This work is read by the teacher but not marked. The teacher leaves occasional encouraging comments after the blog entries, providing guidance on how to improve and what to think about. In the blog posts students are expected to reflect on what they learn in class and consider the questions. So the assessment is doing much more than simply helping to gauge and evaluate the student's progress, it is also helping them to reflect on their own learning, think about their own progress and what they are learning. It has the additional benefit of helping the students learn about blogging, a skill that could be useful to them in the future; it enhances their digital literacy.

At the end of the process the teachers may become aware of various problems on the course. They may have noticed in the students' reflections that there are certain things the students feel they have not learned properly. The teacher might also notice certain shortfalls in their writing. All this information can then be used to change some of the content of the course for the following year. For the teacher this also becomes a form of formative assessment of the course, helping to guide their practice.

Summative and formative assessments

Students when receiving the assessment usually pay most of their attention to their scores and are almost negligent to the instructional comments given by the teacher for future improvement.

(Kwok, 2008: 85)

'Summative assessments' often take place at the end of a unit, module, or a whole course. The focus tends to be on the mark and the idea is to evaluate how well the student has learned what has been presented. Formative assessments take place during a course, module or unit. The focus is more on gathering data about the student's progress and using this data to help them improve. We often read about these two forms of assessment as if they are clearly distinct from each other. However, it is our view that the distinction between summative and formative assessment is perhaps exaggerated, and that if greater use was made of the information from summative assessments, then in reality they too could inform. The distinction between the two types of assessment really develops out of how the information from assessments is used. Summative assessments often come at the end of the course and therefore the information gathered from them cannot always be acted upon since the teacher may not continue teaching the class. The literature often talks about product and process. When we provide formative feedback we are trying to focus more on the process and helping students to produce better drafts or recordings. Focus on the product is providing feedback on the final outcome. What is perhaps more important, is that the formative assessments and summative assessments are well aligned and that what is summatively assessed at the end of a course or unit has been supported by the formative assessments that take place during the learning.

Most teachers no longer view assessment as something that only occurs after the fact. Rather they recognise the benefits of conducting assessment before, during, and following teaching and learning.

(Stoynoff, 2012: 527)

One of the biggest and most obvious changes that has happened to assessment is that there is now much more interest in the area of formative assessment. In other words, we assess students at different stages and provide feedback that they can use to improve, re-draft or change what they are currently working on, but also to help them into their future learning (often referred to as feed-forward). Key to this change is an understanding that assessment is part of the learning cycle. In other words, for students to improve, they need to take the information from assessments and use it to improve their work. This immediately makes the feedback provided from assessments a vital cog in the process. It is the feedback and information from assessments that will help students improve. This shift is not easy. Both teachers and students struggle with providing good formative feedback. Lam and Lee (2010) in their study of process writing and the benefits of formative assessments and feedback found that students still valued the mark more than the feedback they received on formative assessments, and teachers worried about the additional time and energy that would be required to provide feedback and conferencing on drafts and re-drafts. The importance of formative feedback is obvious, but the practicalities of the classroom may mean that it is not done as much as one would hope. Of course, teachers informally provide feedback all the time but providing feedback in various stages of a process can be very time-consuming.

We believe that well designed formative assessments with useful, and well thought through feedback, will greatly help both our students and our understanding of their progress. We believe that it is in this area where teachers in the classroom can have the most impact. Hence our focus in this chapter is on the use of ICT to provide formative assessments.

Washback (backwash) effect

The washback (backwash) effect is the impact that an assessment will have on the teaching and learning. This impact can be very broad. A certain assessment might impact on what a teacher teaches, what the students revise, how motivated the student feels, what skills the students focus on. If an assessment correctly reflects the skills a student needs to be a good language learner then it is likely that any work the students does in preparation for the assessment, or as part of the assessment, will have a positive impact on their learning. Prodromou (1995) highlights the limitations of the positive impact of washback if the assessments the students are given are too narrowly defined, focus too much on accuracy and are time limited. Good assessments, that reflect good practices in language learning, are likely to have a positive washback both from the teaching perspective (what the teachers do in preparation or as part of the assessment) and the learning perspective. Indeed, as we pointed out at the start of this chapter, good assessments will actually offer real opportunities for learning (Tomlinson, 1995).

Peer evaluation/self evaluation

Davison and Leung (2009) offer a four-stage process to guide teachers in organising classroom assessments:

1. Planning assessments.
2. Collecting information on student learning through the assessment.
3. Making judgements about performance.
4. Providing appropriate feedback.

As views on assessment have changed this whole process has become much more inclusive (Bullock, 2011). There is considerable interest in the idea of students self-evaluating and in getting the students to build up a picture of their own learning. You hear terms like reflection, peer evaluation, self-evaluation and self-assessment. All these procedures are attempting to make students better learners, to get them to think more about their own learning, to be aware of their own shortfalls and strengths. The ultimate goal is to make the students more independent learners and hopefully more motivated too. These processes are at the heart of assessment since one of the key goals of assessment is to provide information that will help students in their learning.

A historical review of ELT assessment

A literature review of ELT publications over the past 50 years reveals the shift away from a grammar-focused tradition to real engagement with language in real-world settings (Bachman, online). Until the 1970s, a general pedagogy for language teaching was based on learning lists of vocabulary, grammatical use, reading comprehension and short essay writing. The learning objectives of many courses centred on the mastery of language structures. The related tasks were comprehension questions which involved reading texts and the production of short written answers. This assessed work tended to focus on the accuracy of the written answers in terms of their grammar, correct spelling and syntax. There was often no requirement to show any real understanding of the text. Language was not really viewed from a perspective of communication or use, but rather on the learners' exposure to the mechanics of language. Language was learned about; it was not necessarily used for anything. The modality of most assessment was written and tested procedural knowledge through the memorisation of vocabulary lists and certain types of, sometimes obscure, grammatical forms.

> *My memories of foreign language learning include long lists of vocabulary words and multiple choice, fill-in-the-blank, and discrete item tests.*
>
> (Choa, 1999)

This contrasts radically with current thinking where the idea is to make our language tests and assessments reflect real language use. Summarising what we can summise from a test score, Bachman wrote:

In order to use scores from language tests to make inferences about language ability [...] we must be able to demonstrate how test performance corresponds to non-test language use.

(Bachman and Palmer, 1996: 58).

In the 1960s language teaching and assessment began to shift. Prominent authors such as Hymes (1972) began to consider language learning in terms of communicative competence. This stage is often referred to in ELT assessment development as the 'communicative language teaching (CLT)' approach. This paradigm shift led to changes in the skills we recognised as being important to learn a language and therefore in the skills we needed to assess and test (Morrow, 1979; Fulcher, 2000). This shift has continued and recent reviews of the changing approaches to language teaching have seen an increased acceptance of the key role of communication in learning a language (Waters, 2012).

Before the shift to a more communicative approach to language learning, formal language exams had a very narrow focus. Reading assessment centred on comprehension while writing was little more than the parroting of learned formulas. No attention was paid to learning sub-skills like skimming and scanning, for example. The process of writing and organising a text and planning it was almost ignored; the idea of portfolio assessment and doing drafts and re-drafts was almost non-existent. Most writing tasks were assessed in a similar way to grammar. The assessment criterion was the correct use of the language rather than the appropriate application of content, meaning and ideas. The interest was always on the product and not the process.

Some of the first communicative language tests were designed and developed by the University of Cambridge Local Examinations Syndicate (UCLES), though in the USA focus on oral exams had actually begun back in the late 1950s with the Foreign Service Institute (Fulcher, 2000). We saw quite substantial changes in many of the more formal exams and UCLES introduced a pair-examined oral component, mirroring the changes that were taking place in classroom practice (Taylor, 2006). Firstly, this form of assessment reflected the fact that it was being recognised that we needed to assess the oral skills of our students, but secondly it also reflected the fact that a lot of oral work in the classroom was being conducted in pairs as a communicative methodology began to creep into classrooms.

So, the paradigm shift in teaching and learning a language led to a paradigm shift in what we assessed too. By the beginning of the 1970s assessment had moved towards communication. We learn language so that we can communicate better with others. We stopped just focusing on grammar and developed a wider perspective that viewed language learning in terms of ability to communicate and use the language. The term 'communicative competence' (i.e. our ability to communicate and put our ideas across either in the written or spoken form) became important. New skills were recognised as central to our ability to communicate, including the organisation and planning of text, pronunciation, the ability to paraphrase, the ability to turn take and engage in a conversation. These new skills also needed to be assessed.

Our experience from talking to teachers suggests that perhaps there is a lag between changes in teaching methodologies and the related ways to assess. So, for example, many of the teachers we spoke to in our research for this chapter were using technology in their classes, working in groups and pairs and setting up collaborative activities, and yet their assessments were quite traditional. Sometimes this is because the teacher makes the changes in the classroom teaching but the assessments are set more centrally, as discussed above, and so the teacher has less influence over any changes. Another reason might be that the teacher first wants to see if the experimental ideas they attempt in class work well, and then if they do, they begin to think about how to assess them.

The change in the way we teach and learn languages did not stop evolving with the development of CLT. As we mentioned at the beginning of this chapter, there have been a number of emerging ideas that have impacted on our current view of teaching and learning. Indeed, a lot of teachers do not subscribe to any specific methodology or approach, but rather take an eclectic view of language learning which incorporates the best bits from a range of approaches or methodologies; we often describe the era we are in now as a post-method era (Kumarvalivedu, 1994). There has been a lot of interest in autonomous learning, in making learning more authentic and related to real situations or work-related contexts (often called task based learning) and in social interactions that aid learning (Vygotsky, 1962). The emergence of constructivism has been enthusiastically received by the CLT community since there are parallels in the two approaches. Learning a language is an active, mainly social process where a learner develops and builds his own constructs through interacting and using the language. Language is not handed down to the user from the teacher; rather it is learned and built up through the interactions with other learners (O'Dwyer, 2006).

> The view that classroom knowledge is socially constructed rather than being merely transmitted from teacher to student has made a significant impact in English language teaching.
>
> (Smith, 2001: 221).

Social constructivism has had an impact right across the sphere of education. It fits well with the idea that language is learned through communication and use of the language, rather than by simply learning about the language. Social constructivists see the individual as an active participant in their own learning, bringing to the table their prior knowledge and experience.

> Many studies have shown that students' abilities to understand something new depends on what they already know.
>
> (Mayes and De Freitas, 2004: 15)

Through engaging and working with others, sharing ideas and collaborating, students learn. Of course constructivists are not suggesting that we can't learn from reading or listening (a type of dialogue takes place in our mind when we read or listen to something), but the emphasis does centre around the social impact of learning. Of course, not all writers are totally convinced by the role of social constructivism in ELT (O'Dwyer, 2006), but its general acceptance even in more 'traditional' learning contexts has certainly helped to promote the role of communication in language teaching.

There is no doubt that teaching and learning involves a much broader range of activity than in previous times; teachers are expected to find ways of teaching all four skills, so assessing the learning that takes place has also become more complex. However, it is our view that we have developed a better understanding of the conditions that can help students to learn language, and that we have also developed a better understanding of what effective and useful assessments might include.

A final point to make about new movements within education and within language teaching is that it is not always clear where their roots are. Ideas about the role of autonomous learning, for example, probably go back as far as Dewey (1916), and Vygotsky's (1962) socio-cultural theory originally dates back to the 1930s. We highlighted communicative language teaching as a development within the field of language teaching as it is clearly specific to that field, however, we recognised that many of the developments in education were probably concurrently developing in the field of language education. Where the roots of the movements are, is beyond the scope of this chapter.

Perhaps one way of seeing how far assessment has come is to look at the idea of a language portfolio. We believe that language portfolios are perhaps one of the most serious attempts to provide a modern day assessment method that incorporates much of the current thinking on assessment of language learning. We are not suggesting in any way teachers should be using language portfolios as their main assessment method but it does provide a useful indication of the direction that assessment is taking. As we pointed out earlier, teachers often take a small initial step into the use of ICT in their assessments, and slowly build on this. At the other extreme is perhaps the e-Portfolio, where the student collects together a whole range of digital artefacts that together provide a comprehensive assessment of a student's language ability. These might include video recordings, audio recordings, examples of mind maps, wiki entries, example of articles read, online tests etc., all accessible from one central repository.

What is a language portfolio?

The basic idea of a portfolio is to provide a much wider range of evidence of the language skills of a student. The roots of the idea probably go back as far as the work of Dewey (1916). Portfolios offer students the opportunity to demonstrate what they have learned and experienced with the target language. It can include a whole range of language evidence reflecting a much wider range of skills. It might include tests, readings, written work, essay plans, feedback and reflections. Norton and Widburg (1998: 237) describe a portfolio as 'a systematic and selective collection of a student's work that has been assembled to demonstrate a student's motivation, academic growth and level of achievement.'

In our experience, a lot of teachers struggle with the idea of a portfolio because it is not always clear what to include in them. There is no one definition of a portfolio but the idea is that they demonstrate and reflect the language experiences that the student has had, and through this, demonstrate a broader picture of a student's language ability.

It is not just the products of a portfolio that are of interest. The process of actually developing and finding content for the portfolio often means that both the teachers and the students play a role in the form they take. For example, it may be left to the student to decide what examples of writing or reading to include in the portfolio. In doing this the students 'own' their portfolios and learn and reflect from the process of actually choosing the content for the portfolio itself (Lam and Lee, 2010). This process of selecting and reflecting on their work is key to a portfolio as it adds to the process. At the beginning of the chapter, we mentioned Tomlinson's (1995) suggestion that students should learn from the assessment process itself, and this is certainly one of the goals of a portfolio.

Portfolios are at the heart of what the Council of Europe Language Policy Division was trying to do for language assessment (Cummins and Davesne, 2009). There are similar ideas in the USA with the LinguaFolio and Global Language Portfolio. Each one is slightly different. The European portfolio, for example, is made up of three components:

1. The language passport, which is a record of language learning both inside and outside the classroom. This has personal information like any passport, plus a grid which provides information about the languages that the person speaks and their level, using the Common European Framework of Reference.

2. The language biography which is a diagnostic self-assessment of L2 skills. It is done through a series of 'can do' statements where the student ticks check boxes to demonstrate what they can and can't do in a given language.

3. Finally, there is a language dossier. It is here where the student provides actual evidence of their language ability through a variety of artefacts (Cummins and Davesne, 2009).

The language portfolio includes much of the current thinking regarding assessment. It can be used by a variety of stakeholders; it covers a broader range of language skills including both a focus on process as well as product; the process of actually creating the portfolio can be a learning process itself; it is often negotiated and requires decision making both by the teacher and the student; it allows for self-reflection, encourages autonomous thinking and is hopefully motivating.

Perhaps more interestingly and relevant to this chapter is the e-portfolio. An e-portfolio is a digital version of a portfolio. It is an excellent example of where the affordances of technology can really make a contribution. E-portfolios can be word processed documents; blogs, wikis, mind maps or other specialist tools (for example, Mahara) and can include a wide range of digital assets such as video or audio recordings, saved chat room discussions or forum contributions and a whole range of other electronic artefacts. So the language dossier part of the portfolio can be much richer and cover a much broader range of language skills. The can do statements in the language biography can also be done online. A tool called DIALANG was developed to allow students to self-evaluate. It is similar to the checklists produced in the paper-based portfolio, but has the added dimension that once the students have completed their can do lists, they can click on a button and get some guidance on what to study to improve. Alderson (2005), among others, believes the self-assessment component of a portfolio is a vital element in developing self-reflection.

An obvious key element of an e-portfolio is that they can be distributed and even adapted very quickly. They are also more portable. We tend to think of the needs of a much broader group of stakeholders when we think about assessments. We understand that teachers, students, heads of school, external bodies, visa regulators, university application bodies and employers may all be interested in the language ability of a given student. The variety of artefacts and the broad scope of an e-portfolio hopefully mean it can facilitate the necessary information for a broader range of stakeholders, and since this information is in electronic format, it should also be easily accessible.

An e-portfolio is one example of what can be achieved through using technology to assess students and most of the teachers we spoke to were not doing this. However, they were beginning to incorporate some of the ideas of the e-portfolio into their work. Many teachers started with the simple introduction of a blog, wiki or electronic writing tool as the starting point in introducing technology into their assessments, and then at a later stage introduced more ICT elements. Teachers are looking for ways of assessing a broader range of language skills, to make assessment more relevant and interesting, and provide effective feedback, involving the students in the process and getting them thinking and reflecting on their own learning etc. In other words, they are incorporating elements of an e-portfolio into their assessment processes. So, one of our messages would be 'don't be afraid to experiment' as it is what a lot of teachers are doing.

Case Study 6.1: Recorded group discussions

Antonio is an ELT teacher in Peru. He uses VoiceThread with his students to get them working in groups and discussing certain points. These are high level students and he tries to link what the students do in the class with what he wants to get them to do in their assessments. For example, he might do a lesson about bullying and afterwards the students are put into groups and asked to produce a discussion around bullying. VoiceThread is free for the students to sign up to, and they can then add their voice recordings. This means that several students can work on one topic. They can all add their recording and agree and disagree with what the other students have said and also add their own comments. This makes the discussion very dialogic. To make it easy to find the recordings, the students embed them into a wiki where they can be easily accessed.

Antonio provides feedback on a group basis and sometimes plays back the best recordings in the class to show the other students. Students like the tool as it develops their oral skills and they have to listen to what the other students have said before they make their own recordings. The tool is easy to use; students can record and re-record until they are happy with the recordings they have made.

Focus on technology: VoiceThread

VoiceThread is a free tool. It allows you to upload documents, pictures, video and other digital media and then a voice recording. It is not limited to one voice recording. You could in theory upload a PDF document onto VoiceThread and then all the students in the class could add voice recordings to sit alongside the document. This is exactly what Antonio has done. VoiceThread also allows you to click on a button, copy the code and then embed the VoiceThread into a website, blog or wiki. It requires no coding at all. It has quickly become one of the most popular Web 2.0 tools on the internet.

http://voicethread.com

This snapshot is an excellent example of how technology can support formative assessment. Antonio is looking for interesting ways to get students to develop their oral skills. He links the assessment to what has been covered in the class and the tool he has chosen allows the students to easily add their commentary to a picture, video or document that Antonio has uploaded. The students can also listen to the recordings that other students have created and react by either agreeing or disagreeing with their opinions. Antonio tries to choose a topic that is relevant to the students and one he feels they will have opinions on. He provides general feedback on the overall performance of each group and uses classroom time to highlight good examples by playing back some of the recordings. The feedback is quick and will hopefully feed forward into subsequent recordings.

The example from Antonio also reflects the point we are making about the development of assessment. When Antonio set up the VoiceThread assessments he focused centrally on the assessment task and was careful to choose relevant topics related to what the students had been covering in class time. He paid less attention to the feedback. Now that he has seen that the idea works, he is focusing on improving the feedback he provides to the students. Currently he listens to the students recordings and provides general classroom feedback which he hopes will provide them with guidance on how to improve subsequent recordings, and he also plays some of the best examples in the class. However, he is thinking of new ways to approach the feedback, including getting the students to perhaps provide peer feedback. It highlights the point we are making on the development of ICT practices in assessment being very organic.

ELT assessment summary discussion

In the first part of this chapter we have tried to outline why assessment has changed so much. We have talked about four general areas in education that have influenced our current views on language assessment. Firstly, language assessment has been impacted by the general focus in language teaching towards a more communicative approach to language teaching. Secondly, language assessment has changed because ideas about assessment and its role in education have changed. Thirdly, assessment has been influenced by other changes that have taken place in education but don't necessarily have their roots in language education (though they have been adopted by them). These include issues like reflection, task based learning, social constructivism and autonomous learning. Finally, technology has also influenced assessment. It offers affordances that allow ways and means to assess students that we would never have been able to do even ten years ago.

We went on to talk about e-portfolios as we wanted to provide an example of just how far ideas around assessment have developed. E-portfolios attempt to include much of the current thinking on assessment and they are a good indicator of what can be achieved with ICT. Many of the ideas we outline and discuss in the second part of this chapter could contribute towards the development of an e-portfolio. We wanted to emphasise though, that e-portfolios are not what most teachers are doing, but it is interesting to see that they are being used by the various organisations including the European Union.

Finally, we wanted to give you a snapshot of the sort of practice that today's digitally aware teachers are doing with ICT. We hoped that our example demonstrated some of the points that we developed in this first part. It is exactly this that we want to do in part two i.e. demonstrate real examples of how technology can be used to support assessment and link it back to principles that underpin it.

Technology in assessment

The shift to a focus on a broader range of skills in terms of language learning has meant a subsequent shift in what we assess. This has happened at all levels (for example, formal high stakes exams led by international organisations, tests set at school level or in-class assessments set by the teacher). The range of skills that modern assessments attempt to evaluate is quite broad ranging and reflects our current views on teaching and learning. It might for example include assessing the students' ability:

- to participate in a pair work oral activity
- to skim a text and quickly look for key information
- to tell a story
- to follow instructions
- to plan and organise an article
- to write for a specific group or genre.

We are not only interested in the summative aspects of these assessments. We realise that it is key to assess the process itself and provide feedback and guidance as the students plan, organise and produce their assessments. It is perhaps during the process that we can provide the support and guidance to help students improve most. In doing this we can help them to be more reflective, more independent, better organised and more motivated.

What is key here is that ICT can play a big role in making all this possible.

ICT can promote, facilitate and support our current understanding of assessment. We can now easily record our students speaking using computers, or mobile devices like MP3 recorders or mobile phones. More importantly, we can store, retrieve and share these recordings very cheaply and quickly. We can video group work or pair work interactions and then evaluate and provide feedback. We can get students to write blogs or wikis and provide regular comments and feedback on the development of their written work. We can easily ask the student's peers to provide feedback too. Technology does not only help with what we assess; it can even help us produce relevant materials for assessment. Whether it is recording native or non-native speakers for listening comprehension work or finding interesting and relevant texts on the internet, technology can play a role.

Table 6.1 provides an at-a-glance ELT assessment summary of the tools that the teachers we contacted as we wrote this chapter most used. This is based on feedback from 20 teachers. We have organised the tools along the lines of the four basic skills. We recognise that in reality many of these tools assess more than one skill and that assessments are multi-skilled based, so this is a rather simplistic table. It also includes virtual learning environments that tend to be more like repositories and are sometimes used for e-portfolios.

Table 6.1: At-a-glance ELT assessment mode and tools suggested by teachers contacted for this chapter

What tools are teachers using?	How are they being used?
Writing tools	
Blogger www.blogger.com	Blogger is a free blogging tool from Google. Students can use it to keep diaries, write stories, reflect on classes. Teachers and peers can easily leave comments. Students can develop communities. **Help videos to use blogger** www.teachertrainingvideos.com/newBlogger/index.html www.teachertrainingvideos.com/newBlogger2/index.html
WordPress http://wordpress.com/	Another very popular blogging tool that is also free. Slightly more sophisticated than Blogger it provides all the same elements as Blogger but with perhaps a better look and feel. Versions of WordPress can be downloaded onto your own server, so that they can be customised for a school and plugins added to extend their capabilities. **Help videos to use WordPress** www.teachertrainingvideos.com/wordPress/index.html
Wikis http://pbworks.com/	A great way of providing a platform for collaboration and sharing. Wikis are websites built by groups of students rather than individuals. They allow for collaborative writing exercises where students can edit and review their work and the work of others. Information about the creation of a wiki allows the teacher to easily see who has contributed and who hasn't. **Help videos to use PB Wiki** www.teachertrainingvideos.com/pbworks/index.html

What tools are teachers using?	How are they being used?
Tricider https://tricider.com/en/t/	Quick and simple discussion board that allows students not only to add their own ideas but also to comment on the ideas of their peers. Good for brainstorming, debates, essay preparation and drafting. **Help videos to use Tricider** www.teachertrainingvideos.com/tricider/index.html
Wallwisher http://wallwisher.com/	This website provides a sort of collaborative electronic board where students can add up comments, pictures, video and links around a given theme. Great for brainstorming, preparing essays and projects, and sharing ideas. **Help videos to use Wallwisher** www.teachertrainingvideos.com/wall/index.html
Reading content	
Breakingnewenglish www.breakingnewsenglish.com/	Useful website of reading and listening content that is very topical and related to recent news events. The site includes whole lesson plans built around the content, but the content can easily be adapted to use for assessments.
Listenaminute http://listenaminute.com/	Another source of reading and listening content that can be easily adapted for assessments.
Listening material	
ELLLO English http://elllo.org/	Huge collection of monologues and dialogues from a whole variety of speakers which can easily be used for assessment purposes.
Audio/speaking	
Vocaroo http://vocaroo.com/	Simple audio tool that can allow for five minute recordings at the click of a button. Recordings can be shared via email, embedded in a blog, wiki or virtual learning environment or even downloaded. **Help videos to use Vocaroo** www.teachertrainingvideos.com/vocaroo1/index.html
VoiceThread http://voicethread.com/	Excellent tool that can be used collaboratively. Students can add written or audio comments concerning an image, video or document. **Help videos to use VoiceThread** www.teachertrainingvideos.com/voiceThread/index.html
MailVu http://mailvu.com/	Simple audio tool that also uses the webcam facilities of a computer. Allows for simple webcam recordings in pairs or groups and can be useful for pair work assessments. **Help videos to use MailVu** www.teachertrainingvideos.com/mailVu/index.html
Voxopop www.voxopop.com/	Audio tool works like a discussion board but with recordings. Teachers or students can set up questions and students can add their oral answers, replies or comments. Useful for oral work, discussions, brainstorming, opinions etc. **Help Videos to use Voxopop** www.teachertrainingvideos.com/voxopop/index.html

What tools are teachers using?	How are they being used?
myBrainShark www.brainshark.com/mybrainshark	Versatile tool that allows you to upload videos, pictures, PowerPoint presentations or documents and then add your voice to them and share the recordings via email, or embed them into a blog or Moodle site. **Help videos to use myBrainShark** www.teachertrainingvideos.com/brain/index.html
Virtual learning environments	
Moodle https://moodle.org/	Online virtual learning environment that is used in many higher education institutions. Allows for a huge range of assessment possibilities but has generally been used for writing and feedback. Has chat rooms, forums which can also be used for assessment purposes. Teachers can also create online quizzes and tests that students can use to evaluate their progress and use formatively.
Edmodo www.edmodo.com/	Free online virtual learning environment that teachers can set up on their own by simply submitting their email address. Great for sharing, discussions and brainstorming. Allows for upload of assignments and drafts and quick feedback. **Help videos to use Edmodo** www.teachertrainingvideos.com/edmodo1/index.html
Quiz making tools	
Pro-Profs www.proprofs.com/quiz-school/	A free online quiz maker. It could be used to make formative and periodic assessments.

As we have discussed, the term *constructive alignment* is used when we talk about linking our assessments with the teaching approaches and the learning outcomes of our curriculum (Biggs, 1999). This is a key point about assessment with ICT. It allows us to do assessment in new ways and therefore link much closer to the objectives of the curriculum or course with the assessments we do. For example, if one of the objectives is to help students to brainstorm and prepare better for a report or essay we want them to write, then we can use tools like Wallwisher or Tricider to brainstorm and work collaboratively to develop their ideas. Teachers can easily track which students have made the most valuable contributions to the brainstorming process. These brainstorming activities can be done over time and even at home. The technology offers new affordances and greater flexibility in the types of assessments and tasks we set up. 'For academic staff, the appeal of e-assessment lies in its ability to capture aspects of learning previously considered impossible to assess' (JISC, 2007: 26).

Quiz making tools

The building blocks of learning the English language (i.e. vocabulary, grammar, syntax) are still an important part of the learning process. ICT has traditionally done this part of assessment very well through the use of multiple choice, true or false, ranking, matching and other types of self-assessment exercises and quizzes.

ICT can add value to these types of assessments too. Online quizzes can be provided that students can access at any time, allowing for greater flexibility in the timing and organisation of assessments. Many systems can even automatically mark student input, which has the potential to impact on the timeliness of feedback, provide students with useful knowledge of their progress (at least in terms of grammar, syntax, or comprehension questions) and allow students to repeat the exercises as needed. The success criteria can be set by the tutor to provide the learner with the opportunity to progress to the next level or go to some review resources, depending on how well they did in the quiz. This scaffolding approach can be very powerful for this type of procedural knowledge in ELT. There are a number of free tools online that can easily be used to produce online quizzes and tests. These include Quia and Proprofs, which are both free. Most virtual learning environments also provide quiz building tools. There has been work building more adaptive and intelligent tools where learners can practise discrete skills, but this tends to be other languages, for example, German (Heift, 2009).

Virtual learning environments

Case Study 6.2: Using a virtual learning environment

Yrma G teaches in Turkey. She uses Moodle to support her students' writing skills. She particularly likes this tool as it allows a simple way of getting the students to upload their written work in stages, which she can then quickly provide feedback on.

Moodle allows students to upload individual assignments as files or even to write directly onto a page, which the teacher can access. This allows a simple way for students to submit their work, feedback can be provided and the students can then re-submit. It is also a way of allowing the students to write in stages. They can upload their introduction, then later the main body, etc.

This makes the whole activity more process-based. Yrma can also look back and compare early drafts with the final products. It can be quite time-consuming, but it is very rewarding for the students and by having the content loaded onto Moodle it is much easier to access and provide feedback.

Assessment can be carried out in a more reflective way by responding to students, rather than just correcting. Students are encouraged to go over their work again through questions, recommendations and suggestions where improvements need to be made.

By having the student work drafts loaded onto Moodle, it is much easier to access and provide feedback on the textual use of English. Students are also encouraged to do peer review in the online text discussion boards and this has helped develop friendships as well.

Many education and training organisations across the world are utilising virtual learning environments (VLEs) as mentioned in Case Study 6.2. It is beyond the limits of this chapter to talk about the assessment possibilities using Moodle because it is a very large tool that offers a whole array of possibilities. It is free to download but requires a server to run on, and so often the decision to run a virtual learning environment like Moodle is normally made at institutional level. However, buying server space is not that expensive and it is not that difficult to download and run your own version of Moodle. There are also commercial companies that offer hosted versions of Moodle, so this need not be that expensive.

Many higher educational institutions are beginning to introduce these types of systems into their teaching and learning. However, there are virtual learning environments that are free and not difficult to set up for teachers. One interesting VLE which is attracting a lot of interest at the time of writing is *Edmodo*. You can create as many groups as you want and each group has a code. Students can access their group by simply writing in the code and do not even need to provide an email address. The interface is very much like Facebook and the students have a wall where they can add links, videos, or pictures. The wall can be used for class or group discussions. Teachers can also create quizzes for continual assessment and the feedback can be automated. Students can upload their assignments that the teacher can then quickly access and provide feedback on.

Case Study 6.3: Edmodo is a free powerful VLE

Mouna works in Tunisia with groups of secondary school children learning English. She likes to get them to discuss and share ideas on different topics each week. Mouna uses Edmodo. She sets a discussion topic and each student is obliged to make a minimum of three contributions. The students do this at home. She reviews the discussion and takes notes. In class she often highlights some of the best contributions and explains why she likes them. Each week she chooses the student who has made the best contribution. This is not based on grammar or language but on their ability to communicate an idea effectively. Her focus is to get the students to think less about the grammar and more about what they are saying. She is trying to encourage more fluency in their writing and more focus on the content of what they are trying to say. It is an experimental idea. She has noticed that students write more or less depending on the topic. She is slowly building up a list of the topics that the students seem to like to write about. She is quite happy with her early experiments but wants to find more effective ways of providing feedback on their comments.

Assessment tools that can develop oral skills

One of the areas where the affordances of ICT is perhaps most pertinent is in the area of oral skills. It has always been possible to record students using cassette recorders but this was often cumbersome and didn't allow for easy distribution and sharing. There is now a whole range of ICT tools that can make the assessment of students' oral levels much easier. Many of the teachers we spoke to, and in fact the authors of this chapter, have all been working with a variety of these tools.

Case Study 6.4: Using myBrainShark

I have been making use of myBrainShark over the last three years and it has been a really successful tool to work with. Students can produce their own PowerPoint slides, load them up onto myBrainShark and then add their voice to their slides. myBrainShark then packs the PowerPoint presentation with the audio and creates a link to a file that can easily be shared with the teacher. So students can create PowerPoints on a given topic, record and re-record their voice until they are happy with their recording, and then share their work at the click of a button. Students and teachers can listen to the recordings and add notes/comments as feedback.

I have used this tool with great success. I recently got students to create PowerPoint presentations of six to eight slides where they provided personal information about their families, friends, interests and hobbies. They then added their voice to the PowerPoint presentations and shared them over the internet. I played back their recordings, took notes and provided them with feedback on the work. In class I played back some of the best examples and asked the students why they thought I had selected them.

myBrainShark is particularly useful because there is no need to share big files and it is an online tool. Once the students have uploaded their presentations and added their voice, they simply share the link. The teacher can click on the link and listen to the recordings directly from the myBrainShark server. This tool can also make an excellent contribution to e-Portfolios.

This tool is especially good for English for Academic Purposes students and those doing Business English. Many of these students will be expected to give PowerPoint presentations during their course and this is a great way of getting them to practise. Students are not limited to PowerPoint. They can load up PDF documents, Word files, pictures and even video, and then add their own voice narration.

Students can also share their recordings with other students and in this way get peer feedback.

This snapshot highlights many of the points we made in the first part of this chapter. Here we have a tool that can offer real affordances. Previously, it might have been very difficult for students to prepare for a PowerPoint presentation without actually doing the presentation in front of the teacher/peers and getting feedback. Now students can create them using myBrainShark and then share them quickly over the internet. Feedback is easy and can even involve the students' peers in the process as well as the teacher. Of course, the students can play back their own recordings as many times as they like, and re-record until they are happy with the audio that goes with each slide. This allows for self-reflection and self-evaluation. The teacher could even provide guidelines to the students so that once they have made their PowerPoint presentations and added their voice, they could review and evaluate their own work. Indeed e-portfolios can even include students' own evaluations of their work or peer evaluation as part of the portfolio itself. This can be in the form of a checklist or questions for the students to use when reviewing what they have recorded (Cummins and Davesne, 2009).

Case Study 6.5: Making simple audio recordings

Vocaroo is a very simple tool that allows students to record their voice for up to five minutes and then send the resulting recording as an email. It is perhaps one of the easiest audio recording tools on the internet and works literally at the click of just one button. The students don't even need to open an email client to send the recordings. They simply record, play back the recording and then write in the email address of the person they want to send the recording to. The receiver can then click on the link and listen to the recording. The recordings can also be downloaded onto the students' computer or embedded into a blog by copying the code that is provided and then pasting it into a blog, virtual learning environment, or website.

This tool is great for portfolios and for getting the students to build up a collection of short recordings over a period of a module that can show their development and progress. I have been using the tool to get the students to do regular periodic recordings based on activities we have done in class. So, we use the class time to practise certain speaking activities but the students actually do the recordings at home and then send them to me. Students have to evaluate their recordings and then at the end of the course, choose the recording they are most pleased with and submit this for formal evaluation.

Here are some of the topics I have worked with:

1. Gave personal information.
2. Talked about how they had met.
3. Talked about the friend's personality.
4. Talked about what we they had in common and their interests.
5. Talked about when they last met.

Feedback, peer evaluation and self-evaluation

As we outlined in the first part of the chapter, feedback plays a key role in the assessment process. Good feedback can help students to see their own shortfalls and direct their future learning; it can motivate students and help them to reflect on their own learning. It is important to realise that not all feedback has to come from the teacher. Peer feedback or self-reflection and feedback can also achieve the same goal of making students aware of where they need to focus their own learning. Lam and Lee (2010) experimented with an interesting combination of feedback when they encouraged their students to create paper portfolios. Students were expected to write part of their portfolios in the class and the teacher used this time to provide feedback. Students also had one-to-one conferencing with students about their written work and finally students were expected to peer review each other's work. The students were then expected to choose their best two written pieces and put them forward for formal summative feedback. One powerful aspect of this study was that it really focused the students when it came to the peer evaluations and self-evaluation of their work since the students had to decide themselves which pieces of written work to put forward for formative evaluation.

This approach could easily be applied to oral recordings. Students could build up a series of oral recordings over a course, and self-evaluate their work or the teacher could even set up activities so that peer evaluation takes place. Students then would have to choose their best two recordings and submit these for formal summative assessment. My own experience with getting students to create audio recordings as part of their formative assessments is that they often take a long time to listen to, and provide feedback on, and this may be an innovative way of dealing with the problem and also tightly aligning the formative and summative assessments.

In the table below we can see an example of a form that students could use to help them self-evaluate. After each recording the students should work through the sheet. The idea is to encourage the students to develop their own awareness of their level, their strategies and their shortfalls and in doing so help to make them more reflective and aware of their level. The student then has to pass their self-reflection on to another student who reads the reflection and provides comments. The teacher is then given the self-reflection sheet and can add additional comments.

The students have just recorded themselves giving a presentation about their closest friend. They had to include information about:

- How they first met.
- What they have in common with their friend.
- What types of things they like doing with their friend.
- What it is about their friend's personality they like.
- When they last met and what they did together.
- They could include pictures in the PowerPoint presentation along with the slides.

They uploaded their PowerPoint presentations onto myBrainShark and are now expected to evaluate their own recordings.

Table 6.2: Self-assessment for oral recordings

ELT Student self-assessment form	
Student name: Student number: Class number: Email:	Key: 1 – Very poor; 2 – Poor; 3 – Average; 4 – Good; 5 – Very good.
1 2 3 4 5	My recording was well organised and dealt with the different areas of the discussion in a coherent fashion.
1 2 3 4 5	I was able to clearly articulate and discuss different aspects of my friendship.
1 2 3 4 5	I was able to connect different parts of the monologue and link them together.
1 2 3 4 5	I used a range of vocabulary that reflects my current level of learning.

ELT Student self-assessment form	
1 2 3 4 5	I was happy with the pace of my recording. There were few silences and the monologue flowed well.
Student comments on reflection	
Teacher comments on reflection	

Getting students to work with assessment descriptors is not easy. The language of the descriptors has to be quite simplistic and you need to go through each one and explain to the students what exactly they need to evaluate. When students are reflecting and thinking about their own learning it can be very powerful. Language students can be surprisingly fair when they evaluate and reflect on their own work (Bullock, 2011).

Case Study 6.6: Blogging

Russell's students on his BA Education course are learning to be teachers, but also developing their own level of English. Each week Russell presents different technologies and the students talk about them and how they might use them in their classes. The students usually get a chance to try out the technologies in class and for homework they write about the technologies in their blogs.

Students are encouraged to read each other's blogs and leave comments. They are also encouraged to share their blogs using their contacts so that they can develop the widest possible audience. Russell reads their blogs but does not leave comments. This is something he has decided to change in the future as the students have told him it would be much more motivating if he left comments.

The blogs are assessed at the end, both for the content and for the language. Students seem to get very motivated about their blogs and put a lot of attention into making them clear, easy to read and well designed. Because of this, Russell has introduced the look and feel of the blog as one of his marking criteria.

In some focus group sessions that Russell held with his students, the students emphasised the fact they felt very 'close' to their blogs. They cared about their look and feel and they worked harder on them than they would a normal writing assignment. Many of the students had 20 or 30 friends and connections reading their blogs on a regular basis and this motivated them a lot.

Summary

Testing and assessment has changed enormously over the last 50 years and we believe that most of the changes have been very positive. Technology has played a role in assessment for a long time but with the introduction of the internet, of Web 2.0 technologies and now mobile technologies, the role technology can play is greater than ever.

There will be many teachers out there who are using technology in their assessments, but in general it is still not the case. The large majority of assessments are still paper-based and the use of ICT for assessment, just like the use of ICT for teaching, is still at a very experimental stage. To highlight the point, I have now used blogging as an assessment tool for over 100 students, and yet not one had ever done a blog before as part of their assessment.

Technology often bemuses teaches because it changes so fast. It is 'constantly evolving' (Beatty 2010: 8) and it is nearly impossible for teaching and learning to keep up with these changes. Try not to worry about this. Choose technologies that fit well with your assessment criteria and that will broaden your assessment base and don't worry whether they are the latest thing or not.

Our view is that ICT can offer great affordances to assessment and we encourage you to make use of it, and in doing so hopefully broaden your assessment base. Try it on informal assessments with your class and gather plenty of feedback from your students. Remember, most teachers tend to introduce it step by step. You will certainly change and adapt your assessments as you learn more from using them. Most of the teachers we spoke to said their students were very supportive. It will be a step-by-step process but one that both you and your teachers will find very rewarding.

References

Alderson, JC (2005) *Diagnosing foreign language proficiency: The interface between learning and assessment.* London: Continuum.

Bachman, LF (no date) *Language Assessment: Opportunities and Challenges.* Available online at: www.google.co.uk/url?sa=t&rct=j&q=&esrc=s&frm=1&source=web &cd=2&ved=0CD0QFjAB&url=http%3A%2F%2Fenglishvls.hunnu.edu.cn%2FDownload s%2FLangTst%2Ftst_004.doc&ei=btS3UO31OqPX0QW2mICgCw&usg=AFQjCNFn4zO 27NKnOlts86ky0dV6GIMCTA&sig2=RJlr57WCFkV82Ghs4cjA5A

Bachman, LF and Palmer, AS (1996) *Language testing in practice: designing and developing useful language tests.* Oxford: Oxford University Press.

Beatty, K (2010) *Computer Assisted Language Learning.* London: Longman.

Biggs, J (1999) Teaching for quality learning at university: What the student does. *Higher Education* 40/3: 374–376.

Bullock, D (2011) Learning self assessment: an investigation into teachers' beliefs. *English Language Teaching Journal* 65/2: 114–125.

Choa, C-C (1999) 'Theory and Research: New Emphases of Assessment in the Language Learning Classroom', in Egbert, J and Hanson-Smith, E (eds) (1999) *CALL Environments Research, Practice and Critical Issues*. Alexandria, Va.: TESOL.

Cummins, P and Davesne, C (2009) Using Electronic Portfolios for Second Language Assessment. *Modern Language Journal* 93: 848–867.

Davison, C and Leung, C (2009) Current Issues in English Language Teacher-Based Assessment. *TESOL Quarterly* 43: 393–415.

Dewey, J (1916) *Democracy and Education*. New York: Free Press.

Egbert, J and Hanson-Smith, E (1999) *CALL Environments Research, Practice and Critical Issues*. Alexandria, Va.: TESOL.

Fulcher, G (2000) The 'communicative' legacy in language testing. *System* 28/4: 483–497.

Heift, T (ed) (2009) Technology and Learning Grammar. *Special Issue. Language Learning and Technology*, 13/1.

Hymes, DH (1972) 'On communicative competence', in Pride, JB and Holmes, J (eds) (1972) *Sociolinguistics*, Harmondsworth: Penguin, 1972.

JISC (2007) *Effective practice with e-assessment*. Available online at: www.jisc.ac.uk/whatwedo/programmes/elearning/assessment/digiassess.aspx

Kumaravadivelu, B (1994) The postmethod condition: (E)merging strategies for second/foreign language teaching. *TESOL Quarterly* 28/1: 27–48.

Kwok, L (2008) Students' perceptions of peer evaluation and teacher's role in the seminar discussions. *Electronic Journal of Foreign Language Teaching* 5/1: 84–97.

Lam, R and Lee, I (2010) Balancing the dual functions of portfolio assessment. *English Language Teaching Journal* 64/1: 54–64.

Mayes, T and De Freitas, S (2004) *Review of e-learning theories, frameworks and models*. Available online at: www.jisc.ac.uk/whatwedo/programmes/elearningpedagogy/workshops/session1.aspx

Morrow, K (1979) 'Communicative language testing: revolution of evolution?' in Brumfit, CK and Johnson, K (eds) (1979) *The Communicative Approach to Language Teaching*. Oxford: OUP.

Norton, P and Widburg, K (1998) *Teaching with technology*. Orlando, FL: Harcourt Brace College Publishers.

O'Dwyer, S (2006) The English teacher as facilitator and authority. *TESLEJ* 92/March. Available online at: www.tesl-ej.org/ej36/a2.pdf

Prodromou, L (1995) The backwash effect: from testing to teaching. *English Language Teaching Journal* 49/1: 13–25.

Smith, J (2001) Modelling the social construction of knowledge in ELT teacher education. *English Language Teaching Journal* 55/3: 221–227.

Stoynoff, S (2012) Looking backward and forward at classroom-based language assessment. *English Language Teaching Journal* 66/4: 523–532.

Taylor, L (2006) The changing landscape of English: Implications for language assessment. *English Language Teaching Journal* 60/1: 51–60.

Tomlinson, B (1995) Testing to learn: a personal view of language testing. *English Language Teaching Journal* 59/1: 39–46.

UCLES (2013) Now known as Cambridge Assessment. Available online at: www.cambridgeassessment.org.uk/ca/

Vygotsky, LV (1962) *Thought and Language.* Cambridge, MA.: MIT Press.

Waters, A (2012) Trends and issues in ELT methods and methodology. *English Language Teaching Journal* 66/4: 440–449.

Developing and extending our understanding of language learning and technology

7

Developing and extending our understanding of language learning and technology

Gary Motteram

Introduction

In the introduction to this volume I claimed that computer assisted language learning (CALL) should now be considered an established field, and I gave good evidence for this point of view. It is clear that we are now at a time in human development where digital technologies are making an increasingly significant contribution to language learning in many parts of the world and there are established and high profile journals and conferences where research is presented and discussed.

This final chapter will make an argument that the technologies that we have found presented through the preceding chapters are doing more than simply providing a medium through which teachers can meet the immediate needs of their learners in terms of language development. They are actually enabling teachers to engage in activity that supports language development in more profound ways than has hitherto been realised. The range that we find in the chapters that have preceded this one, and specifically the embedded case studies, show not only that CALL is a broad, well developed and diversifying field, but it also makes it possible for teachers to more easily provide the necessary engagement with language that allows learners to improve their skills in ways that have proved very difficult in the past. This also opens up the possibility for theories presented in fields allied to classroom ELT, like applied linguistics, to be effectively realised in the language classroom. In order to see the significance of these developments, this chapter will use a socio-cultural lens and what I term cultural technical artefacts to show the impact that learning technologies are having on language learning in all the different forms that have been explored in the chapters of this book. The views expressed in this chapter are a significant re-conceptualising of the ways that we have understood the role that technologies have played in the classroom in the past.

In my own recent conference presentations and publications (Motteram, 2012; Motteram, Slaouti and Onat-Stelma, 2013) I have been arguing for a socio-cultural analysis of CALL, particularly with respect to teachers and their professional engagement in the classroom. These arguments have been built on the work that I undertook with Manchester colleagues, Diane Slaouti and Zeynep Onat-Stelma as part of the CUP project which produced 17 case studies of teachers using technology in language education (Slaouti, Motteram and Onat-Stelma, 2008). Three of the case studies from this project are discussed in Chapter 3. The case studies that are included in the other chapters in this book build on the work from this CUP project, and extend it to other parts of the ELT field. While the CUP project was about adult language teaching, other chapters in this book have covered: primary, secondary, ESP, EAP and assessment.

Teachers are central to what happens in the classroom, because they have the knowledge and skills to find creative ways to support learners' language development. They not only have a good knowledge of language, but they have also developed their pedagogical content knowledge (Shulman, 1986) through experience and practice to a level where they can develop a variety of tasks that meet the needs of their learners. However, it is difficult to understand what they do by only considering the teaching practice that we observe. There are a wide range of elements that will be having an impact on the teaching as it plays out in the classroom: the time that they live in, or the place, the phase of education, the choice of a pedagogical approach, whether, for example, mobiles are allowed in the classroom, whether students have internet access at home, the attitudes of the community to the language that they are learning; these are just some of the factors that need to be considered. In one version of socio-cultural theory this is described as an 'activity system' (Engeström, 2001).

This chapter then advances a new socio-cultural account of this discipline by presenting CALL and language teaching in a way suggested in my own writing and hinted at in a recent article by Bax (2011). The chapters that you have read before you reach this one present CALL in the complexity of the real world and also, uniquely, from the perspective of different sub-sections of the world of ELT. It also brings, as I will argue in more detail below, the CALL and ELT activity systems (see below) together and each writer has shown how CALL has impacted on the field of study that they explore. The world of the primary pupil learning how to read (Chapter 1) is very different from the world of a politician in Germany learning (Chapter 4) how to use new media to present his policies to the world in English, and so the activity systems that they inhabit are also different.

The studies that Diane Slaouti, Zeynep Onat-Stelma and I undertook for Cambridge University Press over a two-year period (2006–08) enabled us to see that the decision-making of teachers was central to what made language learning with technology successful in the classroom. This decision-making is undergirded by teachers' cognitions about pedagogy, practice and technology use, the teachers' views of their learners and the learners themselves and their needs and interests, the activity systems that they inhabit.

We can approach the use of technology in ELT in a number of ways, as other writers have done, but in order to understand what is happening now we need to spend some time looking at developments in the past, but as a cultural history.

Cultural history, technical cultural artefacts and activity theory

Why then a cultural history, not simply a history and what are 'technical cultural artefacts'?

Rick Kern, in keynote presentations at seminal CALL conferences, in Lyon in 2010 and Taichung in 2012, and soon to be published in a forthcoming book, has made the argument that the tools that we use for, in his arguments writing, help condition the meanings we can make and the understandings we have of the language that is presented to us. Context and co-text are crucial to meaning and how it is made.

In his forthcoming book, Kern will track the development of writing and show how, over time, different media and the context have afforded different stages of development. One example he gives is of ancient Chinese which in early times was written on narrow vertical strips of bamboo, which it is argued, is still the reason why Chinese is written in this vertical format in certain parts of Asia. He further develops his argument by exploring the development of left to right handwriting of hieroglyphs. The way this writing system developed was conditioned not only by the medium, but also by the situation in which the writing took place, and the needs of the writer. In the case of the development of the left to right handwriting of hieroglyphs, it was the need to have faster ways of writing that was the motivator, so that stocktaking could be conducted in the moment.

In the world of technology a common example of an unexpected consequence of the development of technology that is cited, is that of the development and use of mobile phone-based text messaging (SMS), which was 20-years old in 2012, and as a result got mentioned in the news media. SMS started as a by-product of telephony, but has since become the biggest use for mobile phones with over four billion people able to send text messages today.

> ... the story of SMS shows that the people who effectively invent a technology – in the sense of determining its use and making it viable – are not so much the engineers who design it as the consumers who discover what it's really for.
>
> (Naughton, 2012, online)

Naughton's use of the phrase: '...consumers who discover what it is really for...' is echoing what in the academic world is referred to as 'social shaping' (MacKenzie and Wajcman, 1999). The ways that tools are used by people shapes our understanding of what a tool is for. Tools are not created by technicians and then used in the ways as expected, or even if they are this use has positive and sometimes negative impacts on development. Our technologies are the modern equivalent of the stick, or flint shards, which humans picked up and adapted to do certain tasks in their environment and as a result moved forward their cultural development.

It is tools like SMS, or the word processor I am using to write this chapter that I am referring to when I make use of the term 'technical cultural artefacts.'

When Vygotsky began his explorations that led to the development of socio-cultural theory he was interested in 'semiotic tools', like for example, language. In representations of his theory we often see the term 'tool' used on its own and this is often interpreted in the technological world to mean physical tools: from sticks to computers, and computers is certainly one form of tool that is important. Computers are the sticks or flints for the modern world, in that they can be used by people in ways not originally part of the designed affordances of the tool, but are different from a stick in that they are already complex in nature and already have at least one cultural function in society; they often end up having many. Their use by language teachers does not necessarily change the actual nature of the artefact (although we do see artefacts being changed or modified as the result of their use; see Skype below), but it does change our perceptions of them and our use of them does allow change or development to occur. The social shaping of technical cultural artefacts and the activities they are used for are embedded within the socio-cultural landscape of the moment of time of their production, but later also in the moment of time of their using to meet a particular need at a particular moment. We look back 20 years to the invention of SMS on the mobile phone, this is a historical moment, but we can then track through its development as a tool and its use, in our case, in language education; this is a cultural history.

In Chapters 1 to 6 we can see the current uses made of various tools. One that re-occurs is that of Skype, which was originally created in Estonia to provide telephony on the internet (technically referred to as voice over internet protocol – VoIP). It is now a global brand owned by Microsoft, but for teachers in the world of ELT this tool has opened up a large number of possibilities as we can see in two chapters in the book. In Chapter 2 we find Ayat Al Tawal (Case Study 2.1) using Skype to extend her classroom into the outside world enabling her learners to interact with speakers of English in other parts of the world. In Chapter 4 we find Cornelia Kreis-Meyer supporting a German politician practising using Skype to conduct interviews as he might have to do in the real world (Case Study 4.1). In both these cases additional software is also used to record the conversations for further language discussion and analysis. Here we see Skype being used in ways not envisaged by the creators; the language teaching community is 'discovering what [Skype] is for', it is being socially shaped, but crucially for the arguments being made here, socially shaped by ELT practitioners. Skype as a company has clearly become aware of what language teachers are doing with the tool that they invented for other reasons and recognise the added value to their offering, so we see the creation of https://education.skype.com a website for teachers and learners, where language learning is one of the offerings. Skype and SMS are then examples of 'technical cultural artefacts', they help teachers and learners engage in activity that is necessary for language development and at the same time allow language teaching to develop methodologically.

These technical cultural artefacts are only one constituent of the socio-cultural framework that is represented in cultural historical activity theory (hereafter activity theory) (Engeström, 2001). Activity theory proposes a particular combination of interacting elements that make a difference to the way we understand and interpret the world. Engeström (2001) argues that we are now in the third generation of activity theory that has its roots in Vygotsky's original socio-cultural theory (1978).

In activity theory I am a subject of an activity system and I have agency. I am trying to write a book chapter, the book chapter is the object of the activity system I am a part of; there are certain conventions (rules) that I abide by and some perhaps that I ignore. The choices I make in terms of the way that I write and how I write are a product of the community of practice that I belong to (Wenger, 1998). I am a teacher trainer in a UK institution with a background in TESOL. If I were a lawyer different rules would be in place and I would provide the evidence that I need to present using other conventions.

The TESOL community I belong to has an impact on the writing I do; there are certain expectations. All of this plays a part in how I put marks on this piece of electronic paper (technical cultural artefact). Different people will play a role in the production of this book (divisions of labour). I will ask colleagues to read the chapter and comment on it, copy editors will pore over the text and make suggestions about the way I have expressed ideas and the writing conventions I have used. I may be told to employ a particular convention in terms of a referencing system (another rule). I have mentioned the electronic paper that I am writing on (technical cultural artefact). This technical cultural artefact is exploited by me to enhance my writing, if I did this on paper using a pen, as I would have done when I was at school, then the final result would not be of the same quality. I am very unlikely to have worked and re-worked the text in the same way as I have here (although other writers using a pen may well have done), re-visiting and changing the text numerous times. The word processor scaffolds my writing, allowing me to perform at a higher level than I would have done without it. If I were a touch typist, I might be able to keep up with the ideas in my head rather more easily; I might not lose so many thoughts and perhaps perform even better. While for me there are lots of beneficial elements in using a computer to write, my computer is connected to the internet and at times I go off in search of suitable references or definitions as I type, I then may get distracted by other parts of the web and my flow of writing may be stemmed.

I am, of course, also using Vygotsky's key semiotic tool, that of language. My skill in expressing and representing ideas is also governed by how I was acculturated as I grew up, the schools I went to, the discipline community that I belonged to before I became a teacher of TESOL, the TESOL community that I now inhabit, the fact that I work in a School of Education rather than a School of Languages. You as reader also inhabit your own activity system and for a variety of reasons, your community is likely to be similar to mine, or perhaps differs in subtle ways. Your route into TESOL may mean that the conventions you adhere to are at odds with mine. You may have originally been a scientist and are now a teacher of ESP. This is going to make a difference to the way you view my text, the way you write your own. All of these issues have a bearing on the meaning we make, but also the developments that we make as humans, either locally and personally on a language course we are attending, or more globally in terms of the ways that languages are increasingly learned using a broad range of technical cultural artefacts.

Two activity systems: CALL and ELT

In his 2001 article Engeström suggests that it is between the boundaries of two or more activity systems where we find new developments occurring. In the case of this analysis we are concerned with the activity systems of CALL and ELT and where they interconnect, but also with the relationship between applied linguistics and ELT, and applied linguistics and CALL. Before we come to the boundaries between the different systems we need to say something more about the development of CALL.

Our understanding of Computer Assisted Language Learning (CALL) is tempered by its place in the world, its genesis as a discipline, the general contextual conditions it operates in and the actual specific situation of the class or tasks being undertaken. People continue to debate the use of the term CALL itself, as I have shown in the Introduction, however, in this book we have referred to the discipline as CALL, because, along with the names of the different special interest groups and the predominant journals in the field, this continues to be a common referent.

In the past we have seen a number of attempts to trace a traditional history of CALL. Warschauer and Healey (1998) contend that there were three phases of CALL: behavioural (later changed to structural) (Warschauer, 2000), communicative, and interactive. These were broadly related to the different phases of the development of language teaching methodology (CALL is not a field that exclusively focuses on ELT) and were also allied to different types of computer software, e.g. behavioural methodology being equated with 'drill and practise' software. In their model these historical phases were considered complete, so it appeared to be argued that as the historical phase of the development of behavioural CALL was gone, then such software was no longer being used. Bax (2003) took issue with this perspective and suggested a different route through the history; one that was not compartmentalised and which took better account of the realities of practice. Bax (2003) suggested that we do not see historical phases as such, but developments in which we have a range of tools working together. He proposed the categories: Restricted, Open and Integrated. The main thrust of his argument was connected to the concept of 'normalisation' and in 2003 Bax suggested that there was a move towards a time when in the Integrated paradigm, we would not view technological use as anything but a regular part of the world of teaching. Digital technologies would go as unremarked as the coursebook or the whiteboard (non-interactive). In his more recent thinking (2011) Bax revisited the term 'normalisation' saying that there was a need to reconsider it in the light of our developing understandings of socio-cultural theory. His earlier article had focused too much on the integration of the technology, whereas, as we are seeing here, and in earlier chapters our understanding of the introduction of technology into classrooms is much more complex.

I would like to argue that we have never needed to look at CALL's development in terms of historical phases, but what is more important is how technologies are deployed in classroom practice and how they mediate that practice. We do not need to wait for phases of technological development to succeed others or for technologies to become 'normalised', we simply need to use them to mediate our practice and explore the outcomes.

A cultural history of skills teaching and CALL

I have described a picture of technical cultural artefacts in which we can view them as having become a significant feature of the landscape of our daily lives, and this is a picture that can also increasingly be found in education in the developing, as well as the developed world. In these pictures we see a predominant use of the 'computer' as a mediating artefact, supporting the development of language teaching in a variety of ways, helping learners to make new meanings in new languages. We also see that these technical cultural artefacts can have impacts that are sometimes positive and sometimes more negative, sometimes they can make a difference to the development of the world of language teaching and sometimes they do not. This can all be tracked through research and practice in the field, so I am now going to turn to the impact that technical cultural artefacts have had on what in the ELT field has conventionally been referred to as 'skills teaching'.

The production of written text

I am not going to start in what might be considered a 'traditional skills order', i.e. reading, writing, listening and speaking, where the receptive skill is placed before the productive, because this does not reflect the cultural history of technology and skills and I am also not going to look at all of the skills. I am going to start with the process of producing text with computers because this relates most directly to both writing and speaking, again, exploring the skills in a rather different way to what might normally be expected. We see an emerging cultural history that has been created because of the developments that have occurred with technology and the ways that individuals or groups have used certain technical cultural artefacts over time.

The development of our understanding of writing as a process is an interesting journey because computers allowed language teachers to bring these ideas directly into the classroom. Work by Flower and Hayes (1981), which explored how professionals thought about and prepared for writing and finally wrote, offered a model that showed that professional writing was complex and it went through a series of stages, loosely as adapted to ELT: 'prewriting; composing/drafting; revising; and editing' (Tribble, 1996: 39). Quite early after the initial publication of this process model, research started appearing that showed how computers could be used in the writing class to support this process approach. One of the earliest articles in ELT was by Piper (1987) and this appeared in the mainstream journal *ELTJ* (discussed in the Introduction). This article looks at the positive benefits of using a word processor in the classroom and one of the findings from the questionnaire that was used in the study was that, 'The word processor [...] facilitates the process of moving from a first draft through a process of evaluation and redrafting to a final draft...' (p. 122), confirming my argument. A good summary of the research on word processing over subsequent years was brought together by Pennington in the mid 1990s. Many studies that were undertaken subsequent to Piper continued to confirm her findings that the word processor was better able to model this professional writing process than more conventional writing practices. Pennington (1996: 131) showed that over time learners went through a series of stages that she described as:

- writing easier
- writing more
- writing differently
- writing better.

The affordances of the word processor allow the learners to work towards a text that is both longer than they would normally create when handwriting, more accurate, both because of the correction tools, but also because it is so much easier to go back and correct text. A text which in its final printed form does not show the mistakes that have been made along the way, without having to completely re-write it, and where the engagement in the ideas is of a higher standard, the higher cognitive skills development that is argued for by Vygotsky (1978) is a real development for many second language writers. The word processor is a mediator of the process, but also changes the nature of the writing we do and how much writing we produce. The word processor is also changed from being simply a tool that we use to create and store text to being a technical cultural artefact that allows learners to develop significant language skills. This technology's role has been socially shaped within the field of language teaching, and language teaching has changed profoundly too. In the cases in this book we find writing development continuing with blogs and wikis increasingly being used, in Chapter 1, in Case Study 1.1, and a specialist word processor in Case Study 1.6. In Chapter 3, in Case Study 3.1, we do still find the students developing text with a word processor. They are using this in conjunction with recordings made with the software package Audacity. In our assessment chapter in Case Study 6.3, we see Edmodo being used to encourage writing fluency. The tools created for one reason have been adopted in the domain of language teaching and allow the development of the field.

The process writing approach has not been without its critics who have argued that learners are often left to struggle without input (Badger and White, 2000) and we have seen the development of an enhanced product approach called a genre approach to writing (Badger and White, 2000). In this approach we see an emphasis on the nature of the text itself and the community that produces these texts, these learners are developing the skills to become members of a different community of practice (Wenger, 1998). Teachers in an ESP class focusing on a particular genre, the writing of scientific articles, for example, are doing more than simply teaching language; the writers in the class are having their identity moulded by the processes of writing in a particular way. They are becoming 'writers of science' not simply learning to write in English, the nature of their identity is changing. Since this early research into writing and word processors there has been a revolution in the production of text and because of the nature of the internet, the web and other tools like mobile phones, we find text everywhere and we produce considerably more than we were producing when most text was handwritten. We have seen cultural technical artefacts like blogs being socially shaped and changing the nature of the publishing industry, or wikis being used as malleable repositories for the knowledge base of the world, where a much broader range of people contribute to our understanding of what things mean. We also see this process occurring in language teaching where collaboration is seen as important for language development (see more below on 'languaging').

Working with a word processor in real life can be a solitary process, but this has seldom been the case in language classes. The nature of resources in most schools and colleges has meant that the production of written material has generally been collaborative: two or three students working together in joint activity around a computer (Piper, 1987). Word processing is also an activity that has been found to be effective in getting learners to speak about what they are doing. However, other forms of writing tools have also enabled learners to communicate with each other in text. These include email (Slaouti, 2002), other forms of computer mediated communication (Kern and Warschauer, 2000), but also 'texting' (Cavus and Ibrahim, 2009).

Drawing an absolute line between the uses of text for one form of communication, speaking, and texting for the development of writing skills is difficult in the early stages of the change of use of tools. We have seen research on using text in classrooms as the preparation for speaking, but we also saw early research in the use of MUDS/MOOs for the creation of text-based virtual worlds (Shield, Davies and Weininger, 2000). Text was used to construct and move about the world, but also to communicate via text chat; communication could be synchronous or asynchronous. We see this tradition being continued in Chapter 1 in the discussion of interactive fiction where learners still play games that are text only. With the development of the first stages of the internet and into the Web 2.0 world we now inhabit, research about text has continued to change and develop, reflecting the nature of the tools and their affordances. Each one of these changes sees a modified relationship between the world of ELT and the world of technology; we see new developments at these boundaries. We see an increasing emphasis on collaborative writing either within classes, or across classes, i.e. between different schools, or different countries. We also see the introduction of a number of other tools, a predominant one currently being the wiki, because of its collaborative nature and its ability to see the development of the text over time via the history function (Lund, 2008). In these tools we also find embedded other digital materials and various pieces of multimedia.

Developments from MUDS/MOOS have seen the emergence of highly visual digital games, in which although people make use of a range of tools for communication, they no longer describe the world in the way they did, the descriptive written forms of the old 2D worlds have gone. We also have worlds like Second Life and Open Sim, where learners and teachers can gather and practise language. See Chapter 1, Case Study 1.1 for an example of how Second Life can feature in the classroom. Here also spaces can be built, but these are mainly pictorial and although text-based games can be played, these are not generally how they are used. Here we have a tangible link to the next skill that I want to discuss, that of reading, because digital games require considerable engagement with text as well as production of text via tools like fan fiction (see Introduction for a definition).

Reading

I am turning now to learning to read because this language skill is closely linked to the origins of the web and via the subject we can explore some of the key reasons why we would want to make use of the web in our world of digital language learning, as well as seeing how our cultural technical artefacts are modified through use.

The web had its origins in the desire to have a worldwide system of connected knowledge that was first proposed by Vannevar Bush in the *Atlantic Monthly* in 1945 and then developed further by Ted Nelson who invented the term 'hypertext' in the early 1960s (1965) and first used it in a lecture. However, it was Berners-Lee (Berners-Lee and Fischetti, 2001) who was the real architect of the web, who created the first web server and wrote the protocols to serve web pages as well as the first hypertext mark-up language (HTML), which displayed the documents. As a result, a lot of reading material now arrives with us via some form of screen and many of these screens are linked via hypertext to millions of other texts. This opens up massive opportunities for language learning providing a very large source of authentic input materials. An input oriented approach leads us initially theoretically to Krashen (1985) and there would be enough easily accessible input for every language learner on the planet, but this material needs management to make it comprehensible and learners also need to understand how to approach it effectively.

Three key concepts from the ELT literature are appropriate here: *cognitive* and *metacognitive strategies, autonomy* and *output.* A fourth concept, that of *digital literacy* follows on close behind and this has increasingly become the focus for why people use technology in the language classroom. In order to access the web effectively, to gain maximum language learning from any material or activity, we need to make sure that the learners have the necessary skills to be able to approach and interpret a text. As the web started to have an impact on teaching and learning and specifically on languages, we saw studies that explored the impact of hypertext on learners' ability to read and interpret text. One such study is that of Konishi:

> *Cognitive strategies are direct strategies to deal with the mental processing of a target language. Meta-cognitive strategies are part of the indirect strategies to self-monitor the reading activity of oneself. They also function as a goal setting of reading and revising the use of various cognitive strategies.*

(Konishi, 2003: 104)

In her study of web-based reading, Konishi found that her students used a range of strategies in trying to access the text; they used local and global cognitive strategies to get at meanings in the text, as well as metacognitive strategies to help them organise their activity. Two tasks were explored in this study and we can see that the tasks help to frame and support what the learners do. They helped mediate this process. Strategy research is very closely related to learner autonomy and also to learner training (Hedge, 2003: 92) and much research into CALL and reading has followed this route showing how learners can be supported (scaffolded) to use the internet and other tools on their own. We have seen the development of materials that support and extend the classroom in a variety of ways and we have seen the introduction of the notion of blended learning (see Introduction) allowing more space in the regular classroom to do tasks and activities that are more relevant to the physical classroom. We also see changes in research into reading which range from large reading web-based multimedia reading schemes in mother tongue teaching in the US (Cheung and Slavin, 2012) to the use of mobile devices in the developing world (Hsu, Hwang and Chang, 2013). This last one is a doctoral thesis, showing how new such research is. We see examples of reading practice in our case studies, one in particular is the interactive reading activities that turned into the Bubble and Pebble books in Chapter 1, Case Study 1.3.

This takes us then to *output*. Paran (2012) in his review of the teaching of skills makes the important point that it is really very difficult to keep skills separate:

> *... one issue which needs to be laid out in the open at the very beginning is the continuing, paradoxical separation of language skills. This separation contrasts with our understanding of language use as entailing a relationship between at least two skills (and often more), with our understanding of the importance of context in all language use, and with current views of literacy and oracy. However, from a pedagogical point of view, there are arguments for focusing on skills in isolation at least some of the time.*

(Paran, 2012: 450)

I have mentioned Krashen and the 'input hypothesis' (1985). He argues that people learn language through comprehensible input, but ostensibly through reading and listening. Following criticisms of his core ideas Krashen went on to continue to promote them by focusing on the teaching of reading (2004). Swain, developing work by Long (1981), who argues that input is made comprehensible by learners responding to it by showing that they do not understand and seeking modifications of the input to make it comprehensible, proposed the 'Comprehensible Output Hypothesis'. In an overview of the theory and its possibilities Swain (2000: 100) shows that although input in language learning is important, it is the act of producing language '... which focuse[s] the learner's attention on what he or she did not know, or knew imperfectly.' Swain shows learners engaging in the process of trying out hypotheses and using supporting technologies (in this case a physical dictionary) to construct language that stretches their knowledge that builds the higher psychological constructs of their developing language; what Swain has come to term 'languaging' (2006: 96). This languaging is the external process that leads to the internal construction of a more advanced ability with language. As language teachers we can look at the activity system that Swain has proposed to us and look for ways in our classrooms where we might promote languaging. We (subjects) create new classroom tasks (our object) and taking into account our context, the rules and divisions of labour, we employ certain tools including technical cultural artefacts to try to reach this objective. We have picked up the boundary object of languaging and found ways of encouraging our students to maximise the time they spend on using and negotiating language.

We have seen languaging as a feature of many of the chapters. In Chapter 4, Case Study 4.2, we find the learners working in a company where they make use of different authentic spaces to engage in activities that are relevant to their working lives:

> *For example, if the managers need to give presentations in English, they prepare and give one in the lesson, which is recorded in order to be watched together later to give feedback on language use and other presentation skills.*

This kind of presentation could take place face-to-face, or in a virtual room, depending on what particular skills need to be practised at that time. The recording allows them to see their performance and then negotiate with each other and their teachers about the appropriacy of the language they have used in activity. The video recordings act as a cultural technical artefact to allow them to achieve their objective.

In the second example in this chapter, Case Study 4.3, we find learners in Taiwan using a wide range of digital tools to learn how to create commercials. These are students who are studying advertising, but doing it as far as possible through the medium of English. Here the different tools, for example the blog with different multimedia elements plugged in, acts as an online shop window for their activity to invite comments from course participants and others. Again, this is a situation where these different tools are utilised as technical cultural tools to allow language to be developed, to prepare these learners for a commercial world that is dominated by English. The negotiation with language occurs prior to the materials being put on the web, but they need to negotiate through English to achieve certain objectives and while achieving those objectives they are producing a lot more language than they would in a traditional classroom setting.

It is interesting to note that the semiotic tool of dialogue here is also found elsewhere in the literature on education, technology and learning. In the UK, the most prominent exponent of this perspective is Laurillard, who builds on the work of Pask (1975). In Laurillard's early work (2002) this is termed the 'Conversational Approach' and is aimed at teachers and at the processes of creating learning materials. Laurillard worked for many years at the UK Open University and was a key theorist in the creation and construction of learning materials using a variety of cultural technical artefacts. She uses her most recent book (2012) to lay out these ideas, comprehensively extending them to all aspects of the teaching and learning process. Her basic thesis is the same as Swain's, that it is the combination of both semiotic and technical cultural artefacts, as I have termed them, that promotes advancement in learning. In Laurillard's cases these are cultural technological artefacts.

Conclusions

The increased use of technological cultural artefacts has enabled us to more readily afford the conversations necessary around input texts that help to create opportunities for languaging. We are able to take tools that have been created in other domains of the language learning field, languaging and process writing, and bring these together with technical cultural artefacts like Skype, virtual worlds, word processors, wikis, blogs and many others to improve language development and our understanding of language development. By viewing the field of CALL and its relationship with other parts of the language teaching world through the lens of third generation activity theory and tracing some of its cultural history, we have seen important developments in our understanding of the roles that innovative technologies are playing in altering how we do language leaning in the 21st century. The roles that they are playing are making a significant and important contribution to the development of the field and will make a real difference to how we understand language learning and the role of CALL within it. This chapter and this book has shown that the language learning field is enhanced, but is also being changed by the ways that technology is used by creative language teachers in the many different classrooms throughout the world. CALL has come a long way in 30 years and through the chapters and case studies presented here, we can see just how far, and we will see more in the not too distant future.

References

Badger, R and White, G (2000) A process genre approach to teaching writing. *English Language Teaching Journal* 54/2: 153–160.

Bax, S (2003) CALL – Past, present and future. *System* 31/1: 13–28.

Bax, S (2011) Normalisation revisited: The effective use of technology in language education. *IJCALLT* 1/2: 1–15.

Berners-Lee, T and Fischetti, M (2001) *Weaving the Web: The Original Design and Ultimate Destiny of the World Wide Web by Its Inventor*. Derby, Pennsylvania: Diane Publishing Company.

Bush, V (1945) As we may think. *Atlantic Monthly* 176/1: 101–108.

Cavus, N and Ibrahim, D (2009) m-Learning: An experiment in using SMS to support learning new English language words. *British Journal of Educational Technology* 40/1: 78–91.

Cheung, CK and Slavin, RE (2012) How features of educational technology applications affect student reading outcomes: A meta-analysis. *Educational Research Review* 7/3: 198–215.

Engeström, Y (2001) Expansive learning at work: towards an activity theoretical reconceptualization. *Journal of Education and Work* 14/1: 133–156.

Flower, L and Hayes, JR (1981) A cognitive process theory of writing. *College Composition and Communication* 32/4: 365–387.

Hedge, T (2003) Key concepts in ELT: Learner training. *ELT Journal* 47/1: 92–93.

Hsu, C-K, Hwang, G-J and Chang, C-K (2013) A personalized recommendation-based mobile learning approach to improving the reading performance of EFL students. *Computers & Education* 63: 327–336.

Kern, R (in preparation).

Kern, R and Warschauer, M (2000) *Network-based language teaching: concepts and practice*. Cambridge: Cambridge University Press.

Konishi, M (2003) Strategies for reading hypertext by Japanese ESL learners. *The Reading Matrix* 3/3: 97–119.

Krashen, SD (1985) *The Input Hypothesis: Issues and Implications*. London: Longman.

Krashen, SD (2004) *The power of reading*. London: Heinemann.

Lantolf, JP (ed) (2000) *Sociocultural theory and second language learning*. Oxford: Oxford University Press.

Laurillard, D (2002) *Rethinking University Teaching: a framework for the effective use of educational technology* (2nd edition). London: Routledge Falmer.

Laurillard, D (2012) *Teaching as a design science*. London: Routledge.

Long, MH (1981) 'Input, interaction, and second language acquisition', in Winitz, H (ed) Native language and foreign language acquisition. *Annals of the New York Academy of Sciences* 379: 259–78.

Lund, A (2008) Wikis: a collective approach to language production *ReCALL* 20/1: 35–54.

MacKenzie, D and Wajcman, J (eds) (1999) *The social shaping of technology*, 2nd Edition. Buckingham, UK: Open University Press.

Motteram, G (2012) Re-aligning research into teacher education for CALL and bringing it into the mainstream. *Language Teaching* FirstView Article: 1–13.

Motteram, G, Slaouti, D and Onat-Stelma, Z (2013) 'Second language teacher education for CALL: An alignment of theory and practice', in Thomas, M, Reinders, H and Warschauer, M (2013) *Contemporary Computer-Assisted Language Learning.* UK: Bloomsbury Academic.

Naughton, J (2012) Now 4 billion people know the joy of txt. *Observer*, 6 May. Available online at: www.guardian.co.uk/technology/2012/may/06/sms-text-messages-20th-birthday?newsfeed=true

Paran, A (2012) Language skills: questions for teaching and learning. *English Language Teaching Journal* 66/4: 450–458.

Pask, G (1975) *The Cybernetics of Human Learning and Performance*. London: Hutchinson.

Pennington, MC (1996) *The power of CALL*. Houston: Athelstan.

Piper, A (1987) Helping learners to write: A role for the word processor. *English Language Teaching Journal* 41/2: 119–125.

Shield, L, Davies, LB and Weininger, M (2000) Fostering (pro)active language learning through MOO. *ReCALL* 12/1: 35–48.

Shulman, LS (1986). Those who understand: Knowledge growth in teaching. *Educational Researcher* 15/2: 4–31.

Slaouti, D (2002) The world wide web for academic purposes: old study skills for new? *English for Specific Purposes* 21/2: 105–124.

Slaouti, D, Motteram, G and Onat-Stelma, Z (2008) *The Case-Study Report: Report No. 2*. Cambridge: Cambridge University Press.

Swain, M (2000) 'The output hypothesis and beyond: Mediating acquisition through collaborative dialogue', in Lantolf, J (2000) *Sociocultural Theory and Second Language Learning*. Oxford: Oxford University Press.

Swain, M (2006) 'Language, agency and collaboration in advanced second language proficiency', in Byrnes, H (ed) *Advanced Language Learning*. Continuum: London.

Tribble, C (1996) *Writing*. Oxford: Oxford University Press.

Vygotsky, LS (1978) *Mind in society*. Cambridge, Massachusetts: Harvard University Press.

Warschauer, M (2000) *CALL for the 21st Century*. IATEFL and ESADE Conference, 2 July 2000, Barcelona, Spain.

Warschauer, M and Healey, D (1998) Computers and language learning: an overview. *Language Teaching* 31/2: 57–71.

Wenger, E (1998) *Communities of Practice; learning, meaning and identity*. Cambridge: Cambridge University Press.

Winitz, H (ed) (1981) *Native language and foreign language acquisition*. Vol. 379. Annals of the New York Academy of Science.

Contributors

Dr Anthony 'Skip' Basiel has been a Thought Leader in eLearning for almost two decades. He has won national recognition for eLearning Research and Development projects from the UK Higher Education Academy, the (UK) e-Learning Network and the National Peer Awards. He is an Adobe International Education Leader (Alumnus), with almost a decade of eLearning consultancy in web video telecommunications such as video conferencing, webinars, web video case studies and testimonials. He has worked across the full range of the eLearning design and development spectrum with a focus on evaluation strategies. His Doctorate (2007) explored the pedagogic issues for eLearning design.

Jody Gilbert has taught EAP in Canadian post-secondary contexts for 14 years. He has special interests in content-based instruction, vocabulary development, and reading pedagogy, and uses a range of web-based technology to support learning in the EAP classroom. Jody holds an MA in Educational Technology and TESOL (University of Manchester). He currently works as a Program Co-ordinator at Bow Valley College in Calgary, Canada.

Nergiz Kern teaches EAP at universities in Turkey and the UK. She has worked in different countries for 12 years and taught general, business, technical, and academic English to students of all ages and backgrounds. She has developed and taught blended ESP courses for taxi drivers, aviation maintenance technicians, and city planners. Nergiz has experience in teaching and conducting teacher training online, including in a 3D virtual world. The dissertation for her MA in Educational Technology and TESOL was on increasing EAP student motivation and autonomy through project-based integration of technology and digital literacies skills into a course.

Gary Motteram, editor of this publication, is currently a Senior Lecturer in Education at the University of Manchester, UK. He has an MEd in Teaching English Overseas and an EdD in e-learning. He set up the first ever Master's that linked educational technology and TESOL that still runs on-site in Manchester and worldwide by e-learning. He has presented at conferences and published regularly in the fields of technology in language learning and technology supported distance teacher education. He has recently managed a number of international projects for the University of Manchester, including eChinaUK and AVALON (avalonlearning.eu), and he ran a two year research project for Cambridge University Press exploring what teachers do with technology. His most recent project involvement is the Euroversity (euroversity.eu) network. You can find out more on his blog (edtechandteso.info).

Zeynep Onat-Stelma is currently working in the School of Education, at the University of Manchester. She is teaching in the areas of language teacher education, bilingualism and research methods. She is also currently involved in a research project, Euroversity (www.euroversity.eu) funded by the European Union. Her research interests lie in teacher professional development. She has previously been involved in research projects where she worked with language teachers in different international settings. One of these projects was funded by Cambridge University Press and the other project was funded by the European Union, AVALON (www.avalonlearning.eu). She has also been involved as a tutor on the Language Teacher Training pilot course that has run as part of the AVALON project.

Chris Pim has, over the last 15 years, worked as a local authority adviser for Ethnic Minority Achievement and learners of English as an additional language (EAL). As an ICT and EAL independent consultant, he has worked with numerous schools and government institutions across the country. Chris is also an author, researcher and trainer for a range of publishers including Smart Learning, Education City, Mantra Lingua, Talking Products and Texthelp. He recently updated Smart Learning's 'Years 7–9 Smart Skills Builder ICT' and has written two EAL books: 'How to support children Learning English as an additional language' (LDA Learning) and '100 ideas for supporting learners with EAL' (Continuum).

Diane Slaouti is a Senior Lecturer in Education at the University of Manchester. She works with the Language Teacher Education group teaching on Masters in TESOL programmes and with teachers researching their contexts of practice. Her own teaching experience has given her opportunities to explore technology use in varied adult settings and she now works with teachers to understand how technology is impacting on thinking in the field. The case study teachers in her chapter, participants in a worldwide study of technology in adult EFL for Cambridge University Press, are an example of such collaborations.

Graham Stanley has been teaching English since 1995 and is currently based in Barcelona. He has a Master's degree (University of Manchester) in ELT and Educational Technology. He is a social media consultant and manager of EU projects for the British Council: AVALON (language learning in Second Life), aPLaNEt (teacher development through PLNs) and ITiLT (language teaching with IWBs). His speciality is in using emerging technologies to promote language learning and teaching.

Russell Stannard is a Principal Teaching Fellow at the University of Warwick. He trains teachers in incorporating technology into their language classes. He won the British Council 'Technology ELTons' award and the Times Higher 'Outstanding ICT Innovation Award' for his website (www.teachertrainingvideos.com/). Russell has taught in Spain, where he was the Director of Studies of International House Seville, Greece and the UK. He has also worked extensively in China, Sweden and Italy. He writes a regular column called 'Webwatcher' in the *English Teaching Professional* which he has been doing for 12 years.

Acronyms

BE	Business English
CALL	Computer assisted language learning
CLIL	Content and language integrated learning
CLT	Communicative language teaching
CMC	Computer mediated communication
CMS	Course management system
CPD	Continuing professional development
CPH	Critical period hypothesis
CUP	Cambridge University Press
DDL	Data-driven learning
DGBL	Digital games-based learning
EAL	English as an additional language
EAP	English for academic purposes
EFL	English as a foreign language
EGAP	English for general academic purposes
ELT	English language teaching
ELTJ	English Language Teaching Journal
ESAP	English for specific academic purposes
ESL	English as a second language
ESOL	English for speakers of other languages
ESP	English for specific purposes
GPS	Global positioning system
HEI	Higher education institution
IATEFL	International Association of Teachers of English as a Foreign Language
ICT	Information and communications technology
IF	Interactive fiction
IWB	Interactive Whiteboard
KWIC	Keyword in context
LMS	Learning management system
LSP	Languages for specific purposes
MALL	Mobile assisted language learning

MOOC   Massive Open Online Course

MUDS   Multi-User Dungeon, Dimension or Domain

NA   Needs analysis

NNS   Non-native speaker

PBL   Problem-based learning

PLE   Personal learning environment

PLN   Personal learning networks

ProjBLL Project-based language learning

SIG   Special interest group

SLA   Second language acquisition

SMS   Mobile phone-based text messaging

TESOL   Teaching English to speakers of other languages

TOEFL   Test of English as a Foreign Language

UCLES   University of Cambridge Local Examinations Syndicate

VC   Video conferencing

VLE   Virtual learning environment

VoIP   Voice-over internet protocol